Manpower Agenda for America

Manpower Agenda for America

Eli Ginzberg

McGraw-Hill Book Company

New York

St. Louis

San Francisco

Toronto

London

Sydney

Acknowledgments

Permission to reproduce the following chapters
was graciously granted by:

4, Graduate School of Business, Columbia University; 5,
Southern Regional Council; 7, Chamber of Commerce of the
United States; 11, Edwin Gould Foundation for Children;
12, College Placement Council, Inc.; 13, National Affairs, Inc.;
14, *New England Journal of Medicine;* 16 and 17, Columbia
University Press; 18, American Psychological Association.

Manpower Agenda for America

To the Staff of the U.S. Department of Labor
in appreciation of a constructive collaboration of many years

Preface

Every book should have an objective. Moreover, it should be directed to one or another public. This book has a modest aim: to present a series of analyses of contemporary manpower problems that challenge both the student of ideas and the citizen looking for remedies to urgent social and economic problems.

Our goal is defined by the audience to which the book is addressed —students and scholars who are directly or tangentially concerned with the economics of manpower; businessmen and other employers who are directly affected by changes in the level and supply of manpower and who must act in response to these changes; and politicians and the educated citizenry who have been under increasing pressure to appraise and respond to the powerful forces of automation, unemployment, civil rights, and poverty, in the hope and expectation of reducing the manpower wastes that still plague our dynamic economy.

The chapters which comprise this book were written originally for different audiences, national and international, academic and general, governmental and nongovernmental. Some were speeches; others were articles. Nevertheless, each presentation is addressed to a contemporary theme; each seeks to set a specific manpower problem within the larger frame of economic and social changes; each attempts to use theory to illuminate policy; each is concerned with differentiating the known from what we must still learn. The bibliographical notes and acknowledgments indicate the source of each chapter.

For almost thirty years I have directed an interdisciplinary team at Columbia University which has concentrated on basic research in human resources and manpower. No director can ever know where his contribution ends and that of his staff begins. But this much is clear: the stronger the staff, the greater their contribution. This book has drawn heavily on the work of the senior members of the Conservation of Human Resources staff, many of whom are identified as coauthors in the bibliography.

Although all the chapters were initially drafted within the last two years, the manpower scene is subject to such rapid change that the manuscript has been revised in order to update some of the facts and figures, particularly where more recent data do not appear congruent with the original formulation.

Ruth S. Ginzberg edited the original essays for publication and contributed to integrating the discrete pieces into a unified whole.

Eli Ginzberg

Contents

Manpower Agenda for America

Foreword What Is Manpower?

For many generations, economists and journalists referred to the human element in economic development as "labor" or, less abstractly, as laborers or workers. At the beginning of industrial capitalism, early in the nineteenth century, the term "hands" was frequently used. A term in recent use is "employee," which emphasizes the legal or contractual relationship between the man hired to work and the person who hired him.

Against a history told by such terms as hands, workers, employees, where does the word "manpower" belong?

The older terms were used to designate the large numbers of persons who were hired at the factory gate or some other convenient place and who often were fired with no more concern than had gone into their hiring. These workers represented "labor power." One person was interchangeable with another—although conservative as well as Marxian economists recognized gradations of skill in the work force. But the model they used was of an employer drawing the numbers he required from the large, substantially undifferentiated labor pool and releasing men back into the pool when he no longer needed them.

In addition to the "worker," the early economists made place for one other individual: the entrepreneur, the undertaker, the capitalist, the owner, and later the manager. Here too a change in language reflects the development of theory: to balance the concept of labor, economists began to use the term "management" to describe the functions performed by the small number of men who held supervisory posts. These men were not entrepreneurs or capitalists; they were hired. But they were hired to supervise.

For a long time the division of all who worked into labor and management, or workers and managers, proved satisfactory. Most problems dealing with the human factor in economic life could be treated adequately in terms of this simple twofold schema. Even today, many students restrict their analyses to this schema.

1

But a new term, "manpower," has come into prominence. The President must submit an annual Manpower Report to the Congress. The Senate has established a standing Subcommittee on Employment and Manpower and has held hearings on the manpower revolution. In 1962 Congress passed the Manpower Development and Training Act. The President's Committee on Manpower was established in 1965 to coordinate the policies and programs of the Federal agencies. As a result of a major reorganization of the U.S. Department of Labor, a Manpower Administration was established. The Department of Defense has an Assistant Secretary for Manpower. There is the statutory National Manpower Advisory Committee, with its associated Regional Manpower Advisory Committees, together with state, area, and local manpower committees, all of which have a role to play in connection with the new manpower training programs. The recent reorganization of the administrative structure of New York City led to the establishment of a Human Resources Administration, a key element of which is the Manpower Administration.

The term "manpower" is now broadly used in government. Does it go further? A highly successful business is known as Manpower, Incorporated. Large corporations have begun to establish senior staff positions for "manpower planning." Colleges and universities have introduced courses in manpower and a few have established new professorial titles in the field of human resources and manpower. A new journal entitled *Human Resources* has appeared.

These illustrations suggest an affinity between the terms "manpower" and "human resources." Is there a distinction? The term "manpower" usually refers to human beings who work for wages and those who are out of work, but seeking employment. Volunteers and housewives usually are not included. But since there is a constant shifting back and forth of adults, particularly women, from working for wages to not working, there is no harm in broadening the term manpower, as many have done, to include all noninstitutionalized adults within the ages when people conventionally work.

"Human resources" is a more inclusive term. It covers not only adults at work or capable of working but all human beings who will eventually be able to work as well as those who are no longer capable of being fully employed because of their age. The use of the term "human resources" calls attention to a distinctive and special facet of the lives of people, to their present or potential involvement in the world of work. There are a great many vantage points from which the activities of human beings can be described and appraised. Theologians are concerned about the souls of people; philosophers, about how they think; military strategists, about the kind of soldiers they will make; physicians, about the factors contributing to the health of the population; demographers, about their numbers; ecologists, about the interplay between people and their environment; artists, about man's appreciation of beauty. There is literally no limit to the perspectives from which man can be judged. When he is viewed as a human resource, emphasis is placed on his present or potential capacity to contribute, in association with other resources, to the output of goods and services, that is, to economic development.

Why has the new term manpower been accepted so widely? This nation has always had a manpower policy, even though we did not use the term. In our early days, we encouraged free immigration to speed the settlement of the wilderness and to add to our pool of skilled workers. Government and philanthropic funds were early channeled into education to provide the next generation with a foundation for acquiring competence and skill. With the passage of the Morrill Act during the Civil War, the Federal government acted to encourage "agriculture and the mechanical arts" at state universities. Later the agricultural extension service represented another effort to broaden and deepen the skills of the farm population. Philanthropy contributed to the establishment and growth of health and medical services which were aimed not only at prolonging life and reducing pain and suffering but also at increasing the number of years a man could work. And philanthropy also helped to maintain those without income so that they could work another day.

But the efforts that were made on behalf of education, health, and welfare were not motivated primarily by manpower considerations. However, many of the architects of these important social efforts recognized that they were indirectly strengthening the nation's manpower resources.

In the past, the economy was considered a self-regulating mechanism. The market called forth the resources required to produce what people were able and willing to buy. And if production more than met the demand, prices would drop until demand increased and a new equilibrium was established. The flexibility of the self-regulating market for labor—as for other resources—helps to explain the lack of public concern with manpower. The workers that industry needed were generally forthcoming. In fact, the market mechanism was so subtly attuned that when the demand for labor strengthened in the United States, the flow of immigrants from Europe increased, and when business declined, the number of immigrants declined.

What happened to change the situation?

No one event can be singled out, but several developments, each one reinforcing the other, help to account for the slow but ineluctable change which has forced this country, as all advanced technological societies, to develop manpower programming as a major instrument of national policy.

In brief, the principal events were these: World War I necessitated a balancing of military and civilian manpower needs. Next, the immigration laws of 1920 and 1924 put an end to Europe's serving as our reserve pool for unskilled and skilled workers. The Great Depression of the 1930s revealed that the adjustments between the demand and supply of labor were not automatic. Then, World War II and the cold war which followed illuminated the critical role of scientists and development engineers in assuring national survival and technical progress. The passage of the Employment Act of 1946 committed the Federal government to establishing and maintaining a high level of employment. The civil rights movement was started by the large numbers of Negroes who for so long had been denied opportunities for employment on equal terms with the white majority. The growing recognition of the demands and needs of the American people for various types of services, particularly in the fields of health and education, threw a spotlight on specific personnel shortages.

These are some of the major forces that have helped bring manpower considerations to the fore. There was one other, operating beneath the surface, relentlessly and remorselessly, that may have been even more potent. Our industrial and occupational structure was being radically transformed. We were no longer a nation of independent farmers; we were no longer a nation composed primarily of factory workers. Rather, ours had become an increasingly diversified economy; we had experienced a pronounced shift from reliance on brawn to reliance on brains. The need for workers had been transformed into a need for skilled workers.

Without support and guidance the market cannot be relied upon to produce the numbers and types of professional, technical, and skilled manpower that the economy now requires. While economic considerations play a role in the occupational decision making of young people and in the allocation of skilled and talented adults, it has become increasingly clear that the development of adequate numbers of trained people cannot be left solely to each individual's planning for his own future.

Much more is involved. First, without reliable information about economic trends and occupational characteristics, it is very difficult indeed for even the most intelligent young person to make a sound decision about his future. Second, the effective development of the nation's human potential involves a great many social institutions and values that far transcend the scope of individual decision making. To note only a few: the quality of family life, access to schooling, conditions governing military service, trends in age at marriage and family formation, discrimination in education and employment, the quality of guidance services, patterns of industrial recruitment and promotion, the level of employment, opportunities for training and retraining.

Specifically, an increase in the supply of professional persons required the establishment or expansion of educational and training facilities which were not part of a profit economy but which depended for much of their income on government and philanthropy. Attracting large numbers of scientists and engineers to work on the atomic bomb or on space exploration involved much more than establishing wage and salary scales that were competitive with alternative employment opportunities. The challenge of obtaining the manpower required for the most dynamic new industries, such as air transportation, atomic energy, electronics, health, and education, could not be left to the ingenuity of the employer. He could not go to the market and find what he needed. Whether there would be adequate numbers of physicists, physicians, and electronic technicians for hire depended in considerable measure on the actions previously taken by government to underpin the education and training of various types of specialists. The market still performs important functions, but the market alone can no longer be relied upon to assure the flow of competent personnel which the economy and society requires for growth. The shape of things to come is increasingly determined in the political arena by decisions affecting public expenditures. But since money without trained men is sterile, manpower, particularly trained manpower, has assumed an increasingly important role in the affairs of nations.

One key facet of the emergence of manpower as a central issue of national policy is the complex adjustments required to establish, expand, and support the multiplicity of educational and training efforts required to assure an adequate supply of trained persons. The market alone cannot meet this challenge.

One might conclude that the core of a "manpower agenda" concerns trained personnel. But a manpower agenda, particularly in a democracy, cannot be limited to trained personnel. It must also be concerned with the problems that arise from the fact that advances in technology may be reducing the opportunities of the poorly educated and the unskilled to find or keep jobs; with the limitations of fiscal and monetary policies to provide employment for all who want jobs; with the special difficulties that stand in the way of disadvantaged groups, such as school dropouts, poorly educated Negroes, and farm families, to find profitable employment.

This bifurcation between shortages of talent and skill at one end of the manpower distribution and excessive numbers of hard-to-employ persons at the other may appear extreme when the time perspective is extended to include the next generation of workers. Surely, we might say, those now in school will be able to acquire the fundamentals which will facilitate their making their way when they are ready to work.

But we cannot be sure of this; we recently have learned that usually the children of the hard-to-employ are themselves handicapped in the labor market. This helps to explain why both President Kennedy and President Johnson, in their Manpower Reports, singled out for special attention many more problems resulting from the difficulties which the uneducated, the unskilled, and the poor face in getting and holding jobs than those involving the development and utilization of scientists, engineers, and other critically important categories of professional and technical manpower.

There is an imbalance in the agenda that comprises this book. Although issues involved in the conservation of talent have not been ignored, they have been muted. Most of the chapters are concerned with evaluating the forces operating to turn our productive system into an economy of skill and the problems and difficulties that this transformation has brought in its wake. Since no book, especially one dealing with a subject as broad as manpower, can hope to deal with every facet of its theme, selection is inevitable. The emphasis in this book reflects the concerns that loom large in the public arena.

In the marketplace, one man is not the equal of another. A man with a million dollars to spend is very much more influential than the man with only one dollar. But in a democracy there is a rough equality among men in the political arena, and the politician is sensitive to the needs of the public.

The American people have supported a great many new and

radical efforts to improve the opportunities of children and adults to develop and utilize their potentials. This is a new dimension of our political democracy. The chapters which follow seek to provide perspective on these efforts and to suggest how far we have come and how far we still have to go.

Part One PERSPECTIVES

To understand the responses of American democracy to pressing problems of the day some order of perspective is required. We mut know how the problems arose and why the public selected particular approaches to solve them.

In Part One, the first essay attempts to provide an overview of the slow evolution of manpower policy since the founding of the Republic. This is followed by two essays on the dynamism of technology and its impact on contemporary manpower, from the viewpoints of both employment and skill. We then present considerations of the larger parameters in American society that both contain and shape developments on the manpower front.

In each of these five chapters care is taken to differentiate what actually has happened from what we believe has happened. Manpower is a new field of inquiry, and our misconceptions are likely to be many.

Chapter One The Evolution of Manpower Policy

This chapter will provide historical perspective on the emergence of the nation's manpower policy; it will call attention to the recent challenges that have necessitated new policies; and it will identify certain pressing and unresolved manpower issues. A manpower revolution is under way and it is still gathering momentum.

In this country we have long looked to the marketplace to bring about an equilibrium, an adjustment, between people who want to work and those who hire others to do their work. The marketplace has been the mechanism which has established a balance between the demand for manpower and the supply of manpower.

We relied on a freely operating market longer than any other nation. Moreover, our market was not confined to the continental limits of the United States; it included Western Europe and, at one time, even the Orient. We permitted people of foreign lands to come to this country whenever they thought they could better themselves. And our manpower policy was predicated on this policy of permitting free immigration.

However, immigration was not entirely free. In the second year of this country's independence, Congress passed an act which prohibited the immigration of Negroes, that is, free Negroes. And in the decades following the Civil War we put a stop to the immigration of Orientals.

In addition, some of the Northern states, carved out of the Northwest Territory and of other areas north of the Mason-Dixon line, pursued settlement policies that frequently excluded free Negroes. In fact, there are communities in the Midwest today which continue on their books municipal ordinances which prohibit a Negro from spending the night within their confines.

We had, then, a free market and free immigration, but they applied to white people only. Our early manpower policy was closely linked to our racial policy. Slavery, of course, was a major manpower policy. But our racial policy went far beyond slavery—it excluded free Negroes and, later, Orientals; still later it was transformed into a racial-ethnic policy which discriminated against people not solely because of their color but also on the basis of their national origin.

Our educational policy has had a concomitant manpower dimension. In New England, we were committed early to the idea that all children should have access to free schooling. This commitment to public education became a part of our evolving manpower policy.

Once again we must note exceptions: The antebellum South expressly prohibited the education of slaves; neither the South nor the North paid much attention to the education of the free Negro; and it was not until after the Civil War that most Southern states faced up to the obligation to provide public education.

The extent to which the American commitment to free education was hedged is suggested by the remark of Dr. John Fischer, president of Columbia University's Teachers College, that the public schools have done well for two-thirds of the population. The validity of this assessment can be found in the stark results of the screening of manpower for military service in World War II.

Of the 18 million young American males between the ages of eighteen and thirty-seven who were screened for military service, 700,000 were rejected because they were totally illiterate; another 600,000 illiterates were taken into the armed services, primarily into the Army, and went through special training to achieve literacy. Another 700,000 servicemen were at the borderline of literacy; they could read the word "fire" but not "danger"; they could sign their names but could not write a letter. There were, then, approximately 2 million young men either totally or substantially illiterate in the year 1940, although our nation had been committed to free public education for generations. Nevertheless and despite these shortcomings, education has long been a cornerstone of our national manpower policy.

Another dimension of our national manpower policy has been the development of institutions concerned with the nurturing of talent and competence, a task that has been shared by philanthropy and state governments.

Responsibility for the education and training of professional personnel such as ministers and physicians was assumed originally by philanthropy which provided the funds for the establishment of our earliest colleges and universities. But before long governments of states, especially those without established wealth, found it desirable to enter the field of higher education.

The passage of the Morrill Act during the Civil War indicates that the American people early perceived the important links between a strong educational system, adequate manpower resources, and a thriving economy.

Another facet of our manpower policy has been our science policy, which dates back to the beginning of the country. Originally it was neither very broad nor very deep, but we did have a science policy. West Point was established not primarily for the training of military officers, but for the training of engineers and surveyors so that the opening of the West could be speeded. The Navy has long been involved in the study of navigational science. The first American Nobel Prize winner, Albert Michaelson, was an Annapolis graduate and worked for the U.S. Navy, although he was a professor at the University of Chicago when he received his award. The National Academy of Science dates from the Civil War. Since then it has played a role, albeit a modest one, in advising the Federal government. We have long had a science policy.

No modern country can exist without a military manpower policy, and we have had one since the Congress first authorized an Army of eight men. We resorted to the draft during the middle of the Civil War and again, after a false start, in World War I. The story of the last quarter century in the procurement of military manpower is familiar to all of us.

We have identified seven strands as the key elements in the nation's manpower policy:

The free market
Immigration
Racial policy
Basic education
Higher education
Science policy
Military manpower policy

Despite these seven elements, we cannot say that the American people were deliberately engaged in the design of a manpower policy during these 150 years of their history. This was not so. Rather, our manpower policy slowly emerged as the country began to respond to a series of challenges. To these we now turn.

We first established limitations on the inflow of immigrants when American trade unions, with employers' acquiescence, decided that our economy no longer needed hordes of unskilled laborers. Tremendous numbers of unskilled laborers had entered the United States between

1900 and 1910. This was the period of our largest immigration. During World War I we were able to expand our economy even though the large inflow had ceased. Although racial and nationalistic considerations entered into the development of a restrictive immigration policy, rising doubts that the economy could continue to absorb large numbers were at the heart of the new restrictions.

A second development was the Depression of 1929, which actually lasted until 1941. Despite all President Roosevelt's efforts, despite the experimentation and initiative of the New Deal, unemployment never dropped below 10 percent during the 1930s. The economy did improve after 1933, but, as a study of the long-term unemployed in New York in 1939 and 1940 revealed, conditions were still unpropitious at that time.[1] The New Deal did help to undermine, alter, and shift sole reliance for employment expansion from the free market to other mechanisms. Indicative of the difficulty of changing the established structure and ingrained attitudes was the unwillingness of the American Federation of Labor as late as 1932 to support unemployment insurance. The AFL held that the Federal government had no right to enter this arena. Yet the Depression wore down the opposition, and the country did succeed in establishing a social security program by the middle thirties.

The next facet is military manpower. The first peacetime conscription in the country's history was legislated in 1940. Men inducted into the Army at that time were to serve for only one year. In September, 1941, Congress agreed, by one vote in the House of Representatives, to extend this term of service. That is, three months before we entered World War II, Congress came within one vote of destroying our mobilization base.

Since 1940, except for about a year and a half from late 1946 to early 1948, we have had a Selective Service System in operation. During this period we had hoped to come to agreement with the Russians, but by 1948 we were confronted by the take-over in Czechoslovakia and the Berlin crisis.

The science policy of the United States underwent a metamorphosis during World War II. In the Roosevelt Museum at Hyde Park is a letter from Albert Einstein to President Roosevelt in which the great physicist warned about the danger of neglecting the military implications of the recent developments in nuclear physics. Einstein asked that the President invite some of his wealthy friends to a meeting at

[1] Eli Ginzberg and Associates, *The Unemployed*, Harper & Row, Publishers, Incorporated, New York, 1943.

the White House at which he, Einstein, would speak. He wanted them to contribute millions of dollars for research in nuclear weapons. Einstein was right to push the issue; he was wrong with regard to the sums required. We spent not $10 million on nuclear development, but over $2 billion.

World War II saw the burgeoning of a new and vital science policy. The National Institutes of Health, with the Cancer Institute in the lead, got under way in 1938, but significant Federal support for health dates from the post-World War II period. Today the Federal government spends about $1¼ billion annually on research on health and about $16 billion on all forms of research, development, and testing.

In 1946 Congress passed the Employment Act, thereby institutionalizing the reforms of the New Deal. Our experience during the 1930s permanently negated the theory that we could rely solely on the free market to keep the economy strong. The Employment Act, passed overwhelmingly by both houses, legislated that thenceforth it would be the responsibility of the Federal government to establish and maintain a high level of output and employment. It committed the Federal government to playing a major role in keeping the economy at a high level.

These five responses played an important part in the shaping of our manpower policy: a change in immigration laws, an underpinning of the free market through social security and other New Deal legislation, military manpower policy, science policy, and a new economic policy. The Depression and World War II were the two major challenges which elicited these new responses.

These earlier challenges were followed by some of more recent date. They will be reviewed chronologically.

First, racial policy. The Supreme Court's decision in the Brown case in 1954 reflected several recent developments: our new position in international affairs, the increasing urbanization of American society, and our growing sensitivity to the gap between our democratic commitment and our democratic performance. Mainly for these three reasons, we finally moved definitively to alter our racial policy.

When the Army was finally desegregated in 1950–1951, manpower considerations were the deciding factor. The Army, facing difficulties in finding individual replacements to send to General Ridgway in Korea, inquired whether he was concerned about their racial composition. The general indicated that he was not at all concerned; that he wanted and needed men who could fight. This led to the desegregation of the forward battalions. We had moved a little earlier to desegregate various training centers at home.

Until the combat units in Korea were desegregated, Negroes were not used at the front. The Army had learned that it could not develop satisfactory fighting units by using exclusively Negro troops; such units would lack the required range and depth of skill. But the consequence of using Negroes only in supporting units was that more white men would be injured and killed. When the conservatives in the military and the Congress finally understood this, it was easier to gain support for the policy of desegregation.

The current level of unemployment is down, not up. The unemployment record of recent years, however unsatisfactory in terms of our raised expectations, is better than it used to be. The difference is that in the past we did not count the many who were underemployed, particularly those on Southern farms. However, during and after World War II, many of these people moved to urban centers in the North and West where they frequently remained unemployed but where they were counted.

The economically disenfranchised, alienated poor, who were hidden as long as they stayed on the farm or in the mountains, are very visible in the central cities. And they become even more prominent when they riot or threaten to riot. Much of the new legislation in favor of Negroes and poor whites is aimed at keeping this new threat in check.

In 1958 we made a second major commitment of Federal support for education. The first had been the Morrill Act during the Civil War. The second was the National Defense Education Act in response to sputnik. When we realized that the supposedly backward Russians had bettered us in the space race, we rushed to remedy our shortcomings in engineering, mathematics, foreign languages, and other fields associated with national security. We acted under a Republican President who basically did not want to move in this way. He believed that the Federal government should stay out of education, but he was propelled by events to move into this new and untried arena.

In 1961 we passed the Area Redevelopment Act, which was another new commitment for the United States. For several years the Democratic majority, with Senator Paul H. Douglas in the lead, and President Eisenhower had sparred over such bills; and none was ever approved during that period. However, one was finally passed under President Kennedy.

After four years of experimentation in which relatively modest sums were spent in a great many depressed areas, the ARA came to an end. But several new pieces of legislation were enacted which sought to make a more effective attack on the problem of declining and stagnant economic areas and regions. These acts have attempted to enable unemployed persons to find jobs in the vicinity of their homes; however, no decision has yet been made to pursue this policy whole-heartedly. So far, the longtime adjustment between the supply and the demand for labor has been effected by the movement of people from areas where jobs are scarce to where they are plentiful. It remains to be seen whether we can change this long-established and reasonably successful approach to one that has much to commend it if it can be implemented bringing work to the unemployed.

In 1962, Congress passed the Manpower Development and Training Act to provide training and retraining for unemployed and underem-ployed persons. We shall soon have spent almost $1 billion under this act to train and retrain the unemployed. Over 700,000 persons have been or are in the process of being trained or retrained. The placement record is commendable. This experience will be valuable in the years to come as the nation accelerates its training efforts.

An important part of the act relates not to training per se, impor-tant as it is, but to its Title I, which introduced a new dimension to Federal manpower policy. Before the act was passed, the President, according to the Constitution, had to submit an annual State of the Union message and under law he had to submit an annual budget and an annual Economic Report. Now, under Title I of the Manpower Development and Training Act, he must submit a fourth document— a Manpower Report—in which he reports on the resources, require-ments, training, and utilization of the nation's manpower. Congress, aware of major changes in our economy and society, now looks upon manpower as a major national resource that requires annual appraisal by the executive as a prelude to continuing legislative action.

The next important change occurred on the educational front. It involves Federal support for vocational, general, and higher educa-tion. The last seven years have seen a tremendous burgeoning of gov-ernmental action in these three areas, the most spectacular being the long-delayed breakthrough in 1965 in Federal support for elementary and secondary education. American history is replete with the efforts made by Republican Presidents, starting with Garfield and continu-ing through Harrison, to pass a Federal bill to aid education. The Republicans, understanding the Civil War legacy of millions of illiter-ate and impoverished Negroes, appreciated the need for major Federal intervention. They came close to getting such a bill passed, but it foundered repeatedly on the two obstacles that have plagued every Congress and President up to the present. It foundered on the opposition of the Catholics, who were interested in developing a parochial school system with, they hoped, governmental support. And it foundered on the opposition of the Southern states which believed that Federal monies would reestablish Federal control in the South. For eighty years this coalition remained intact, even though it early became clear that public monies would not go to parochial schools and that the Federal government would not reoccupy the South.

The primary reason that we finally have monies flowing into education from the Federal government (they are now at a level of almost $6 billion a year, up from less than $500 million as recently as six years ago) is that the country has come to understand that employability depends increasingly on an educational base. When the Manpower Redevelopment and Training Act of 1962 was passed, this was not fully appreciated. But within one year amendments were passed which took cognizance of the fact that many people cannot be taught a skill because they are illiterate; they cannot read simple instructions or do simple sums. The amendments enabled the unemployed to undertake basic education prior to or in conjunction with their training for a skill. The reforms in vocational education are also directed specifically at improving the employability of many young people and adults who cannot profit from academic studies.

The poverty program is a further illustration of the growing awareness and increasing concern of the American public that too many people are living on public asistance or living in misery without public assistance. San Francisco, for example, is certainly not the most depressed city in the United States, but there are Negroes in San Francisco whose families have been on relief for three generations. Some are the grandchildren of migrants who came into San Francisco from Mississippi, Alabama, and Louisiana at the beginning of World War II and who got jobs, good jobs, in the shipyards. Many of the migrants had been illiterate farmhands. The shipyards closed down in 1945. San Francisco has very little general manufacturing which could use such unskilled and semiskilled labor. These former shipyard workers were unable to fit themselves into the white-collar employment sector. They went on relief. They brought up their children on relief, and there is now a third generation growing up on relief. The riots at Hunters Point in 1966 brought this festering sore to the public's attention.

Congress became concerned before rioting broke out in the urban areas. The poverty program, which was started modestly in 1964, has been expanded to its present (1966) level of about $2 billion.

The most exciting facet of the many different approaches undertaken by the Office of Economic Opportunity is the Community Action Program, which has sought to make a place for the poor in directing the efforts to alleviate their own plight. That this approach has found difficulties is not as surprising as its success in many areas. The Office of Economic Opportunity has experimented along a great many different axes, from Operation Head Start to programs aimed at involving older persons in providing assistance to other older persons who need specialized services. While it has had considerable funds at its disposal, they have been far from sufficient to meet the very many needs of those who live in poverty. Moreover, insufficient time has passed to design, implement, and evaluate many of these new efforts. The answers still lie in the future.

To recapitulate, the first challenge to which the nation has responded recently has been the challenge of the Negro. Many Americans believe that anti-Negro policy and slavery was a matter which involved the South alone. In point of fact the first colony which enacted legislation on slavery was not Virginia but the Commonwealth of Massachusetts in 1639. Since political power had been in the North and West from the very beginnings of our country, and was underwritten by the victory of the North in the Civil War, the North and the West together could always make their opinions prevail. However, the point is that the Civil War aside, which was fought over the integrity of the Union and the control of the West, they did not hold views with respect to the Negro that were at marked variance with those of the South. When Lincoln issued the Emancipation Proclamation, he indicated that it was an emergency war measure and did not free the slaves. His adopted state of Illinois denounced him through its Legislature, stating that he had committed one of the most dastardly acts in the history of mankind!

The economy has been performing very well since 1940, and this performance has prevented the emergence of major manpower problems. Yet the very technology which has been responsible for much of our gains has also brought some troubles. Briefly: We have a continuing surplus of people on the farms; it has been reliably estimated that we need only about 3 million persons rather than the 5 million who are still attached to the farm labor force. Next, recent technological advances help to explain the slow growth of employment in manufacturing, which in turn has made it more difficult for many noncollege youths to find a satisfactory opening into the world of work. And the failure of technology to advance in many of the service fields probably is responsible for the presence of so many low-paying jobs, the holders of which have such poor career prospects.

A third challenge is that presented by the in-migrants to the large cities. Reference was made to San Francisco; Los Angeles is another example. In New York City three-quarters of the white population are native-born New Yorkers, in the case of Negroes less than half are— the rest are in-migrants. These people carry into the cities the consequences of the deprived circumstances of their youth, which in most instances they spent in the rural and urban South. Each of the metropolitan areas in the North that has attracted large numbers of in-migrants faces tremendous difficulties. Chicago is potentially the most explosive city in the United States; two-thirds of a million Negroes are concentrated in two very constricted ghettos. The President, in an unusual statement for a Chief Executive, has warned that there may be more explosions such as occurred in Watts.

The fourth challenge relates to the expansion of educational and training opportunities. We are moving slowly to improve the educational, training, and retraining opportunities available to young people and to adults. But if we contrast the opportunities provided by the poorer states in the Deep South with those available in the more affluent states of the North and West, we are struck by the very wide differentials. A rough measure of the differential in opportunities is about 100 percent after allowing for the fact that the price level on some items is lower in the South than elsewhere. If particular subgroups are compared—if we compare, for example, Negro children— the differential might be nearly 300 to 500 percent!

Of course, the North has its own problems. The flight of the white middle class to the suburbs has had the effect of undermining the opportunities of the poor, the in-migrants, the people who most need help. The flight has helped to erode the tax base at the same time that the city must provide more services. It is questionable whether New York or any other large city will be able to extract itself from its present predicament unless new relationships can be established among various governmental levels. Unless the Federal and state governments and suburban areas carry more of the financial load, the central city is likely to lose its vitality and become the depressed area of tomorrow. No city can continue to provide an environment of economic opportunity during the day if the wealthier people disappear to the suburbs at night and pay their taxes there.

The fifth challenge comes from the poverty front. We know we need more money. Two billion dollars—the current spending level of the poverty program—can provide only modest services for a maximum of 3 million to 4 million people. Current government estimates suggest that at least 30 million people need help. But it is not solely a question of money. Only through considered action are we likely to learn more about the dynamics of poverty and what is required on the psychological and sociological fronts to institute effective remedial efforts.

This brief review of five contemporary challenges—the Negro, technology, metropolitanism, education and training, and poverty—has helped to illuminate both our strengths and weaknesses as we have sought to fashion a manpower policy more responsive to the times. On each front we have made some progress, but a great deal remains to be done. Among our greatest shortcomings is our failure to assure that every young person who comes of working age is prepared to work and able to work effectively and that jobs are available for all adults who are able and willing to work, even if they are not well endowed physically, emotionally, intellectually.

Five conclusions can be distilled from the foregoing analysis:

1. In consonance with our national tradition, heritage, and style, we have operated pragmatically with respect to manpower policy. We have encountered problems and we have responded to them one at a time. Somehow this approach has generally worked out well, although periodically we have found it necessary to stop and put the pieces together.

2. While we have responded primarily to real challenges—unemployment, defense, race, and poverty—there has been a dynamic factor in the equation. The expectations of the public have kept changing. During the Depression of the 1930s we accepted the fact that the unemployed were selling apples at the street corner to earn a pittance. Today we no longer consider this a civilized or even an efficient way to cope with unemployment. We no longer tolerate a 7 percent unemployment rate, a rate which did not concern us only a few years ago. In a dynamic democracy, standards change. We are responding not only to the challenge of reality but also to our changing expectations.

3. Although this analysis has focused primarily on the actions of the Federal government since we are considering the evolution of national manpower policy, in a democracy manpower policy always involves the individual and the family from which he comes, the employer, the trade union, and many other institutions. A comprehensive analysis must make room for them.

4. Our economic system is called capitalism. It got its name from the fact that capital was the scarce resource. Capital is still a scarce resource, but in the future human resources may be the strategic factor which will determine both our security and our economic progress.

5. This much is clear: No democracy can look to its future with equanimity unless it provides opportunities for all of its people to develop their potentialities and to utilize them.

Chapter Two Dimensions of Technology

The economists used to make the problem of technology simple; they used to stipulate that technology was a stable factor. The only way they could analyze the economy was to eliminate technology from their model; they undertook analysis solely in terms of market mechanisms. They realized that if they took account of technological changes, their whole system would become very complicated. Consequently, they swiftly assumed that technology remains stable. There was quite a gap between academic economics and the real world!

There were, however, a few economists who understood that it was not sensible to study economics under such an assumption, and they put technology into the middle of their considerations. Thorstein Veblen was one of these economists. He argued that a real understanding of the economy can be had only through an analysis of technology. He even pushed this a step further back—to developments in science and advances in knowledge. He believed that the basic capital of a society is in the accumulation of knowledge from which technology itself is derived and on which the economy rests. He also made some interesting reflections about private property. He said that all scientific knowledge, the real basis of all wealth, is public property. Technology, he said, represents a private expropriation of property in the public domain.

Just as there is a doctrine of theological eschatology, so there is a group of eschatological technologists. In the 1930s, they were called technocrats. They had a picture of the world in which everything was going to be different because of technology. The more extreme variant of the present cybernetics group is closely related to these eschatologists of an earlier day. They are certain that the world will soon be very unsettled by the tremendously rapid and fundamental changes in technology that are taking place.

The technocrats and the cyberneticists have been vigorously attacked by many professional economists. These critics say that technology is the mainstay of economic growth and prosperity and higher per capita income. The recent report of the National Commission on Technology, which in addition to professional economists had employers, labor leaders, and public members, came out on the side of the optimists. They concluded that while technological changes frequently have brought difficulties in their wake for particular groups of workers, industries, or regions, on balance technology is a boon. Moreover, the difficulties and disturbances should not be exaggerated. In a world still grossly deficient in output, all people need and want the additional output that technology makes possible.

To argue that technology can be ignored because it is relatively unimportant is foolish. To argue that currently technology is operating in a manner uniquely different from the way it has operated in the past and that historical evidence can be therefore disregarded is also foolish.

The following evidence cannot be brushed aside as unimportant. All of this nation's food is grown by less than 6 percent of the labor force. The prospects of growing most of our food in the future in test tubes is no longer science fiction. The impact of technology on agriculture is beyond dispute.

One who has seen the open-pit mining in the West, in which large machines slice sections off mountains, or has seen the oil wells in the Gulf of Mexico pumping hour after hour without a single man in attendance, will not be inclined to question the impact of technology on the extractive industries.

Manufacturing is a less clear case, but not for the informed observer who is acquainted with automated steel mills or automated engine plants. Wherever large amounts of standardized output are required, the new machines perform wonders. But only part of the manufacturing sector is involved in standardized output. At the opposite extreme is the manufacture of such items as women's dresses in the high-price range, where each garment must be unique. Here the potential of automation is much more limited.

The services also provide a mixed picture. Despite the enthusiasm of many for what the computer can do to revolutionize medical practice by making diagnoses better and faster and the enthusiasm of others for the role of the teaching machine in the reform of education, it is likely that neither medicine nor education will in fact be significantly mechanized. But other services are already far down the road: banking, insurance, telecommunications.

What do the data on employment reveal? First, that total employment in the goods-producing sector of the economy has been substantially static over the past thirty-five years, and secondly, that there has been a pronounced upward drift in the occupational structure from blue-collar to white-collar work. Both these trends may still be reversed, but only if the major forces operating during the past few decades are altered.

If the past is a clue to the future, it appears reasonably clear that agriculture, mining, and manufacturing will not absorb the large numbers of new workers who will soon be entering the labor force. We shall be fortunate if these sectors are able to maintain their relative positions. It is likely that they will not. Therefore, the whole task of absorbing the additions to the labor force will be placed on the services. Since the services consist of such a hodgepodge—from shoe repair to Telstar—we can expect labor-saving devices to be used wherever large amounts of capital can be profitably absorbed, such as in communications and routine record keeping; we should not anticipate much change, at least in the short run, in the labor/capital ratios in such fields as education, medicine, and recreation. In these fields, the pattern of work involves one person doing something to or for another individual or a group of individuals. The individual worker plays a crucial role, and even with technology to help him, his reach is relatively limited. With the most modern techniques and the best organization, a nurse can take care of only a limited number of patients.

It is easy to be impressed and overwhelmed by exposure to a completely automated garage in which your car is returned to you in six seconds. One man can operate a 300-car establishment. He need not even speak English. Moreover, all the accounting is done automatically.

However, the cautious economists are correct in warning against generalizing from any one or a number of startling examples. The weight of the evidence is still greatly against widespread replacement in many service fields of men by machines.

We have seen the machine reduce employment opportunities absolutely and relatively in every sector of the economy except the services. And the new technology is pressing strongly against some of the services. We may not run into serious problems in the near future but we cannot use history to shore up our confidence. The record of the past should put us on guard.

Related to technology, but worthy of separate consideration, is the heavy investment this nation is making in research and development; currently, it is in excess of $20 billion annually. This is a new phenomenon that is largely the outgrowth of our experience in World

War II and the cold war that followed. One reading minimizes its significance. But James E. Webb, the head of the National Aeronautics and Space Administration (NASA), reads it differently. He believes that the annual $5 billion expenditures on space programs are having an important spillover for industry. There are two ways to assess what this development means for the economy.

One way is to look for short-run results. It is hard to believe that Mr. Webb could have had these in mind, for they are very hard to find. But there is a second approach—one that focuses on long-run consequences. With this lengthened perspective one does indeed find that many critically important advances in air travel, electronics, nuclear power, and medicine are unquestionably spillovers from military research and development efforts of an earlier day.

In 1965 Congress passed a "sleeper bill"—that is how the President referred to it—which established a technical assistance program for small industries so that they might enjoy the benefits of scientific and technological advances. It may one day parallel the highly successful agricultural extension service.

Another interesting innovation is the effort, spearheaded by the state of California, to involve leading aerospace companies in using their advanced systems approaches to help solve urgent community problems, such as urban transportation, smog, and similar conundrums. Reference can also be made to the burgeoning interest of General Electric and some other large corporations in contributing to the planning of new cities on the outskirts of established centers.

Expanded research and development has brought about a greatly increased demand for scientific and technically trained manpower. Most of this manpower is paid by government funds even when it is employed by private companies. We are a defense economy. In 1958 President Eisenhower, in an effort to avoid requesting an increase in the debt ceiling, directed the Air Force to spend its R&D funds more slowly. Within sixty days, most of the presidents of the large universities with government contracts and most of the aerospace companies were in Washington, warning the government of their untenable position. They did not have sixty days' working capital to keep their research teams together. This emphasized how dependent this crucial sector of the economy is on governmental financing. The extent to which the economy has been transformed is indicated by the fact that two-thirds of all our scientists and development engineers are supported by dollars that do not come from profits and are not directly related to making profits.

One important manpower consequence of the rapid growth of expenditures for science and technology is the extent to which the skills of many trained people become obsolescent. Much human capital is destroyed. Another important manpower consequence is the liquidation of a large number of unskilled and semiskilled jobs—work that machines can do better and cheaper.

While these two manpower implications of the new trends in R&D are not to be minimized or downgraded, it is not necessary to agree with Hannah Arendt, who contends that fewer and fewer people are playing a role of any importance either in the economy or the larger society. But then, the mass of mankind never played important decision-making roles. The peasants worked in the fields and the laborers tended the machines in the factories. They never wanted to play critical roles; they were not trained to play such roles, and they were not frustrated because they failed to play such roles. Today, however, the average young person enters the labor force with about thirteen years of formal education in back of him. He hopes to have some modest influence on the outcome of affairs, if only through his trade union or the ballot box.

One way to look at the problem of skill obsolescence is to consider the parent of a sick child. The parent would not want him to be treated by a Harvard Medical School graduate of 1945, even if he were the honor man in his class, if he had not added to his knowledge in the interim. It is interesting that physicians, who spend more time in school than any other group, were the first to recognize the dangers of their skills becoming obsolete and the need to take corrective action through further education and training.

The university presents further understanding of this problem. The university remits to its professors about half of their effective time so that they can stay intellectually alive. Many do not do so, but not because the university fails to provide the opportunity. Interestingly, American industry has little if any understanding of the rapid rate at which its trained manpower becomes obsolescent because it does not have the opportunity to replenish its store of knowledge.

In a large corporation such as Du Pont, a man can move from the laboratory to sales or manufacturing; but it is questionable how many would make such a move if they had the option to remain alive and productive in their scientific work.

While it is not necessary, or even essential, for everybody to remain in the field within which he was trained, it is highly doubtful whether any society, even one as affluent as ours, can justify the erosion that takes place among its trained manpower because of a failure to offer opportunities to remain intellectually virile and alive.

Another way to assess the impact of technology on the economy is to focus on regional development. We see that valuable new resources become available as a consequence of new technology—such as the ability of the lumber industry to use the scrub pine of the South. We also see the opposite: We see that nuclear power has put coal on the defensive. However, there are circular factors involved in technological change. Put on the defensive, the coal industry has done much to modernize itself, to cut costs, to keep and even expand its markets.

A final dimension of these broad extensions and impacts of a changing technology bears on the alterations that have taken place in the relationships between the profit sector, nonprofit institutions, and government. This has already been suggested by the large proportion of scientists and development engineers who are supported outside the profit sector. In former days, the dominant view of the economy was that of Herbert Hoover, who saw government as extracting hard-earned dollars from private employers, to be spent, not very usefully or economically, by a swollen bureaucracy of government officials. His was a simple bifurcation between the productive private sector and the wasteful public sector.

But his is no longer a satisfactory model, if it ever was, of the American economy. A more realistic model starts with three sectors—profit, nonprofit (the key nonprofit institutions are colleges and hospitals), and government. Government, in turn, has three parts—Federal, state, and local. The operations of the economy depend on a great many circular relationships among these several sectors. For example, business gets its trained manpower largely from governmental and nonprofit institutions. It does not assume responsibility for the education of its managers. The great chemical, petroleum, electrical manufacturing industries are dependent on the university. The industries select people only after they have been educated and trained in college and graduate school. The basic technology on which they depend is likewise heavily based on advances in science, which are largely made in the universities, and on development, which is increasingly determined by the flow of government dollars.

So the old—and still widely accepted—theory that the dynamism of our economy is located in one single sector is not borne out by the facts. We think of our most dynamic industry, the automotive industry, as the quintessence of private enterprise. But this industry is completely dependent on public highways, an exclusively governmental domain. If the story of the automotive industry is written correctly, much of the credit will go to those executives who succeeded in developing broad public support at state and Federal levels for colossal highway programs. This was the *sine qua non* for the rapid development of their industry.

While the economists and other academicians have been slow to recognize the new circularity in the American economy, many practical people, even conservative ones, understand the new situation. For instance, the state legislature of Kansas recently sponsored an economic survey which resulted in a report recommending that the state establish some professorships at the State University at $25,000 per chair. Now, no civil servant in Kansas earns that much, not even the governor! But the report argued that it was essential to attract technological concerns if the state were to prosper and that this first required the shoring up of the university. When the conservative legislators of Kansas see the interrelationships among universities, technological industries, and general economic growth and development, we can conclude that the new model is fast gaining acceptance.

Now that we have delineated these broad perspectives on technology, what can be said about the future role of work in our society? A first point is the major shift that is under way from brawn to brains. Immigrants used to get off the boats from Europe, and, though they did not know a word of English and had never been in a factory, they could get a job immediately. Recruiting was literally done on the docks of New York City! Many newcomers were hired on the spot and told to report to work the next day. If a man looked healthy and strong, an employer needed to know no more about him.

Today, relatively few jobs depend on muscle. Rene DuBois made an important point about adaptation when he pointed out that for fighter pilots in World War II eyesight was of critical importance. One had to have eyes in the back of his head! But in the new planes, operated by electronic controls on the instrument panel, a certain amount of astigmatism is helpful!

Advanced technology has contributed to larger and more complex corporate structures. If technology has had a major effect on changing skill requirements at many levels of the organization, it has also intensified pressures at the top. Those at the top confront one decision after another, decisions that have such compelling importance to the organization that they must be made at the top. Key decisions must constantly be made about new investments, new products, about the shape of the R&D program, about locating plants. These decision cannot be decentralized. But once they have been made, the rest of the decisions come much easier. In fact, those of a more routine nature are being taken over by machines. If this development continues, and there is no reason for it to stop, increasing numbers in middle management—those who used to worry about inventory controls, those who used to be concerned about sales data, and others in similar positions—are likely to fade away.

The fact that power tends to flow to the top means that the big rewards are reserved for those who hold key positions. As long as a man looks forward to achieving one of these preferred posts he is likely to work very hard. But many learn, some soon and some later, that they are out of the race. Hence the few up front, or those gaining on the leaders, will be very busy, while most of the others are not likely to put forth any special effort.

The next question relates to the increasing professionalization of the work force and the problems that this raises. Most companies with large research and development programs still operate their laboratories on the same principles that they followed so successfully in manufacturing. That is, the research scientist is expected literally or figuratively to punch a clock and to stay put in the laboratory from nine to five. The laboratory, like the plant, is closed on Saturday and Sunday. These firms treat their scientific and technical personnel in the same way they treat workers on the assembly line. Management can insist that the research staff come in from nine to five, but unless it can assess their productivity other than by the clock, it is not likely to control their output.

The more the economy becomes dependent on educated and trained manpower, the more important the question of appropriate standards becomes. Continued reliance on simple quantitative measures is likely to result in gross errors. To illustrate: We think of a person as a high school or college man. But this gross distinction leaves much to be desired.

Students who graduate from the best high schools—private or public —actually know more than graduates of the lower half of the colleges of this country, which boasts 1,800 institutions of higher learning. For instance, a graduate of the Bronx High School of Science in New York or Phillips Exeter Academy knows more English, mathematics, and history, can write better, and can think better than many college graduates.

The growing importance of quality as a measure of performance is associated not only with the growth of professionalism but also with the pronounced shift of the economy toward services, which today provide employment for 2 out of every 3 workers Therefore, the challenge to develop more effective criteria is increasingly urgent. We talk about hospitals, but the difference between a poor hospital and a good hospital may well be the difference between life and death. We have professors, even at the same university, whose contributions, however they are measured, bear no resemblance to each other. One man is an important research investigator and inspiring teacher; another has contributed very little and what he teaches has little value. But both are professors and may even receive identical salaries!

We see then that an advanced technological economy confronts the question of how to measure and evaluate the quality as well as the quantity of the services that are being produced. Most international comparisons of economic performance are meaningless unless one can take into account these qualitative aspects of output. It is easy to add up bushels of wheat, tons of coal, barrels of petroleum; but how does one compare the quality of housing, of education, or of health services?

The growth of knowledge and technology reflected in increasing specialization has had an interesting impact on the way in which young people get prepared for work and life. To take an extreme case: Several years ago a study was made of the members of the American Psychoanalytic Association to discover the age at which they had completed all their formal training and were fully qualified to practice. The results were unbelievable. The norm, which included time out for war service, came to 40.5 years. No wonder that analysts charge high fees!

While we can acknowledge the need for training in depth, it is not difficult to see that the system is very much awry when a man must stay in school or training for over thirty-four years, which leaves him less than twenty-five years for his working life. Many scientists have finished their productive work before these analysts have begun to work on their own!

If, as appears desirable, men should start their careers earlier, then a correlative problem arises. Who will be responsible for their continuing education and training? Unless provision is made for them to stay alive, intellectually and professionally, there are clear dangers in the path of contracting and shortening their initial preparation.

Another aspect of the trend to professionalization should be noted. American business now employs large numbers of college- and university-trained personnel who have real commitments to their disciplines —chemists, physicists, engineers, economists, even a few sociologists, anthropologists, mathematicians, and others. The basic assumption of American corporate life is that an employee should be faithful to his employer. In turn, the employer has certain responsibilities to his employees. The matter is more complicated in the case of professionals. One comes up against the problem of double allegiance. The better the professional, the deeper his allegiance to his profession. We have not begun to grapple with the host of complex problems that are inherent when business hires more and more university-trained men who have been brought up to be sensitive to the demands of their discipline long before they enter into an employment relationship.

Another interesting development on the work front is the extent to which many skills that the individual possesses are limited to a specific environment. A former Assistant Secretary of Labor remarked that he felt very secure because he could always earn his livelihood. If he lost his job, he had his kit of tools: He could go out and make a living. A phenomenon of corporate life is the specialized skill that men acquire from operating in a particular organization—a skill which is not necessarily transferable to another environment. A man gains understanding in the depth of personalities, the distribution of power, the way in which the work is carried on in that organization.

When a man has worked for a corporation for twenty years and has reached a markedly high level, it is nerve-racking for him to know that if he is let go, he will have relatively little to offer another employer. This is the vulnerability that many confront.

Another question is: What do these occupational and work trends imply for the trade-union movement and for the political structure of the country? The trade unions' strength was founded on blue-collar workers in manufacturing. The problem that they face today is that these occupational and industrial sectors are losing ground. And to date the trade-union movement has experienced difficulties in organizing white-collar workers. But it is too early to write off the expansion of the trade unions into the white-collar area. We may be in a transitional period, waiting for the old leaders, who have little or no sensitivity for or capacity to organize white-collar workers, to retire or die. But in the years ahead, considerable organization of white-collar workers appears likely. The outstanding potential, interestingly enough, is in the governmental sector.

The Federal government has passed rules and regulations permitting its employees to organize, as have a considerable number of states and cities. It should be recalled that government, in total, has approximately 7 million civilian workers—a large pool of potential union members.

Whether the white-collar workers will join unions in large numbers will depend on whether they believe that they can do better for themselves through collective bargaining than through individual negotiation. As more people go into white-collar work, and as there is less mobility for individuals at the lower levels, the more likely it is that they will turn to unions.

The fact that so many white-collar workers are women—in fact, women who work part time—makes the problem more difficult. And American industry is often smart enough to offer the unorganized a little bit more than the organized. But even in the face of substantial difficulties, it is likely that white-collar unionism will grow.

The question of retirement should be considered in light of recent technological trends. Since rapid advances in knowledge, science, and technology lead to skill obsolescence, one must anticipate increasing pressure from corporate management for earlier retirement. While there may be a few older people who have special value to their employer, management's preference is for younger people. It can gain by trading off high-earning people—there is a connection between earnings and age—for youngsters who have been exposed to new knowledge and trained in new techniques. This suggests that there will be more and more pressure to retire older people earlier.

Many men, apparently responding to this threat, are beginning to make changes under their own momentum. Several foundations and universities have begun to explore the problems connected with changes in mid-career.

This phenomenon of early retirement from one's principal employment, though not from the labor market, should be juxtaposed to what has been said about the pluralistic economy. It is likely that the next years will see greatly enhanced mobility among the three sectors: from business to nonprofit, from nonprofit to government, from government and nonprofit to business. There are many members of university faculties who at fifty-five have little to offer students at home but who could make a contribution abroad. This applies also to business executives and government officials. Moreover, if they make the change in time, they are likely to be stimulated by new exposures and experiences.

The term "manpower" includes of course womanpower. Hence, some consideration must be given to developments on that front. We are in the middle of a major revolution in womanpower. Half of all the women in the United States aged forty-five to fifty-five are at work. As recently as World War II, the only married women who worked were Negro women, impecunious widows, and women without children. From a tradition that held "Women should stay at home," we turned things completely around during World War II with the slogan "It's your patriotic duty to come to work." Many observers were naïve enough to assume women would return to the home once the war was over. Of course, they didn't.

Many women live a long time; women know this. Hence, many of them work in order to qualify for Social Security benefits. This is just one of the many reasons why they work, but it is an important reason. The next decade will probably not be as favorable for women who seek employment as the last decade. Although women currently account for only one-third of the labor force, more women than men have of late gotten jobs. This reflects an unusual demographic development (the low birth rate of the 1930s) and the facts that more men have gone on for additional education and others have had to serve in the military. In the coming decade, there will be many more young men competing for jobs. As more married women work, employers will be faced with a new problem. In seeking to hire or move a man they may have to consider also what they can do for his wife. We have long recognized that the family is the key unit with respect to consumption. It may soon develop, especially among the better educated, that family considerations will loom large in matters of employment. The military, the universities, and certain other employers are already aware of this fact. Columbia University lost its distinguished president of Barnard College because her new husband was berthed on the West Coast and no comparable academic assignment was available to him in the New York City area.

An important generalization recently substantiated again by our study in depth—*Life Styles of Educated Women* [1]—is that the more education a woman has, the more likely it is, other things being equal, that she will be working or will soon return to work. With ever more women acquiring higher education, the likelihood is strong that more and more of them will in the future be closely tied to the world of work.

This analysis of the several dimensions of technology and its extensions can be brought to a close with a brief consideration of the im-

[1] Eli Ginzberg and Associates, Columbia University Press, New York, 1966.

pact of recent changes and of changes that are likely to come on certain basic value constellations.

New technology offers a society several options. It can maintain its output of conventional goods and do some new things, such as going to the moon. Or it can expand its output of conventional goods and provide three cars per family. Or it can opt for more leisure. There is nothing preordained about the allocation: new goods, more old goods, more leisure, or any combination thereof.

Historically, the United States used about 40 percent of its increased productivity in the form of shortening its hours of work. The gains of technology were divided: three-fifths went to more goods; two-fifths to more leisure.

Since World War II, while we have cut the total amount of time that a man works during the course of a year, mostly through longer vacations, the conventional hours of work per week have been only modestly reduced. The unions have been more interested in overtime pay than in leisure. But it is likely that if unemployment should again begin to mount, the unions will change tack and the average hours of work will begin to decline anew.

If that happens, male workers will not necessarily be the ones who gain the most. A shorter workweek will make it easier for many married women to combine home and job, and more will be drawn into the labor market. Several astute Catholic observers of the problem, desirous of keeping married women at home, have shown little enthusiasm for a reduction in the normal workweek.

In the past, we thought about jobs and income as being very closely related. Economic growth was characterized by more jobs and more income. While these relationships between jobs and incomes still exist, they are being loosened.

The ties among growth in output, income, and employment are not as close as they used to be. Some critics believe that technology has solved the problem of output and that the government should send everybody who does not have an adequate income a check to ensure that he can be an effective consumer. Others, while they do not believe that the production problem has been solved, do think that it is a good idea to send poor people checks, the amounts to be determined by a negative income tax. They believe that this is a more efficient way of dealing with the problem of relief than by conventional welfare programs.

If it were solely a matter of ensuring that poor people have enough money to keep their families alive and intact, there is much to be said in favor of one or another scheme which results in the government's sending checks to those in need. But although a man cannot live without consuming, he is not really alive if he is only a consumer. A man requires a more positive and meaningful relation to the society of which he is part. He cannot have this through a government handout. He needs the opportunity to work and to support himself and his dependents. If the problem of work is solved, the problems of income will largely take care of themselves. But if the problem of income only is solved, the work problem remains.

Philosophers worry a great deal about what people will do with their increased leisure. But these worries may be unnecessary. Why should not every man, not only those with wealth, have the opportunity to live two lives—one on the job, one off the job? Most ordinary people have strong interests—interests centered around their home, their church, politics, sports, fishing. They find no difficulty filling their hours. The fear that the "lower classes" will not know what to do with their free time must be reconciled with the ever higher levels of education of the American public. Unless our major efforts on the educational front are a failure, they should go far to help solve the leisure problem, if there is a problem.

An interesting aspect of broadened options is the case of married women. We used to talk about the home-or-job dilemma, or about the constraints under which the educated woman lives because she has to cope with so many routine tasks at home. But the reality is quite different. More and more married women do not face such sharp alternatives, nor are they hemmed in by constraints. Instead, they confront multiple options. They can work full time or part time, they can work for a time and then withdraw from the job market and return later on, or they can stay at home for a number of years and then begin to work. There are other patterns that may suit them even better. A rich society is a society which offers its members multiple options.

Similarly, a rich society offers opportunities to all. We talk a great deal about education, and we say that we are committed to education. But we tolerate very large differentials in expenditures for education between poor and rich children. If we were really serious about our democratic commitment to equality of opportunity, we would have to narrow substantially the differentials which now exist. The issue is not a minor one, since education has become the open sesame to better jobs and a better life. Governor Nelson A. Rockefeller of New York has commented on the fact that he is the grandson of two high school dropouts. But he was quick to add that he would not recommend that young people follow in the path of his illustrious forebears.

The issue is simple. While few if any of the great captains of industry of yesterday were high school graduates, and even fewer were college graduates, the restructuring of our society has vastly constricted the opportunities for the unschooled man to make his way up the income ladder. A few do, but only a few.

On the Negro issue, we must note that for 350 years our democracy has been for whites only. We were committed to keeping the Negro on the periphery of American society. Every President of the United States from Washington to Taft wanted to send the Negroes home to Africa; Lincoln was no exception. They saw no possibility of absorbing the Negro minority in white America.

Slavery was initially instituted as a system of social control, only secondarily a system of economic exploitation. It was inconceivable to the early colonists that these strange, un-Christian, illiterate people could be absorbed. There was no place in America for the free Negro. Even today we are still busily erecting barriers between the white majority and the Negro minority.

Currently, the whites are in flight to the suburbs and exurbia, anywhere to escape the Negro. But slowly more and more people are beginning to recognize that escape is no answer and that we must learn to live together.

A basic question that has not been considered is who should pay the cost of technological change. If workers are going to lose their skills and lose their income and lose their seniority, they clearly have a claim for compensation. It is inconceivable that a rich society would permit all or even most of the costs of technological change to be borne by those least able to carry them. The fact that we have experienced so many difficult strikes, many of which grow out of adjustment to technological changes, underlines how far we still have to go before we find effective solutions.

We have seen that technology has impinged on a great many different fronts. We have sought to assess some of these impacts. Many are still to be revealed. But one conclusion stands out: A flexible society can accommodate to the changes that technology brings in its wake if it holds fast to the fundamental principle that old institutions must be modified if the new is to be successfully encapsulated. Moreover, there is no certainty that change will prove beneficial. This depends on whether intelligence and courage prevail so that old institutions will become more responsive to the needs of the citizenry. In that event, technology will be a boon, not a bane.

Chapter Three

The Economic Consequences
of Automation

N
o one who has even a fleeting acquaintance with the volumi-
nous and ever-growing literature on automation will contest
the assertion that this is a subject about which we apparently
know relatively little, since so many experts hold diametrically opposed views. It would appear that the less we know about a subject,
the easier it is for experts to adopt strong positions.

But there are certain problems subsumed under the concept of automation—we use "automation" here as a synonym for "technological
change"—about which leaders in industry, labor, and politics must
make decisions with inadequate or even contradictory information.
Men of action cannot wait until all the evidence is in and has been
carefully sifted. If they wait, they lose the opportunity to affect the
shape of things to come.

The intellectual disorder characteristic of the literature and the inevitable pressure on men of affairs to adopt policies on automation
places a special responsibility on the scholar. He must contribute to
the clarification of the issues, knowing that in the world of action
leaders must choose among alternatives on the basis of the "weight of
the evidence." Leaders cannot stand by, immobilized, because scholars
have not reached a definitive assessment.

This reference to the relations between the academician and the
man of affairs indicates the framework within which this chapter will
be developed. It has a fourfold objective: to set out the special characteristics of the American experience which underlie the positive
stance of American society toward technological change; to review the
major interrelations between technological change and economic development; to call attention to some neglected or misunderstood relations between the two; and to point up some dimensions for policy.

Early in our history, visitors from abroad remarked on the pervasive
efforts of Americans to economize in the use of labor. Throughout
most of our history, we have been a country rich in land and natural
resources and poor in labor supply. Therefore, we have continued a

search for improved ways to economize in the use of human power.

Certain aspects of American experience reinforced this trend. The large distances between farms and the isolation of the frontier forced men to find solutions to their own problems. Because of the circumstances of pioneering, many Americans became gadgeteers—not because they had special gifts, but out of sheer necessity.

As our nation—a nation of immigrants—developed, the most recent arrivals were likely to serve in the least desirable jobs, those that demanded the hardest labor and paid the lowest wages. But the development of the American economy proceeded at such a rapid pace that even the most recent immigrants did not have to remain indefinitely at the bottom of the job hierarchy. We did not have a hereditary class of hewers of wood and drawers of water. Many with even limited aptitude could advance up the ladder.

This relative scarcity of labor led to high wage levels, a cause and result which had caught Adam Smith's attention as early as 1776! This was a further prod to employers to find ways of economizing in their use of labor. This relative tightness of labor supply continued to be characteristic of most of our economic development. Trade-union contentions that high wages are an incentive to employers to develop technological improvements and thus help keep the American economy dynamic cannot be dismissed merely as propaganda for a higher standard of living. They contain considerable truth.

Our country, like others characterized by rapid industrialization, was marked by substantial economic and social mobility, and early developed regional, and later national, habits and patterns of consumption. Although people with different incomes live differently, many manufacturers found it possible to establish a standardized product. This fact, reinforced by the continental dimensions of the American market, especially after 1890, created an increasingly favorable background for the expansion of industries capable of serving the mass market. Henry Ford's genius was to see the potentialities of this market and to exploit it through technological and managerial innovations.

Before they became lenders, Americans were borrowers. For many decades, we used the fruits of European science and of European applied research. Large investments were made in American industry from abroad; we were able to attract many persons of talent and skill; and Europe served as our labor reserve.

One additional aspect of our history of industrialization: For the last hundred years, our educational efforts, particularly at the college and university level, have been directed in considerable measure to teaching the "mechanical arts." We have educated—more specifically, we have trained—large numbers of engineers and other technologists. From the outset of their working lives, these men have been dedicated to the proposition that it is a worthy aim to contribute to the increased efficiency of American agriculture and industry. Theirs has been a very pragmatic concern to get work done better, quicker, cheaper.

Each of these factors which have contributed to the positive stance of America toward technological change would have been less potent had it not been for the overriding consideration that prior to the Great Depression, workers were seldom worried about being displaced by new or improved machines. Rarely did they consider the machine to be their enemy! One tentative generalization may be ventured here: Social acceptance of rapid technological change requires not only the prospect of profit for the employer, but also freedom from fear of unemployment on the part of the worker. Through most of its history the American scene has provided these two favorable preconditions.

We now turn to certain hard facts about the relations between technology and economic development. The first point is that agriculture represents that sector of the American economy that has been most affected by technological change. In many parts of the Midwest, a considerable number of wealthy farmers leave home in November for a warm climate and return in time to plant their crops in March. One American farmer today feeds sixteen other American workers; our agricultural sector produces large surpluses As a consequence of the mechanization of agriculture as well as other changes, the outflow of population from the farms has been very rapid, but it has not been sufficient to bring about a balance between agriculture's manpower needs and requirements. There are still large numbers of underemployed persons in rural areas.

The government has long played a crucial role in accelerating agricultural productivity by research, training, and some of its market support policies. But despite the expenditures of very large sums, government has not been able to eradicate large centers of rural poverty. The lagging growth of urban employment during the decade following the end of the Korean War has made more difficult the relocation of the surplus farm population.

Mining and the extractive industries now account for a very small proportion of the American labor force—less than 1 percent. Since the end of World War II there have been marked increases in mining productivity along with sharp declines in total employment, particularly in bituminous coal. The trade-union leadership reached agreements with the larger employers which resulted in the accelerated mechanization of the industry, with correspondingly large increases in wage rates for those who remained employed. During the decade of the fifties, total output in the industry declined by 22 percent, while average daily employment dropped from 416,000 to 150,000, or by about two-thirds. Average tons mined per man, per day, or per year almost doubled, and average gross hourly earnings increased from $1.94 to $3.12.

It is easy to argue, as many do, that the longtime head of the mine-workers, John L. Lewis, pursued a wrong policy and that he is largely responsible for the plight of so many unemployed and underemployed mine workers. But it is questionable whether in the face of new and improved sources of fuel and power, the industry could have kept four-fifths of its market without rapid mechanization. Low wages and slow mechanization would not have provided a viable solution. While only a very small proportion of the total labor force is engaged in mining, there is no blinking the fact that rapid technological improvements have eroded the base of many mining communities and have resulted in misery for adults and children alike. Here, too, the recent relatively slow expansion of urban employment has hindered the successful relocation of many unemployed workers.

Manufacturing has long been considered the strategic axis of highly developed economies. Therefore, the impact of technological changes on the manufacturing sector of the economy should be carefully noted. At the end of World War I there were about 10.5 million employees in manufacturing; this was approximately 40 percent of the entire labor force employed outside of agriculture. The postwar depression of 1920–1921 reduced this figure to 8.1 million. Once the economy recovered from that decline, manufacturing employment returned to between 9.5 and 10 million, and only exceeded this level in the peak year of 1929, when it was back at the 10.5 million mark. We see then that the highly prosperous New Era between 1923 and 1929 was marked by no gain in manufacturing employment. It is worth noting that the term "technological unemployment" dates from the late 1920s, when many workers were left without jobs because of shifts in the economy. The depressed 1930s formed an economic hiatus: Total manufacturing employment, like many other key indices, was no different in 1939 from what it had been in 1929! For a quarter of a century, from 1914 to 1939, manufacturing employment fluctuated around a high of 10.5 million. However, output per man-hour more than doubled in this period.

Between 1939 and 1943 the number of employees in manufacturing expanded enormously, from 10.3 to 17.6 million. Except for 1 million, all of the increase was accounted for by the durable-goods sector, which experienced a gain in employment of 136 percent!

Although the American economy did not suffer a depression at the end of World War II, a marked readjustment reduced total manufacturing employment to 15.5 million in 1947. After that year, it grew slowly, reaching a peak in 1953 during the Korean War of 17.5 million, a slightly lower level than that of a decade earlier. After 1953, manufacturing employment decreased again. It was not until 1965 that employment in the manufacturing sector exceeded the two earlier peaks of 1943 and 1953. Although the data indicate that there has been no significant increase in manufacturing employment since 1943, they do not take into account the increase in the total labor force; nor do they tell us that the number of blue-collar workers in manufacturing has been declining both absolutely and relatively. We see, then, that manufacturing as a source of employment, particularly for blue-collar workers, has declined even more than the absolute figures indicate.

Although jobs for unskilled and semiskilled production workers have declined substantially, rapid increases in output have taken place. Between 1947 and 1963 the value of output of durable manufactured goods in constant 1954 dollars increased by over 72 percent, while employment increased by 15 percent. With respect to nondurables, the corresponding figures are an increase of 50 percent in output and 3 percent in employment. In each instance, the proportion of nonproduction workers increased: in durable goods from 16 to 27 percent; in nondurable goods from 17 to 25 percent.

Several unequivocal conclusions can be drawn from these few data. Manufacturing employment did not grow significantly from World War I to 1939, nor from the peak of World War II up to the present. However, over the entire span, manufacturing output per man-hour increased significantly.

Through the use of new and improved machines and through other improvements manufacturers were able to meet all the market demands for their products with only minor increases in employment. To increase their total output between 1947 and 1963 by $95 billion (in constant 1954 dollars), or by more than 58 percent, they added 1.5 million employees, or only slightly over 9 percent.

To complete the picture of the goods-producing sector, the experience in construction should be reviewed. Here we find a more substantial gain in employment in the period between 1947 and 1963: from about 2 million to 3.1 million, or by more than one-third. Between 1950 and 1963, the value of new construction in constant 1954 dollars increased from over $35 billion to $53 billion, or by over 48 percent. During this same period, employment increased by about 700,000, or 30 percent. Clearly new and better technological and other methods resulted also in increased efficiency in construction.

The rate of technological and related forms of progress in the goods-producing sector of the economy (including agriculture) can be summarized in these terms. In 1929 there were approximately 24 million persons attached to the goods-producing sector of the economy who turned out about $122 billions of output. In 1963 slightly more than 25 million persons turned out $311 billions of output. Both amounts are in constant 1954 dollars. The nation produced a tremendous increase in real goods without any significant increase in employment. To obtain a considerably smaller absolute increase in the value of services (from $60 to $181 billion), it was necessary to expand employment in the service sector from 23 to 43 million persons. We have moved from a goods to a service economy *only* in terms of employment, not in the value of output. The service sector accounted for 33 percent of GNP in 1929 and in 1963 accounted for 37 percent.

What general conclusions can be drawn from these developments? The first and perhaps the most important is that over the last 3½ decades advances in technology and other factors contributing to higher productivity enabled the goods-producing sector of the American economy to turn out a greatly enlarged output without any significant increase in employment. The important point to note is that it was not only a few industries which showed this trend, but the goods-producing sector as a whole.

Secondly, the rate of technological and related change was sufficiently rapid in certain industries, such as agriculture and bituminous coal, that significant groups of workers, and even more, their children, found little or no employment opportunities in these traditional fields.

Thirdly, the prosperity during the 1920s and since the end of World War II was distinctive in that in both periods employment opportunities did not expand at a rate sufficiently rapid to provide jobs for all who were dislocated by technological and other changes as well as for the new entrants into the labor force. The American economy came to be characterized by "underemployment prosperity."

Fourthly, since 1929, the service sector of the American economy has been characterized by a considerable absolute and relative expansion particularly in terms of employment, but also in output. Productivity in services increased rapidly: A doubling in employment was matched by a three-fold increase in output. In round figures, there has been a 50 percent increase in the total American labor force since 1929; almost all the gain in employment occurred in the service sector.

Lastly, the record demonstrates that during most of these decades rapid technological changes were associated with rapid growth in output and employment. Although the chronic underperformance of the American economy during the 1930s cannot be ascribed primarily to technology, it was probably accentuated by the difficulties that agriculture, mining, and manufacturing faced in seeking to adjust to a host of major changes. However, there is considerable evidence that the rate of technological change has increased since World War II, particularly if adjustment is made for the improvements in the quality of services. Finally, while the ability of the economy to adjust and grow rapidly has been striking, the fact remains that its performance with respect to output has been even better than with respect to employment. This indicates the special need for caution as we look ahead.

Transportation and public utilities, trade, services, finance, and government are the conventional subdivisions of the service sector. The first category, transportation and public utilities, most clearly resembles manufacturing. It is worth noting that this category today accounts for no more employees than it did immediately after World War I. It has expanded its output substantially, but solely through the use of better capital equipment and other improvements. Each of the other four fields, however, has shown marked growth in employment, a growth that became manifest right after World War I and which leveled off or declined slightly (except for government) through the depressed 1930s and accelerated again after the end of World War II. In the more recent period from 1947 through 1963, employment in trade grew by about 3 million, or 30 percent; business and personal services by about the same number, or roughly 60 percent; finance by 1 million, also by about 60 percent; and government by 4 million, or about 75 percent.

Looking ahead, we can find some comfort in the trend in services, since employment opportunities in this sector are likely to continue to expand in response to the increased needs and desires of the population which will result if per capita real income continues to grow. However, if past trends continue, employment will lag behind gains in output. The rate of growth of employment in trade has been considerably more modest of late, and while further increases in employment are likely, they may not be spectacular. Finance, which includes real estate and insurance, has experienced a rapid rate of growth, but in absolute terms it is the smallest of the service components. Moreover, it is the one most immediately affected by the computer revolution. This suggests that the number of new jobs which finance is likely to provide may be more modest in the years ahead. This leaves government. Most of the growth of employment in this sector since the Korean War has been in state and local rather than Federal government. This has largely reflected the expansion of the school population and the increased needs and desires of the burgeoning population for other public services. Since our population will continue to grow rapidly, it is unlikely that the trend toward increased state and local government employment will be reversed, though it may slacken somewhat.

We will not speculate here about the complex factors which will determine the rate of growth of the service factor of the American economy in the years ahead, either in terms of output or employment. Ours is a narrower focus. We are concerned here about the probable impact of technological and related changes. Passing reference was made earlier to the computer revolution. We are undoubtedly still in the early stages of that revolution. No one can foresee the rate at which existing labor inputs will be further economized or new jobs created in response to the potentialities created by the new technology. But if the record of the goods-producing sector during the last half century can be used as an indicator, it is likely that wherever the computer or other major technological breakthrough is effective, the gains will be primarily in output, not in employment opportunities. While a part of the service sector is likely to undergo rapid and far-reaching technological changes, it is likely that employment in other parts, such as education, medicine, trade, recreation, and personal services, will not be seriously affected by machines, at least not in the near future.

The following observations may shed some additional light on the complex interrelations among technology, the economy, and the trends in employment. Since the service sector now accounts for 37 percent of GNP and over three-fifths of all employment, it is inevitable that more and more management effort will be devoted to improving the use of labor resources in this sector. Additional managerial effort will probably lead to greater reliance on capital and to tighter controls over the expansion of employment. One illustration: The Federal government has recently completed an exploratory study of productivity in several agencies. Another illustration is the ever-mounting criticism about the "wastes" in the use of educational and medical personnel.

Another important relationship is that between the rapid growth of the service sector during the post-World War II period and the corresponding growth in the number of women in the labor force, particularly married women. Much of the new female employment has been in other than full-time jobs. This has been a boon to many employers as well as to many employees. But in the years immediately ahead, the American economy will face a rapid increase in the size of its labor force; the number of young men who are entering the labor market for the first time will be double the number who entered during the early 1950s. And they need full-time, not part-time, jobs.

Another facet of recent experience is the fact that during a period of sustained prosperity—and the American economy has been free of major recessions since the onset of World War II—management practices slacken, and many people are kept on the payroll who under a profit squeeze would be let go. This is confirmed by the aggressive steps which the large oil companies took in the late 1950s to separate redundant employees, even at the managerial level. There is also confirmatory evidence in the steel industry.

There are additional difficulties in a shift in employment from manufacturing to services. Three in particular should be noted. The first is that many parts of the service sector need people with substantial educational background, but many of those who are entering the labor force for the first time or who must seek new jobs do not have the foundation to acquire advanced skills. This has created the paradox of multiple vacancies in the face of large numbers of unemployed.

The second difficulty derives from wage differentials. Many who have lost their jobs in manufacturing, mining, or transportation were able, when they were employed, to earn between $3 and $4 an hour. The only jobs that they can obtain in the services pay half that amount. Small wonder that they hesitate as long as possible before accepting such a cut in earnings. To make matters worse, the personnel function is being constantly professionalized, with the consequences that artificially high standards of selection tend to be institutionalized and major reliance tends to be placed on formal written tests which discriminate against those with limited education.

Thirdly, the flight of many middle-class people from the cities has meant that the need for many services in the urban centers has declined—yet the older sections of the city have numbers of workers with little skill who might be employable in the services. And with few or no houses for the poor in the suburbs, many demands for services there remain unmet. This has led to a new balkanization of the labor market, to use Clark Kerr's phrase.

These are just a few of the complex phenomena that have come to characterize the American economy during the past several decades. Many have been identified only recently, and few have been studied with the thoroughness that they warrant. It would be foolish to see technology as the primary cause of all these difficulties, but it would be equally foolish to ignore its influence.

While the goods-producing sector of the American economy did not experience any significant increase in employment during the last quarter of a century, the economy as a whole continued to expand rapidly in terms of both output and employment. Although there were many years in which the economy did not meet the criterion of full utilization of human resources, the shortfalls could be considered within bounds except for the Great Depression. In general, out of every 20 persons in the labor force, only 1 was without a job.

Since we can say that the American economy has performed so well during most of the period since the end of World War I, we might conclude that there is little reason for concern, and even less for policy innovatons. But both conclusions would be unjustified.

The first point to consider is that the dynamism of the American economy since 1940 has been greatly affected by World War II and the cold war. Expenditures for defense, atomic energy, and space have been critically important in helping to maintain a rapid rate of growth. In the absence of a deterioration in international affairs, the President is committed to an early leveling of and, it is hoped, a reduction in, these expenditures. It remains to be seen whether the resources eventually freed by a stabilization of the defense sector will be bid for and used by the private sector or by the expanding civilian sector of government. Expenditures for defense are very large, both absolutely and relatively, and the transition to peace activities may prove much more difficult than is now anticipated.

Two points should be made in passing: Congress generally responds more favorably to requests for additional appropriations for defense than for civilian purposes; and the defense sector seldom faces a drying up of demand, since the products, even if unused, are characterized by rapid obsolescence. The Armed Forces always want the newest equipment. Without these large defense expenditures the relative decline of employment in manufacturing might have been even more rapid than it was. In brief: Any leveling off, and certainly any reduction, in defense expenditures must be carefully planned to ensure that the released manpower is absorbed either by the private sector or by alternative public programs.

Related to the foregoing, but distinguishable from it, has been the transformation which has taken place in the entrepreneurial structure of the American economy. The shift in employment from goods to services and the dynamic part played by the defense and defense-related activities of the Federal government has had the consequence that the not-for-profit sector (government and nonprofit institutions, particularly educational and medical) has accounted for most of the growth of net employment since 1929. Although we continue to talk about our free-enterprise economy, in point of fact it has been very much transformed since Herbert Hoover was elected President in 1928. One-quarter of our GNP, and possibly up to as much as two-fifths of total employment, are accounted for by economic activities generated outside the private profit-seeking sector. This means that the future growth of employment may depend to a marked degree on the strengthening of the not-for-profit sector and on its improved articulation with the profit sector. The foregoing suggests that since technology is proving to be so potent in increasing output without raising employment in the goods-producing sector, the continued growth of employment as a whole depends on the effectiveness with which the institutions concerned with the production and distribution of services perform. Government and nonprofit institutions loom very significant in this regard.

The United States has experienced great changes from one decade to the next in the numbers entering the labor force. The post-World War II years saw an unusually small number of young male entrants, reflecting the low birth rates of the depressed 1930s. The numbers seeking civilian jobs were further reduced by the elongation of schooling and the enlargement of the Armed Forces. The outlook for the years ahead is quite different. Many more young men will be seeking employment.

The multiplication of manpower programs since 1962, many directed at youth, have been in response to these new demographic pressures.

The thin flow into the labor market of young people during the earlier postwar years (1950–1960) helps explain why there has been relatively little pressure exerted by the trade unions to lower the conventional hours of work. But in the face of the demographic revolution which is upon us, the nagging unemployment of recent years has lately caused many unions to take a more aggressive position with respect to a reduction in the conventional hours of work. This is sound as well as overdue. While a reduction of hours cannot completely sop up the excess unemployment which has long characterized the American economy, it is a useful step in helping to bring about a better long-term balance between work and workers. In the past, we took out between a third and two-fifths of our increased productivity in greater leisure. With our technological progress continuing apace, a further reduction in hours would probably be salutary. A shorter workday and workweek and a larger number of three- and four-day weekends should help to stimulate the growth of the economy and employment by encouraging the expansion of the education and recreation industries, among others. From a dynamic viewpoint, the economy requires shorter work hours for sustained growth.

Another reason for looking with favor on a downward adjustment in the average hours of work is the certain fact that people will have to devote more time to further education and training if they are to keep their skills vital. Continuing adult education began in the United States with people at the top of the occupational hierarchy—with professors and physicians. In recent years, industry has greatly expanded the scale and scope of its several training programs for line and technical management as well as for its skilled workers. Several major unions have found it essential to sponsor elaborate and continuing training programs for their journeymen—witness the electrical workers and the plumbers. In a technologically advanced economy, it is desirable to make several time adjustments: Total working time should be reduced, because leisure is a precondition for welfare; more time should be available for education and training; less time will be required to turn out the nation's goods and services.

Rapid advances in technology tend to be associated with accelerated advances in wage rates and fringe benefits for those who succeed in holding on to their jobs. However, there may be a widening gap in opportunities and income between those with jobs and those without. Some American economists believe that in the recent past there has been considerably less than an optimum diffusion of the gains from advancing technology among the population as a whole. The recent modest steps of the Council of Economic Advisors toward establishing criteria for wage increases is evidence of this concern. But the trouble-some issues have scarcely been identified; they have certainly not been probed. And we are still far from a consensus about what public policy in this arena should be.

In recent years, sporadic efforts have been made to deal with the costs of automation within the context of collective bargaining. Al-though for a long time most collective bargaining agreements have made provision for protecting seniority, the order of dislocation inci-dent to major technological changes has been the focus of recent efforts. All the evidence is not in, but the burden of opinion now ap-pears to be that these "private" efforts to cope with automation, while desirable and to be encouraged, are much less effective than their proponents had originally hoped or expected. Private planning and financing can ease the impact of automation. Retraining and reloca-tion allowances can help some of the dislocated to find new jobs more readily. But if the numbers who are thrown out of work are large, or if their skills are no longer in demand, or if many of them are handicapped in other ways, such as by limited education, then indeed private resources will not be adequate to the task.

Consequently, it is to government that we must look for the range of institutional supports which will be required to cushion the ad-verse effects of automation. The United States has moved energetically in the last few years to fashion a great many new instruments to cope with the effects of automation and other change-producing agents in order to establish and maintain a better balance between people and jobs.

The United States is putting more and more behind the education-and-training solution to underemployment prosperity. It is fairly certain that a high proportion of those now without jobs cannot be fitted back into the economy because they do not have the skills or competence to meet the changed demands of the job market. While the economic advisers to both President Kennedy and President Johnson have adhered strongly to the belief that the shortfall in employment is primarily the result of deficiency in general demand, the Congress, carefully hedging its actions, has written new legislation aimed also at correcting the imbalance in the demand and supply of labor—an im-balance rooted in difficulties that go beyond a weakness in general demand.

It is too early to reach a definitive judgment about the new pro-grams. As suggested earlier, the numbers of unemployed youths who now stand on street corners in the slums of metropolitan areas are being reduced, at least for a time. But whether their experiences in various types of training programs will enable most of them to find a permanent place in the economy remains to be seen. The answer depends on the rate at which technological changes will be introduced in the years ahead, the changes in the skill requirements incident to these changes, and particularly on the rate at which the total number of jobs in the economy expands. With the substantial increases in new entrants into the labor force that loom ahead, only a substantially expanded rate of new job creation, considerably beyond the average of the 1950–1965 period, holds forth much hope.

This brings us face to face with the one challenge that the United States, as a matter of policy, has sought to avoid confronting directly until now—whether to use the Federal government as an employer of unemployed and underemployed workers. Perhaps the closest parallel until the legislation of 1966 has been the accelerated public works program. The best-informed view about this program is that the cost of thus employing a man is very high and his job is likely to be only temporary. Further, many jobs cannot be made available for unemployed men if they have little or no skills in the construction trades. The program has been a boon to mobile construction teams, but they have not been the ones who have been unable to find employment in recent years.

When we consider all the facets together, there is no ground for undue optimism. While all the new approaches to job creation have some merit, it is not clear that the American economy will be able to produce enough net new jobs in the years immediately ahead to furnish employment for all who will want and need jobs. In the face of such multiple problems as the continuing shift from goods to services with its inherent difficulties; the possible levelling off of the defense budget; uncertainty about the future trend of the not-for-profit sector; the upward drift in skill requirements and specifications; continuing technological progress; the danger of a downturn after the long period of substantially uninterrupted economic expansion—it will be a significant accomplishment if the American economy can maintain the average rate of job expansion established during the past two decades. But significant as this would be, it would fall short of what we need.

The swelling numbers of young people reaching working age requires a step-up in the rate of new job expansion. Our increasing dissatisfaction with an unemployment rate of 4 percent also demands an acceleration of employment expansion. Some experts believe that the American economy has demonstrated such great strength and flexibility in past decades that it will be able to meet and solve these new challenges without great stress or strain. They believe that sound fiscal policy and amicable government-business relationships will suffice and they are confident that both preconditions have now been established. They are convinced that despite continuing rapid technological changes, the market has sufficient flexibility to make the necessary adjustments, including the required shifts on the labor front.

This optimism, however, glosses over too many of the difficulties that stand in the way; the required adjustments will not come so easily. We may experience a widening gap between the potential labor force and the available jobs. Our underutilization of manpower is not currently 4 percent, as it is reported, but very much more when allowance is made for people who are forced to work a short week, those who have involuntarily dropped out of the labor force, the large number of young people who are marking time in school or on street corners and who are not yet counted as job seekers, married women who would welcome an opportunity to work, the underemployed population on the farms, the self-employed who barely support themselves, and the many handicapped persons who are not counted in the labor force.

The optimists have not faced up to the implications of providing work opportunities for all these groups. They know that an economy that is running in excess of $740 billions annually is able to provide financial support for those who are unable to support themselves. And they ask: What more can we expect?

One answer is that a responsible democracy should seek to provide employment for all who are able and willing to work, even if this requires special conditions which recognize that many will not be able to meet the standards of the competitive market. An urbanized democratic society cannot look with equanimity on its security and progress if a significant minority has no status in that society. Without work a man is alienated.

Chapter Four The Passing of an Economy That Never Was

There has always been a sizable gap between what Americans do and what they think they do. This is nowhere more evident than in the area of economics, where, if anything, the distance between belief and reality has widened perceptibly in the last few years.

The assumption is widespread that the United States economy is primarily responsive to the lure of profits and the dictates of competition. It is, but not to the extent commonly believed. While profits remain important and competition is pervasive, ever more output and employment takes place in the not-for-profit sector, which encompasses the economic activity of government and nonprofit organizations. Some of the nation's most important and largest efforts—for example, those related to defense, education, health—are carried out in it. A brief look at the data will help confirm this fact.

In 1929 GNP amounted to $104 billion, of which $91 billion, or 87 percent of the total, was accounted for by the private sector. The not-for-profit sector was divided as follows: Government accounted for $9 billion, or approximately 9 percent, and nonprofit enterprises for just under $4 billion, somewhat under 4 percent.

In 1963, when GNP stood at $584 billion, the private sector's share was $424 billion, or about 73 percent of the total. Its relative position had slipped about fifteen percentage points in the intervening thirty-four years. Almost all of the shift was accounted for by an increase in the role of government, which jumped from under 9 to over 22 percent during this period. The increase in the nonprofit sector was much more modest—from 3.7 to 5.1 percent.

It should be noted that the foregoing data understate the true figures. Various national income accounting conventions tend to minimize the role of government and nonprofit institutions and *pari passu* tend to exaggerate the role of the private sector. The figure of 27 percent as the not-for-profit sector's share of 1963 GNP may be several percentage points too low. In any event, in terms of dollar output, the not-for-profit sector surely accounts for more than a quarter and possibly for as much as a third of the total GNP.

The dollar value of output is a crucial measure of a sector's contribution, but it is not the only one. In the Western world today, employment is an equally important, if not more important, measure. Let us look therefore at the transformations that have taken place in employment since 1929. In considering employment in the not-for-profit sector, we must calculate first the number of workers who are directly on the payroll of government and nonprofit institutions and then add to this number those in the private sector whose jobs are a direct consequence of the expenditures of the not-for-profit sector—for instance, those on the payrolls of aerospace companies that are engaged solely in producing defense materials for the U.S. government.

This is what we find: In 1929, employment in and for the not-for-profit sector accounted for 15 percent of total employment. By 1960, the proportion of employment accounted for by the not-for-profit sector had more than doubled. The share of this sector, as previously noted, is surely not less than one-third of total employment and may well approximate two-fifths. This means that at least one out of every three Americans and possibly as many as two out of every five are currently employed outside of the private sector or have jobs in the private sector that depend directly on purchases made by the not-for-profit sector.

The share of total employment of the not-for-profit sector increased in each of the last three decades, though only slightly between 1940 and 1950. Once again it was government that accounted for most of the gain: Its share rose from about 10 percent in 1929 to 25 percent in 1960. In the same period employment in nonprofit institutions increased from 4.5 to 6.8 percent of the national total.

Another way of assessing the impact of the not-for-profit sector on jobs is to review its contribution to *net* changes of employment during the three decades under consideration.

Between 1929 and 1940, when total employment increased from 46.2 to 48.5 million, the not-for-profit sector accounted for 184 percent of the net change. This means that, in addition to providing the net increase of 2.3 million, the not-for-profit sector compensated for the decline of more than 2 million jobs in the private sector. Between 1940 and 1950, total employment showed a net increase of slightly more than 10 million, of which the not-for-profit sector accounted for about 27 percent. In the decade of the fifties, employment increased by about 8.5 million, with the not-for-profit sector accounting for over 85 percent. This last figure means that during the fifties the private sector provided only 1 out of every 6 new jobs, and the other 5 reflected the expansion of either government or nonprofit institutions. It is this last statistic, perhaps more than any other single figure, which indicates caution in assigning the private sector primary responsibility for the recent growth of the American economy.

These statistics indicate some of the important qualitative characteristics of the recent transformation of the American economy. But such statistics are the result of the actions of men within a complex set of institutions and markets. Let us therefore consider some of the important institutional changes that underlie these transformations.

To start with government. Its rapid growth during the 1930s was the result of the Federal government's response first to the Depression and secondly to the subsequent reforms of the competitive economy. The period since 1950 has witnessed a twofold expansion. The Federal government's expenditures for defense have increased substantially, while state and local governments have very rapidly expanded services for a burgeoning population.

In 1950 all levels of government spent about $59 billion. Thirteen years later, in 1963, the figure was slightly in excess of $152 billion, or an increase of $93 billion in current dollars. Two functions, defense and education, accounted for about 56 percent of this large increase: Expenditures for defense jumped from $18 to $55 billion and for education from $10 to $25 billion. The only other function for which there was a large absolute increase in expenditures was highways, for which outlays increased from slightly under $4 billion to almost $10 billion. The rest of the increase reflects the efforts of all levels of government to provide more adequate services under established or new programs for a rapidly increasing population.

Since it is commonly believed that the Federal government has been largely if not solely responsible for the growth of the governmental sector, it should be pointed out explicitly that while the Federal government led the way for many years, it has now yielded the lead to state and local governments, which recently have accounted for *slightly more than half* of all government expenditures.

With regard to nonprofit institutions, the major functions responsible for their expansion were education and health. Between 1950 and 1960 expenditures on higher education rose from about $2 billion to over $5.3 billion for operating purposes alone, a sizable increase both absolutely and relatively.

Total outlays for health and medical care have increased since 1950 from $12 billion to about $40 billion today. The voluntary non-profit hospitals together with the nonprofit Blue Cross and Blue Shield plans have provided the fulcrum for this expansion. In the decade between 1952 and 1962, total expenditures of all hospitals increased from about $4.5 billion to over $10.1 billion, while those of the nonprofit hospitals rose from $1.9 billion to just under $5 billion.

The rapid expansion of the government sector has occurred not only through the activities carried on by the conventional agencies, i.e., the Department of Defense, boards of education, etc., but also by newly created and expanded special-enterprise structures. One need only consider the Tennessee Valley Authority, the large number of turnpike authorities, various port authorities, the San Francisco Bay Rapid Transit District, the Southern Regional Educational Conference, the great many housing and urban renewal authorities, and other instrumentalities to appreciate the extent to which all levels of government and particularly state and local governments have increased their ability to meet the demands of their electorates for new or improved services through the establishment of new forms of enterprise structures. These structures have become so large and extensive that when Robert Moses, a New York civil servant, was at the height of his activity in the middle 1950s, he had the best claim to the title of the nation's outstanding entrepreneur!

The recent establishment of the Communications Satellite Corporation, the proposal to set up a new government-private corporation to purchase surplus agricultural land in the vicinity of growing urban areas, new approaches to government-business technical cooperation—all indicate that governments are likely to be drawn increasingly into additional types of economic enterprises which they will carry out either on their own or in collaboration with the private and nonprofit sectors. The United States has surely not come to the end of this road despite the fact that government makes a move now and again to get out of "business" by selling one or another of its enterprises—be it a bankrupt bus line or a hotel in a recreation area.

Though educational and health agencies predominate in the non-profit sector, religious institutions receive annually over $5 billion in contributions, which suggests the scale of their operations. And the economic activities carried on by such diverse nonprofit institutions as cooperatives, research organizations, museums, and trade associations add up to a significant total.

As the recent report of the Rockefeller Brothers Fund on the performing arts suggests, the scale and scope of nonprofit organizataions is likely to grow in the future, in response to consumer demands for services that cannot be readily produced and sold by private enterprises and where there are limitations to government's assuming the dominant role.

The vast growth in the demand for services—particularly those supplied by government or nonprofit institutions—has already substantially altered the relationship between the goods-producing and service sectors of the economy. Although the dividing line between these two is sometimes sharper in the statistics than in life, and although it is easy for shifts from goods to services to take place without the output undergoing any significant change (as when an employer decides to buy services from others which he had previously provided himself), the fact remains that the last decades have seen a continuing shift in favor of services.

Let us recall in this connection the data presented in Chapter Three which showed that in terms of constant 1954 dollars, the United States secured an increase of $189 billion in the goods-producing sector between 1929 and 1963 without any significant net increase in employment. A shifting of millions of farmhands into industry, as well as the increasing productivity of manufacturing labor, made possible this large increase in output. On the other hand, a considerably smaller absolute gain—$120 billion—in the output of services required the net addition of 20 million workers.

The burden of these figures is unequivocal. During the last $3\frac{1}{2}$ decades, technological and other improvements have been sufficiently rapid to enable the American economy to turn out all the goods that the market was able to absorb—including the specialized demands of the Federal government for defense—without any significant increase in employment.

Are there any significant relations between the growth of the not-for-profit sector and the shift of the economy (in employment terms) to services? We believe that there are. It is not correct to say, as do the proponents of "The Triple Revolution," that the American people are surfeited with goods and that before long machines by themselves will be able to produce all the goods that are needed, and more. This is nonsense. But it is true, as the rapid expansion of demand for education, health, and recreation makes clear, that a more affluent, more urbanized society tends to need and desire more services.

Many of the services which people need and desire cannot readily be produced by any of the three G's—General Motors, General Electric, or General Foods. While an occasional academician has gone so far as to advocate the abolition of public education, the American people have not really been interested in such an answer to the expansion of government, except in a few communities which sought for a time to evade the Supreme Court's decision on desegregation. Nor have they seriously considered the suggestion that the way to control the rapidly rising costs of good hospital care is to encourage an expansion of proprietary hospitals. Not even the two Hoover Commissions, which were very sensitive to the encroachments of government on the private sector, recommended that our national parks and other recreational areas be turned over to private enterprise for development. And the most rabid opponents of urban renewal have stopped short of advocating that condemnation powers be given to private enterprises.

Much of the improved amenities that the American public needs and wants can be provided only by governments and nonprofit institutions. This is not to say that they must do the whole job. Far from it. But the needs and desires of the public cannot be met without their contribution. This is at least a partial reason for the rapid growth of the not-for-profit sector during the last $3\frac{1}{2}$ decades.

Interestingly, this recent spectacular advance has caused many persons (1) to forget that the United States economy has always had a not-for-profit sector that worked hand in glove with the private economy and (2) to assume that this not-for-profit sector will continue to grow at the same rapid rate as it has in the recent past.

These people forget that the development of transportation, for example, a strategically important sector, has always involved government, sometimes alone as in the case of the Erie Canal, sometimes in collaboration with private enterprise as in the instance of the land grants to the railroads. Nowhere is this complementary relationship between government and the private sector more significant than in the development of that mainspring of our economy—the automotive industry.

To take another example: There is general agreement that one of the strengths of American management is the high proportion of college- and university-trained technologists and executives in its ranks. These people were educated and trained in nonprofit and government institutions. It is difficult to see how the large corporations, especially those which are research-and-development based, could operate without a steady stream of such well-trained personnel. Here is another piece of evidence of the complementary nature of the three sectors.

What about the future? Will the profit sector continue to shrink and the not-for-profit sector inevitably expand? The conservatives fear this eventuality, but many liberals argue that unless it comes to pass, the economy will suffer from a new form of resource underutilization which may be called "prosperity underemployment." We made passing reference earlier to the aerospace companies, to the Communications Satellite Corporation, to various types of port and throughway authorities. A closer look at these enterprise structures would reveal that the United States economy and society have demonstrated considerable innovative skill in the design of new forms for meeting the demand for new types of goods and services. There is nothing very "governmental" about a turnpike authority that raises its funds on the capital markets, pays the going rate of interest, hires personnel competitively, and fixes its rates so that the users pay all costs and even a sum to cover future improvements.

Another illustration: New York City built Shea Stadium and then leased it on a long-term basis to a private group, the New York Mets, for a rental fee that is set to cover all the costs. The Houston Astrodome is a similar instance, except that in that case the citizens first voted a special bond issue.

Karl Marx prophesied many years ago that it was inevitable that capitalism would reach a point where the system would blow up because of inherent contradictions. More recently, critics on the right have read the signs to mean that if the profit sector continues to shrink, the system of private enterprise is doomed; while those on the left have maintained that unless the not-for-profit sector expands, the United States economy will suffer ever larger shortfalls in output and employment.

But our look at the record reveals a different and considerably more reassuring situation. We find that the United States now has long had a three-sector economy—profit-seeking, nonprofit, and government. We see that they are independent. We see that the distinctions among them are frequently more legal than economic. And finally, we see that the vitality of our economy depends upon continuing innovation in enterprise structures in each of the three sectors as well as in their interrelationships. The United States will be able to maintain its dynamic economy as long as it is willing to experiment and innovate. But it must not become immobilized by using models of an economy that never was and never can be.

Chapter Five

Manpower and the South

There are many aspects of present-day life that can be placed in perspective only after they have been considered in historical context, for the forces of the past continue to exercise an influence on the present. The problems of the South have been particularly conditioned by its history—a history markedly different from that of the rest of the country.

The main thrust of the economic development of this nation was from east to west, from the Atlantic to the Pacific. While the economy of the South, antebellum and postbellum, played a part in this larger national destiny, it did not share fully in it—surely not in the many decades between the Civil War and the outbreak of World War II. During these critical eighty years the South was an appendage to the body economic. Many of the economic problems that confront the South today—manpower surpluses, retarded industrialization, scarcity of capital, lower-than-average per capita income—can be appreciated only against the background of its longtime isolation.

Along the historical axis it is important to note what William H. Nicholls demonstrated so convincingly in his book *Southern Tradition and Regional Progress* [1]—that segregation as a way of life was a major drag on economic development because so much Southern energy and competence was used to holding the Negro down and apart rather than to improving the terms of life for all.

To continue along the same route a little longer: The fact that the South was for so long a cotton-growing area dependent on various types of family farming established an early nexus between the production of babies and the production of cotton. The family with the most hands, even very young hands, had the edge over others with fewer children. However, times changed. The South became less dependent on cotton, but the babies among the farm population have kept coming. Even with very high levels of internal migration and out-migration, the South still has more people than jobs.

[1] The University of North Carolina Press, Chapel Hill, N.C., 1960.

The shortage of jobs is of long standing. The early textile mills were erected, frequently with community funds, to provide work for the redundant workers whose plight was clearly visible in the older parts of the South as early as the 1880s. However, in this effort the Negro was ignored, and the pattern was set: Manufacturing jobs were not for Negroes. The mill towns of the South became towns for whites only.

The failure of the South to catch up with the accelerated industrialization of the country which gained momentum after the Civil War, together with the erosion of its farmlands caused by overuse and poor management, helped to widen the gap which separated it from the rest of the country until it became, in the words of President Franklin D. Roosevelt, the nation's number one economic problem. Indicative of the plight of the South in the 1930s is the finding of Morton Rubin that the wage scale on the plantation was about the same at the outbreak of World War II as it had been sixty years earlier.[2] And Gunnar Myrdal observed that in the 1930s getting on relief in the North represented a major economic advance for many Negroes from the South.

Insufficient work and wages for the white population and even less for the Negro population is one way of summarizing the long depressed period between the Civil War and World War II. But we must take account of another dimension: A poor economy yields low tax revenues, and low tax revenues result in public services that are inadequate in range and quality—education, health, vocational training, and others—all of which are directly or indirectly connected with the acquisition of skills which in turn will help determine what the laboring man is capable of earning. And so the South was caught up in a cycle of public as well as private poverty; and each reinforced the other. This was the classic syndrome of a conservative, agriculture-based, low-income class society, poorly positioned to attract capital and industry and getting in its own way by preferring stability in race relations to economic advancement and a higher standard of living.

The location of the South was the cause of much of its special problems. It was for a long time largely inaccessible except along the principal railroad and river routes. But the automobile began to change all that. It contributed much to opening up the South and helped to expose the South to new influences at the same time that it provided greatly improved opportunities for many Southerners to get out of their constricted environments. While there had been a steady

[2] *Plantation County*, The University of North Carolina Press, Chapel Hill, N.C., 1951.

out-migration of Southern talent for many years—to the great detriment of the South—it was not until World War I that a large number of Negroes began to leave. The outflow of both whites and Negroes continued at a more modest scale during the 1920s, but the adverse economic conditions of the 1930s resulted in a much-reduced flow.

Northern industry had been moving South for a long time, but on a small scale; and its net impact on the Southern economy had been modest. Some firms moved because of the low wage rates; others were attracted by proximity to raw materials. But with a weak Southern market, and with transportation costs relatively high, the South was not able to surmount its comparative disadvantages.

What, then, accounted for the South's economic takeoff? How did the South finally break out?

The Great Depression finally wrote finis to the old South, as it did to so much else. The protagonists of states' rights were among the greatest beneficiaries of the New Federalism, which pumped large sums into the South and otherwise helped to stimulate its economy through new systems of relief, agricultural reform, flood control, the expansion of rural electricity, and a host of other expansionary programs.

Then, World War II laid the groundwork for major changes in the South. First, the tremendous military bases created many new employment opportunities and introduced new streams of income. These, in turn, increased the demand for land, housing, improved food, and services.

Equally important, for the first time in our history there was a strong demand for the labor of Negroes outside the South. In World War I several hundred thousand Negroes had obtained jobs in the North. But they had made relatively little progress thereafter. The Negro's position in the labor force began to change significantly only with World War II.

Without attempting to date the agricultural revolution exactly, we can say that World War II gave it further impetus. The demand for milk and other dairy products generated by the large populations at the military bases, together with rising incomes in the towns, encouraged farmers whose land could no longer raise a profitable cotton crop to sell to others or to shift over to dairy and cattle farming. And the postwar period, characterized by higher per capita incomes and changing food habits further intensified the shift, reinforced as it was by valuable tax incentives.

On the industrial front there were several important developments. The chemical industry, which requires much space and much water, came increasingly to the South. The Federal government located its big hydrogen plant in Aiken, South Carolina. The largest plant expansion of Eastman Kodak took place in Tennessee. The petrochemical industry developed the arc from Houston around to New Orleans and up to Baton Rouge which offered not only cheap space and ample water but also easy access to raw materials and good water transportation.

Rising incomes also stimulated the expansion of consumer-goods industries. Moreover, the continuance of a wage differential in favor of the South has facilitated the expansion of electrical manufacturing and other durable goods.

Governmental expenditures, agricultural reform, and industrialization reinforced each other, and together they had sufficient momentum to enable the South, after its longtime doldrums, to escape and take to the road of economic development.

In every region, and particularly in the South, there are several subdivisions. On the grossest of scales, we must distinguish among the rural areas, the small towns, and the growing cities. The quality of life differs substantially among these subdivisions—especially for the Negro. In the Delta he is still very much a prisoner of the whites; in Atlanta he is almost a free man.

An interesting phenomenon in the South is the shift in the recent past from farm to nonfarm living. In 1950 there were roughly 9 million people living on Southern farms, and 9 million others were living in rural nonfarm communities. In 1960 only 4 million people were living on farms, and 13 million were living in rural nonfarm communities. Many millions of people, then, have left the farms and are living in small towns. Much of the underemployment that previously was concentrated on the farms is now concentrated in the small town. And much of the explosiveness on the racial issue is centered in these small communities.

In this connection it should be noted that the South has roughly the same proportion of small Standard Metropolitan Areas—cities such as Charlotte and Savannah—as does the rest of the country. But if one focuses on the major metropolitan areas and disregards Florida, one finds that only 5 percent of the South's population is concentrated in large urban centers, in contrast to a third of the population of the country as a whole.

This phenomenon of retarded urbanization shows up in many ways. There are first of all only three large Southern metropolises—Dallas, Houston, and Atlanta. This means that there are few complexes with a population which has a variety of skills in depth. When a major space operation was put into New Orleans, the problem of recruitment of trained manpower long plagued the several contractors. Neither Louisiana State University nor Tulane University had produced large numbers of scientific and technical manpower over the years, and many of those who had graduated had drifted off.

Another view of the South's changing manpower situation can be had by reviewing certain broad trends. In the postwar period (1950–1960) almost a million net new jobs were added in manufacturing in the South—the Southeast and South Central regions combined—but very few Negro males obtained factory employment. The outside figure would be 10,000, and it may have been as low as the Census suggests—only 1,000! The South has long recognized four classes of manpower—white men, white women, Negro women, and Negro men, and substantially in that order. Southern employers just do not hire Negro men if they do not have to.

During the first two decades following 1940, the industrial expansion was not sufficient to use the surplus manpower, and Negro women and Negro men at the end of the queue were not hired. However, a recent study by the Equal Employment Opportunity Commission shows that in the last five years Negroes have been hired in substantial numbers in the textile plants of North and South Carolina as whites have moved on to better-paying jobs.

The employment problems of the South are compounded by the fact that many of the profitable industries which establish plants in the South and which pay a decent wage do not use much manpower. This is true of the chemical industry. Moreover, there are no jobs in these plants for poorly educated whites and Negroes. Jobs for unskilled workers do, however, open up as income begins to flow. And secondary jobs are important for the growth of the economy. Rashi Fein has published some interesting studies [3] about the manpower import versus the manpower export of the South by quantity and quality. There is no way to start modern plants in the South except by bringing trained people into the area. Fein shows that the South's position has been eased because it has been able to import skilled people. Nevertheless, the South historically has lost, and continues to

[3] *Southern Economic Journal*, July, 1965.

lose, a large part of its manpower potential. A rough estimate suggests that since 1940, the South has exported $3 billion to $4 billion worth of trained manpower!

A related point is whom it loses and whom it retains. There is no question but that the South loses a high proportion of the best-qualified Negroes. In Houston, for example, discrimination results in a nonfit between the Negroes and the community. The abler Negroes leave, and the poorer Negroes come in from the countryside. This is a double loss from the point of view of the city. It is interesting to read the literature put out by the various Southern chambers of commerce; one would never know from these publications that there are any Negroes in the South—there is seldom a word on the subject.

Since agriculture long provided a major source of employment, we must consider the additional problems precipitated by the continuing heavy displacement of the poor sharecropper and poor self-employed farmer. The magnitude of the agricultural revolution in the South is substantial. In many parts of the South farms are valued at between $100,000 and $200,000. These farms can be best run by college-trained men, managers who can supervise the operation and maintenance of such large and complex investments. However, in a poor area, such as the South, agriculture conventionally serves as a kind of social security system. A man can at least survive on the farm. He may live in a shack, his family may not have enough to eat, but he can survive. Today, many poor Negroes are being forced off the farm. For many of them, however, joining the migrant stream represents a step up in the world. They can earn more, bad as migrant labor conditions are, than they were able to earn at the lowest rung of tenant farming in Mississippi, Alabama, and Georgia.

Now, an interesting development in the South that has directly helped the whites but not the Negroes is the erection of many new manufacturing plants in rural areas. A white man, with the help of his wife and adult sons, can continue to run his farm; he may even improve it once two or three members of the family have become wage earners in the nearby plant. Such a family is not doing badly! But Negroes do not have such opportunities; they are generally not hired by these local plants. Not all the white men get jobs either. Thus there is still much unemployed and underemployed labor in the region.

However, Negroes do profit indirectly from these new plants. As whites become two-car families, more service stations open, and some Negro men are taken on as attendants. Negroes also find jobs in other service occupations. Obviously there is a spillover effect, and the expansion of the service industry has helped the Negro to improve his circumstances.

For the long pull, the progress of the South will depend in considerable measure on the quality of its manpower. While the South has been making gains, the rest of the country has also been moving ahead. Relatively, the South is in only a slightly better position than it formerly was. It still lags very badly.

Take the question of educational expenditures—which are the key to trained manpower. The South spends not much more than half of the amount per pupil spent by the rest of the country. The South is doing much better than it used to do; it is even doing better for the Negro. But the problem of closing the gap between the white and the Negro, between South and North, remains.

There are continued and rapid changes in the job requirements of the Southern economy. Consider the space operations in Texas, Florida, and Louisiana. Many companies have an unfilled demand for technicians. Few technicians are trained in the South. It is easier to import scientists and engineers by making them sufficiently good offers. However, the experts hold that the South does not have one first-rate university. The strongest are the University of North Carolina, Duke, and Vanderbilt. It has not been easy to recruit able persons, especially if they are natives of the North or the West, to work in an area where there are so few good universities. The absence of strong high schools and junior colleges is a further drawback. With respect to junior colleges, Florida has a major effort on the way. North Carolina has been moving in the same direction of expanding its system of junior colleges, but the region continues to lag. This is serious, since much of the industry that is moving into the area, and the other types of industry that the region would like to attract, is quite sophisticated and requires more technically trained manpower.

What are some of the policy considerations that derive from this analysis? Because of the South's own long opposition to Federal aid to education, its school system, like the school systems in many other parts of the country, is seriously undernourished. We will continue to have a badly lagging, substantially undereducated South until we do considerably more than as yet appears likely. The South has been making a serious effort on the educational front, but its effort simply does not yield enough gains.

Our agricultural policy is predicated on the trickle-down effect. At a recent conference on farm manpower the participating economists concluded that, on the whole, farm policy has done nothing for the people who most need help. In fact, it has had a negative effect because it raised the price of land relative to the price of labor and thereby added to the woes of the farm laborer.

At the moment, the defense-space effort continues to provide broad support for the economy of the South. Houston, Cape Kennedy, Michaud, Marietta—these names tell the tale.

The South would be particularly vulnerable to a defense cutback, although the area has recently been helped by the Navy's moving down into the warmer waters; Norfolk, Charleston, and the Florida port cities are increasingly important naval bases.

We now have an Appalachian policy, and that is primarily a Southern policy. We may not know what we want to do with Appalachia, but we have decided to build roads; and an injection of jobs and money should help. According to various state plans, Appalachia is supposed to be used for vacation purposes. If the region is to prosper, the plans must be broadened. Every depressed area cannot turn itself around solely, or even primarily, on the basis of tourism.

But Appalachia aside, there are some booming places in the South. In the Charlotte area, Negro women have finally broken into manufacturing, and they have broken in at $60 to $80 a week. It is, of course, revolutionary for Negro women to get jobs in Southern manufacturing at such wages. If the economy in some parts of the South remains tight, many underemployed whites and Negroes will finally find jobs.

What has been and what is likely to be the impact of civil rights on employment? No matter how slowly race relations improve or how difficult it is for changes to be negotiated through commissions, the enforcement of Federal contracts, and similar instruments, a few more jobs here and a few more jobs there are being opened up. We must not minimize the cumulative influence of these modest changes wherever the Negro population is not too large. Where it is substantial, such gains are too little and too late.

We must give attention to the rural nonfarm population living in very small towns. These communities may be the holding area for large numbers who have been displaced from the farm and who have not found a place for themselves in the urban economy.

The peculiar cheek-by-jowl economy in various parts of the South should also be noted. This can be clearly seen in the area between New Orleans and Baton Rouge. Here are some of the most deprived whites and Negroes in the world—the Bayou population. Many of them cannot speak English; they have never been to school or attended for such a short time that they learned little; their health standards are unbelievably low. They live next door to the most advanced of all industries—the space industry. But there is no direct relation between these people and the neighboring plants. Of course, such contrasts are not limited to the South. Just consider Harlem and Columbia University, or the White House and Georgia Avenue in Washington, D.C.

The next point is that Negroes in the South will continue to depend on segregated colleges for a long time, and these segregated institutions need a tremendous amount of shoring up. Foundations have finally begun to put some money into them, but the gap between what those institutions are and what they should be is great. They continue to produce a Negro leadership with inferior education. Of course, the situation will improve, and many graduates of these colleges will continue their education up North. However, those who leave are not likely to go back to work and live in the South.

These policy observations can be reformulated as questions. First, how advantageous is it for the American economy to have regions that are at different stages of development? Does such imbalance itself contribute to the dynamism of the economy? Does the imbalance provide a stimulus for investment?

Second, how can an effective birth-control program be launched and carried out in the rural South? After all, most Negroes are Protestants, and state governments in the South need have no inhibitions on the birth-control issue. However, it is impossible to have white people tell Negro families about birth control. Negroes have suffered so much that they might conclude that they were being asked to exterminate themselves!

Third, what is required to make the affluent states understand the error of their failing to help raise minimum standards in the South? If California, Illinois, and New York understood that what goes on in Alabama, Georgia, and Mississippi is their problem too, they might support more liberal grants-in-aid to the South.

Fourth, can the trade unions contribute to the modernization of the South? It is interesting to note the little data that are available on the present status of the trade-union movement in the South. That in itself tells much. The Federal government alone is not going to be able to modernize the South. We need many kinds of institutions for this task and the trade-union movement still has to find a way to contribute.

Finally, how can the Federal government continue to help the Negro? Housing remains a very difficult area, as does school integration. The problem of employment, while not easy, may present fewer obstacles.

We have a paradoxical situation in the South. We see an area that has only recently rejoined the Union, an area undergoing rapid changes in all facets of its life, an area that has begun to deal with its fantastically complicated racial problem. More than half of the Negro population continues to live in the South, although out-migration continues heavy. Between 1960 and 1965, several hundred thousand Negroes relocated outside the region. Moreover, the South is the home of almost all of the country's Negro farmers, who are among the most impoverished and disadvantaged people in the country.

In seeking to speed its own advance, the South must pull the submerged Negro minority with it. It is doubtful indeed that the South has the leverage to carry this off unless it receives major Federal assistance.

In the 1930s the Federal government rescued the South from total collapse; in the intervening decades it has done much to help the South turn itself around. But the South will become a full partner in the Union again only if it receives much more help—help over a considerable period of time. For it must eradicate the roots of poverty, both white and Negro.

The claims of the South for such help are strong now that the North and West have learned that their problems are the South's problems once removed. A nation, like a family, must use its resources in behalf of all its members.

Part Two PATHOLOGY

The story has yet to be written about the forces that helped to catapult the seamy side of the American economy onto the national stage in the early 1960s. Nagging unemployment was one factor; the persistence of depressed areas another; the mounting impatience of the Negro a third. The plight of the elderly was a further factor; increasing relief rolls in the face of rising per capita income was a troublesome dilemma. But none of these phenomena was new; each had existed for a long time, many in aggravated form. The journalists who discovered "poverty" and the politicians who responded to their challenge helped to place it high on the national agenda.

In consonance with our history and tradition, once we recognized the problem of poverty, we wanted to do something about it. We have come to recognize during the past few years, however, that the causes of human misery run deep and that remedies are hard to find.

The chapters in Part Two are efforts at clarification. They will attempt first to delineate the principal factors that contribute to various types of manpower waste and secondly to draw connections and point out linkages between some forms of social pathology.

They have one other aim. The enthusiastic reformer believes that changes in the environment, particularly the availability of more material resources to cover previously neglected human needs, are the answer to pathology. In the long run he may be right.

This cautionary approach is not a reflection of pessimism or cynicism. It is grounded in the conviction that nothing is gained and much may be lost if too much is claimed for the contribution of full employment to the reduction of the many types of social pathology. We do not have to consider jobs and incomes a cure-all in order to acknowledge their very substantial contribution to economic progress and social betterment.

In the chapters which follow we have sought to identify the many barriers that block the escape of people from poverty, that transmit the evils of unemployment from one generation to another, that confound the search for simple cures for juvenile delinquency.

There are many faces of poverty. Youngsters who are born and bred in poverty are more likely to live in poverty as adults than are their more fortunate mates. We know that if parents cannot give their youngsters a proper start in life, their children will be severely handicapped. This is a prelude to continuing difficulties. The generational aspect of poverty was pointed out as early as 1890 by Alfred Marshall, the distinguished economist. The vicious cycle describes the phenomenon of poverty.

Unemployment is another precondition for poverty. If a man loses his job and then uses up his savings and stretches his borrowing power to the maximum, he soon moves from the status of a worker without a job to that of a poor man. The transition from unemployment to poverty is gradual but often unavoidable.

In a modern society men live by the exercise of their minds and skills. To develop their intellectual or technical abilities, they must have training. Therefore, limited education is another factor which is likely to be associated with poverty. Without a minimum amount of training, a man cannot find a minimum job.

A fourth cause of poverty is the inability to work because of poor health. In this country, we have a disturbingly large number of people with one or another physical or emotional handicap which makes it impossible for them to support themselves and their dependents. Some help has been made available for people in poor health in recent years through permanent disability insurance, but a large proportion of this group is not covered or does not qualify.

Another cause of poverty is old age, when a man is no longer able to earn his livelihood. "Old age" is a flexible term and can range from under thirty to over ninety, depending on the other characteristics of the individual and on the demands of the employer. For the military, it means about forty, since a man with twenty years of military service is eligible to retire. In certain sports, old age arrives much earlier. In some careers, age is not necessarily a barrier to work. The presiding judge of the Eighth Circuit Court of Appeals in the 1950s was ninety-three years old. Nevertheless, an older man with limited education and skill is likely to encounter difficulties in seeking employment. Social Security benefits, when added to the savings of a lifetime, make it possible for many older people to live without public assistance, but many others slip into old age without adequate economic resources at their disposal.

Another characteristic of many caught in circumstances of poverty is a large family. Until recently the minimum wage in the United States was $1.25 an hour. If a man worked forty hours a week, his gross weekly earnings might have been $50. If he worked full time during the entire year, his annual earnings might have been $2,600. According to the standards of the Welfare Department of the City of New York, a man with five children needs $5,000 a year to live at a subsistence level. Therefore, an unskilled man with a large family is likely to face poverty. In New York City today there are 10,000 fully employed people who do not earn enough to support their families adequately, and another 10,000 people who earn so little that their families are eligible to receive free food.

There are ethnic and racial characteristics of poverty. A majority of the 20 million Negroes and of the 5 million Spanish-speaking people in the United States are at or close to the bottom of the income scale. In percentage terms, the most impoverished group in this country are the Indians; the Spanish-speaking are next, followed by the Negroes. These groups, particularly the Spanish-speaking, are handicapped because they do not share the dominant culture. Moreover, they have limited access to public services, to schools, to jobs. The result of discrimination is often poverty.

Location, especially the accident of where one is born, is another important cause of poverty. The poor farmlands of the United States, particularly in the Southeast, are the breeding ground and major center of poverty for both the white population and Negroes. There are few jobs available in this area, and those who stay find it difficult to eke out an income. Those who leave with a limited education and no skill find it difficult to earn a living in the urban centers to which they migrate.

Whether or not we accept Freud's teachings, we now know that most youngsters who grow up with their natural parents have certain advantages. Most white boys and girls grow up in such families. Only 1 in 10 white youngsters reaches the age of eighteen without having lived until then with both his parents. However, not even 1 of every

2 Negro children who reach eighteen has lived with both his parents. While many children who are brought up in foster homes or by one parent are successful adults, the odds are against them.

The tenth face of poverty is the pervasiveness of low wages and intermittent employment in many sectors of the economy, particularly agriculture and consumer services.

These then are ten faces of poverty:

Born into poverty
Unemployment
Poor educational opportunities
Poor health
Old age
A large number of dependents
Minority status
Location in a depressed area
A broken family
Low wages and intermittent employment

Nobody knows how to cure poverty. All that we can hope to do is to reduce it as rapidly as possible.

Our list of factors does provide the direction for preventive and remedial action. In our society, the key to a family's standard of living is the man's job—often supplemented by his wife's job. Unless a man is able to work, to work regularly, and to work at a wage that will enable him to provide for his family, he cannot escape the boundaries of poverty. Therefore, our efforts to reduce poverty must begin by expanding the total demand for labor and by eliminating as rapidly as possible jobs which do not offer a living wage. While the United States has lately been more venturesome in using fiscal and monetary policy to expand its rate of growth and the level of employment, we have not yet undertaken the policies and programs which could assure that all who are able and willing to work will be given an opportunity to do so.

The recent legislation of Congress establishing staggered minimum-wage increases from $1.25 to $1.60 an hour was a move in this direction. But not all jobs are covered, and, in any case, it will be 1968 before the $1.60 level is reached. Whether this will be a reasonable floor at that time will depend on, among other factors, the rise in the price level between now and then.

The most important factor in the control of poverty is employment at a reasonable wage. However, in many families, because of age, illness or desertion, there is no active wage earner. These families present the problem of providing them with incomes that they can escape from poverty and so that the children can escape. In most states this implies an increased level of public assistance and more reasonable standards of eligibility. On both grounds our standards are below what should prevail in an affluent economy. The recent increases in Social Security benefits, together with the inclusion of additional groups, will ease the income problems of many older people. But the fact remains that even the new levels will not provide sufficient income for millions of older persons unless they have accumulated sizable savings. We need further upward adjustments in benefits.

High-level employment and higher public assistance and Social Security benefit payments would go far in preventing many families from falling into or remaining in poverty. But a comprehensive attack requires much more private and public intervention. Above all it requires a strengthening of our educational and training systems. Whether a man can get and hold a job, especially a good one, depends primarily on the skills and competences he has acquired, and this in turn reflects the opportunities he has had to become educated and trained.

Since education is largely financed by state and local government and since there is great unevenness in the ability and willingness of the states to raise money for educational and training purposes, differences persist in the opportunities that children and adults confront. Those who live in circumstances of poverty are more likely to live in states and counties which are poor; this means that they and their children are unlikely to have access to the range and quality of public services which would enable them to extricate themselves from their predicament.

States and cities with higher per capita incomes also find it difficult to provide adequate schooling and training opportunities for their more impoverished citizens. To run a good school in a slum area requires money, but money alone cannot provide the answer. Therefore, many young people and adults who were born, reared, or are now living in the more affluent regions of the country often cannot acquire the education and skill which alone would enable them to get and hold a good job. This much is clear: Unless our society uses every agency of government and the community to improve the quality of education and training available to the children of the poor and to those adults who have not been able to find a place in the economy, the next generation will be trapped as was the last. A man without basic schooling and without some type of skill has less and less prospect of making a secure niche for himself and his family.

Large families and broken families are both likely to be poor. The two are not unrelated. A man who finds that he cannot support his dependents, even though he tries, may desert his family—particularly if he realizes that their income may even be enhanced by his desertion under the perverse laws prevailing in many states.

But even if we succeed in introducing more humanity and more logic into our system of public assistance, it must be recognized that family limitation is an important factor in the reduction of poverty. After many years in which politicians were intimidated by the Catholic electorate, our legislators have started to take remedial action. But we cannot expect too much too quickly. Control of the number of children in a family has always been best achieved by families with a good education, an adequate income, and comfortable living quarters. All three of these conditions are missing in poor families. If the health and welfare authorities devise new and skillful methods of communication, support, and encouragement, more and more young women living in poverty may be encouraged to practice birth control. But birth control is not a panacea and cannot be expected to make more than a modest, if important, contribution to the reduction of poverty. To the extent that it is successful it may not only reduce the numbers born into poverty but also reduce desertions, thereby enabling more children to grow up with both parents.

Much of the nation's poverty is concentrated in the Southeast and Southwest on farms which cannot support the large numbers who live on them. Every year tens of thousands of "surplus" farm dwellers leave for the city in the hope of a better future. Poorly educated and otherwise poorly prepared for urban life, most of these migrants find the urban environment a major challenge. While some are able to make this transition more or less easily, many others flounder.

We have paid very little attention to the needs of migrants; little help is available to them in their preparation for eventual transfer, and little is done to assist them once they move. These people want to escape from their background of poverty, but they need help in order to succeed. They need to acquire at least the foundation for a skill before they move so that they will not join the ranks of the unemployed, and they need orientation and specific services that will aid them in negotiating the complexities of the modern metropolis. To permit the least-prepared to cope with these challenges on their own or to force them to seek help from their relatives and friends who themselves are at the bottom of the ladder compounds the problems of a successful transition. Here is one of the gaping holes in our system of social services.

We noted the prevalence of poverty among ethnic and racial minorities. It is not enough that this country is in favor of civil rights. We cannot approve of civil rights in principle and ignore them in practice. One of the most intractable problems in the entire field of poverty prevention and control is white hostility to the Negro. In the past the more affluent members of the white community were able and willing to assist other whites, immigrants and migrants, who were in need of help. But no one rushes to extend help to the Negro.

While we have argued that a significant impact on the causes of poverty will require much larger expenditures than we have yet been willing to commit, money is not the only requirement. Poor white people and poor Negroes need more income and better public services—but they also need the encouragement and support which can be provided only by the members of the middle class. And this support and encouragement must go beyond words to actions, to actions that will influence where the poor can live, where their children can go to school, where they can play, where the family can worship. Only if the more affluent members of the community acknowledge the poor as fellow citizens will the resources, financial and human, be forthcoming. The final test is whether the well-to-do consider the poor worth the effort.

Chapter Seven Poverty and the Negro

We have seen that the problems of poverty include the influence of education, illness, age, and rurality. In this chapter we will consider specifically poverty and the Negro. Why have we singled out the Negro for special consideration?

We know that a great many Negroes are included in each of those groups in our population who are poor because they have had inadequate education, or because they suffer from serious illness or disability, or because they are old, or because they live in agricultural regions where the economic base has eroded. In fact, all the Negroes who live in poverty or near poverty are included in one or more of these groups.

However, there is justification for focusing attention on the Negro *qua* Negro in addition to studying the illiterate, the sick, the older person, and the marginal farmer. Although the first Negroes were brought to the Colonies almost 350 years ago, color itself has not yet been eliminated as a major economic disability. The probability that a man will be impoverished as well as the probability that he will escape from poverty is not the same for the black man as for the white man. History makes it much more likely that the Negro will be poverty-stricken and that the attitudes and behavior of the white community will make it much more difficult for him to escape from this condition.

However, since there is overlapping between categories—that is, between the condition of race and most of the other determinants of poverty, we will attempt to avoid redundancy. Certain characteristics and conditions are likely to impoverish any man, white or Negro. We will not consider these forces and situations in this chapter.

We will however call attention to those circumstances and conditions from which Negroes suffer disproportionately, in order to understand the poverty that afflicts them. Only in this fashion will we be able to escape, at least in part, from what would otherwise be the trap of circularity: Persons with little education are much more likely to be impoverished than those with more education. Many Negroes have a limited amount of schooling; many Negroes live in poverty. So far the question of race can be canceled out in the equation. But if a disproportionate number of all those with limited education who live in poverty are Negroes, we have noted a fact that is apparently related to the question of race. And race would be relevant if we find that of all those with a particular economic disadvantage, such as limited education, a disproportionate number are Negroes.

The interaction among the factors that contribute to reducing families to poverty or keeping them at that level makes it impossible to ascribe a specific weight to the factor of race in cases of Negro poverty. But it will be possible to call attention to the factors that are particularly important in keeping so many Negroes on the lowest rungs of the income scale. After these factors have been identified we will be in a better position to weigh alternative policies aimed at reducing the proportion of Negroes at the bottom of the economic ladder.

Following are the major factors that appear to play a differentially important role in keeping such a high proportion of all Negro families on a poverty or near-poverty level.

1. The majority of Negroes are born and continue to live in the South —primarily in the Southeast, that region of the country which since the 1880s has been characterized by a relative manpower surplus. This means that Negroes are particularly handicapped in obtaining employment within the region in which they live, since they must compete not only with white males but also with white females. Less than 30 percent of the total white population live in this area of relative labor surplus, while the comparable figure for Negroes is 60 percent.

2. Approximately 1 out of every 4 Negroes continues to live on a farm or in a rural nonfarm area. This is a slightly higher proportion than obtains for the white population. To this must be added the fact that almost all of these nonurban Negroes live in the Southeast, the area with the least profitable agriculture. Only 37 percent of all whites who live in nonurban areas, however, live in the low-income South.

3. The last quarter century has seen an accelerated migration of Negroes off the Southern farms into the cities of the South, North, and West. World War I stimulated the outflow that had been under way for some time previously, but the major migration dates from World War II. Although economic opportunity in the cities was certainly the major magnet that drew so many Negroes off the farms, another important factor was the agricultural revolution that caused the de-

cline of the cotton culture in favor of dairy and cattle raising in the states of the Old Confederacy.

This economic revolution was accompanied by a revolution in skill which greatly reduced the requirements for unskilled labor. Many Negroes left the farms where they could no longer eke out even a marginal livelihood. Among them were men and women who joined the migrant farm labor force on the Atlantic Coast. Hard as it is to believe, they actually improved their economic position by this shift. The fact that history had placed the overwhelming majority of Negroes on Southern farms and the further fact that in recent decades this sector has had less and less need for their labor represent major handicaps that they have had to surmount before making a place for themselves in the expanding sectors of the economy.

4. Although migration off Southern farms and from Southern cities, particularly between 1940 and 1953, was one road which many Negroes took to improve themselves, it must be pointed out that, other things being equal, the migrant is likely to be at a disadvantage relative to the population settled in the communities where he relocates. More whites than Negroes tend to migrate across county and state lines, and Negroes comprise a disproportionately large percentage of all migrants with less than a high school diploma. This means that even if the employment market is better in the communities in which they have relocated, they are likely to find themselves at the end of the queue because of less adequate preparation for jobs.

5. Many Negro migrants were handicapped because they came from states and areas where they had had access to education and other developmental opportunities much inferior to those available to the population among whom they were relocating. Therefore, it is not only the stresses and strains connected with relocation that handicap Negroes in their new environment, but also their poor education and training compared with the standards prevailing in their new communities.

6. The factors that result in migration in the first instance, and migration itself, tend to be associated with a high incidence of broken families. This is particularly true with respect to the Negro. We noted earlier that less than half of all Negro youngsters reaching eighteen had lived with both of their natural parents throughout their childhood and adolescence. The comparable figure for the white population is around 90 percent. Even after we make allowance for the survival among Negroes of the extended family in which grandmothers are often willing and ready to rear their grandchildren, this is an

excessively high degree of family disorganization. It is particularly burdensome for Negro boys and young men who grow up in a completely female household and who have no close male relative. We must admit that this high order of family disorganization is a great affliction to many Negroes as they struggle to make a place for themselves in white America.

Related to the problem of family disorganization is the carry-over into the present generation of sexual patterns that militate against family stability. It is important to recall in this connection that prior to the Civil War colonial and state law below the Mason-Dixon line did not permit Negroes to marry or allow the Negro male to protect his marriage bed and that until recently Negro girls in many parts of the South were fair prey for white youths. As W. J. Cash pointed out in his classic study, *The Mind of the South*, ". . . efforts to build up a taboo against miscegenation made little real progress." [1] However, the relevant fact is not that many Negroes continue to follow a sexual pattern that is relatively uninhibited, but that large numbers have adopted the standards of the middle-class white population.

A disproportionately large number of Negro children are still born out of wedlock—more than ten times the proportion of white children. This suggests that many of them will be brought up under adverse conditions which will make it difficult, if not impossible, for them to acquire the values and behavior patterns associated with independence and self-support.

7. What a person is able to make of his potential and his life depends in considerable measure on the guidance and support that he receives during his formative years, primarily from his parents. We have noted that a disproportionate number of Negro children grow up without having both parents available to help them. What of those who do live with both parents? Many Negro parents are unable to provide adequately for their numerous offspring; they simply do not earn enough. Moreover, most of them are unable to prepare their children for an environment in which white attitudes and white behavior toward Negroes will be markedly different from what they themselves experienced. Undoubtedly many Negroes are caught in constricted circumstances today because they were unable to take advantage of the opportunities that were opened up to them in an earlier day. It is likely that their children will also find it difficult to grasp quickly the new opportunities that are becoming available to them.

[1] Doubleday Anchor Books, Garden City, N.Y. (Copyright 1941 by Alfred A. Knopf, Inc., New York.)

8. This gap between established attitudes and the new reality has many manifestations, and none is more relevant than the continuing high birth rate among rural Negroes. For a long time farmers knew that a child was a good economic investment. At least there was no reason to consider him a liability, particularly in the cotton culture of the South, where even very young children were customarily used as farmhands. Parents knew that many owners preferred to rent their farms to large families. There was no reason, therefore, for a Negro farmer not to have a large family.

But times have changed. Children must attend school, and even if they are available for work there is little for them to do in the new type of farming now prevalent in most of the South. But the children keep coming. The Negro farmer knows little about birth control; the whole concept is alien to him. And when the proponents of birth control are whites, as they usually are, the Negro is likely to balk at taking their advice. The highest birth rate in the country is found among the Southern Negro rural population. The hold that poverty has on so many of them will not be broken unless they leave the farm or, if they remain, unless the average size of their families shrinks appreciably.

9. The probability that children will become self-supporting, responsible citizens, that they will be able to care for themselves and their dependents, is heightened if their parents can give them a good start. We have seen that many Negro parents are unable to do this for their children. In addition, there are related factors which are very important: the opportunity to attend good schools, to receive proper medical attention, and to enjoy other opportunities in childhood, such as healthy recreation. But, as we have noted, a disproportionately large number of Negroes live in the South, and the rural areas of the South are conspicuous for their inability to provide adequate public services. Moreover, the Southern Negro is further handicapped since he can avail himself of much less than his share of many of these services. Nowhere has the heavy hand of segregation and discrimination been more in evidence than in limiting the Negro population to the least desirable of these inferior public services.

Although the South has come a long way since conditions called forth the comment of the late Charles S. Johnson of Fisk University to the effect that the whites in Mississippi had been educated off the backs of the blacks, the fact remains that in the North as well as in the South Negro children have generally had access to schooling that has been inferior, and sometimes grossly inferior, to that available to white children. Similar discrepancies have long existed in both North and South with regard to Negro and white access to medical and hospital care. Once again the Southern Negro has been particularly disadvantaged, because total expenditures were much lower in the South and the racial barriers much higher. And the Negro farm population was the most benighted.

In a different arena, closely associated with poverty, are the very limited opportunities available to Negroes in most areas of the country for obtaining vocational education. Negroes are differentially handicapped here even after allowance is made for the fact that opportunities available for vocational education for the white population are also far below a desirable level. To take a single illustration of many both in and out of the Deep South: Until recently, Dallas offered about twenty different vocational-education programs for white high school students to every one or two that it made available to Negro students.

The intensity with which many Southern white parents fought the Supreme Court edict to desegregate their schools was not exclusively a reflection of racial prejudice against the Negro. It also reflected an acknowledgement of the inadequate system of segregated education, and their fear that desegregation would result in a leveling down in the education available to whites.

10. So far this analysis has been concerned primarily with the South because such a high proportion of Negro families at the lower end of the income scale—those with less than $3,000 annually, approximately 72 percent of the total—live there. But the circumstances of the Negro in the North and West are hardly sanguine, and the outlook is bleak as a result of the recent migration. As background, it is necessary to stress that *de facto* and, until recently, often *de jure* segregation has prevailed throughout most of the North, with its heaviest weight on housing, education, and employment. As a result of the postwar housing shortage and the flight of middle-class whites to the suburbs, the Negro masses are today often crowded into various sections of the central city and confined to a ghetto-like existence in which they are often exploited by both Negro and white landlords and merchants.

The urban services available to recent Negro migrants—especially education and medical care—may be considerably better than those to which they had access in their home communities. But the Negro ghetto in the large city is frequently bereft of the supporting social structures and family ties which gave some order and cohesion to their early lives. Moreover, both the city-born Negro and the Negro migrant are likely to be able to obtain services which are not one but several levels inferior to those available to white families in the middle- and even lower-income range.

11. The flight of the white middle class from the city to the suburb has meant a substantial weakening in the base of support for public education. The more affluent schools in the suburbs sometimes spend up to two times as much per pupil as do the schools in the central city, in which most Negro youngsters are enrolled. While the ratio may vary, this differential pattern is duplicated in most of the major centers of Negro population.

We have heard *ad nauseam* that young people who drop out of school are seriously jeopardizing their prospects for employment. But too little attention has been paid to the *reasons* that so many young people, particularly young Negroes, drop out of school. We know that one important reason is that the school does not appear to be meaningfully related to their present or even future lives. The overwhelming proportion of the dropouts are one, two, or more years behind the grade appropriate for their age. It is likely that they do not have the basic reading, mathematical, and comprehension skills which will make further learning from books possible. School is a day prison where they are forced to sit until the three-o'clock bell rings. If we look back of this inability of so many young people to cope with junior and senior high school, we find that several factors are responsible. These include inadequate stimulation and support at home and despondent and defeated teachers and administrators.

The substantial isolation of the Negro community from its white neighbors means that many Negro children are not properly stimulated during their preschool years, and enter school with major handicaps. These handicaps are surely remediable, but the school authorities must have the desire and the resources to remedy them. All too many have lacked one or the other, and sometimes both.

It was long the proud boast of American educators that the public school system would turn the children of immigrants into real Americans. In large measure this boast was justified. But the aim of the Southern segregated school was to keep a wide social distance between white and Negro; and the result of the *de facto* segregation in the North was not much different. Put as simply as possible, for all too many Negroes the public school has failed to perform its basic task of providing the tools that alone will enable them to escape from the poverty and other constraints that held their parents prisoners.

12. This brings us to the all-important and closely related area of

employment. One reason that so many Negroes are little motivated to do well and continue in school is that they see all about them proof that a Negro does not get his just deserts. Many an educated Negro has been forced to take a menial job. And legend has tended to exaggerate the facts.

While discrimination in employment has at long last begun to ease, it will be a long time before it can be disregarded in assessing the economic position of the Negro and his prospects for the future. During the last several decades the American economy has seldom had enough jobs for all who were capable and desirous of working. Less well prepared than the average citizen for work, the Negro was doubly handicapped in competing for employment because of the preference of most employers for white employees. In addition to prejudices of employers, the Negro has had to contend with the barriers created by many unions, particularly craft unions; thus large segments of the occupational structure have been closed to him.

As recently as a decade ago there were no production jobs in Southern industry open to the Negro except in a few border states, and then only in a few enterprising concerns. Although the situation has improved somewhat in the interim, progress has been very modest. In the North, the rate of improvement has been considerably more rapid—although one recent government report showed that of about 200,000 employees in sales positions in firms doing business with the Federal government, 200 were Negro!

13. One of the most serious consequences of the fact that Negroes are so low in the occupational hierarchy is that very few Negroes are able to give others a helping hand. Many people find a job through a relative or friend. But if all of one's relatives and friends are prohibited by law or custom from entering desirable fields of employment —this opportunity does not exist. The slow but steady and, in some cases, rapid decline in employment discrimination against the Negro will dissolve this particular handicap—*if* Negroes obtain the education and training which will enable them to qualify for jobs, and *if* the fields where there have been breakthroughs continue to expand.

14. Another handicap that Negroes have faced in recent years has been the fact that a considerable number who succeeded in obtaining employment in the meat packing, steel, rubber, automobile, and other major industries suddenly were displaced by machines or through plant relocation. Many of these men were former farmhands who had succeeded in working up to semiskilled jobs paying $2.50 and even $3 an hour, which meant that they and their families had been

able to move a considerable distance from their poverty-stricken back-grounds. But when they lost their jobs, they were in a poor position to get new ones. They had only a little education, and they were skilled at only one machine or process. Consequently, many fell back into poverty. Recent government figures show an ominous decline of several percentage points in the labor force participation rates of Negro men between the ages of twenty-five and fifty-five. A consider-able number of Negroes have stopped looking for work.

15. Our economy is called a system of private enterprise because it depends on individuals in many different sectors to take the initiative in setting up goals for themselves and in pursuing them. This goes for employers, farmers, laborers, investors. But to set goals and to work toward their accomplishment requires confidence in one's abilities and confidence in the integrity of the business system and the larger so-ciety. Yet it is just this self-confidence and confidence in the larger community that so many Negroes do not have.

Their history and experience are replete with evidence that they will not be treated fairly. Until recently, a Negro in one of the rural communities of the Deep South who succeeded in accumulating even a modest amount of money put his life in jeopardy, since many poor Southern whites cannot tolerate the idea of a Negro's being substan-tially richer than they. Times are changing, but the oppressive history which has stalked the Negro in the United States continues to influ-ence the attitude and behavior of a great many Negroes. Confidence is important for the success of an enterprise system; the toll that lack of confidence takes is very high even if it cannot be quantified.

The foregoing can be summarized by sketching three major con-stellations of poverty that characterize large numbers of Negroes. The Southern farm constellation consists of many Negroes, with very large families, living on poor land, often subject to eviction because of changes under way in Southern agriculture, without access to ade-quate educational and health services, with little confidence in them-selves or in the white community because of the longtime deprivation of their rights and the systematic exploitation to which they have been exposed.

The Southern urban constellation has these characteristics: A large number of poorly educated Negroes have moved off the farms into the rundown areas of the city where they pay relatively high rents for dilapidated housing; city-born and migrants continue to be excluded from many preferred types of employment, particularly industrial employment; while they have access to better public services than the farm population these services are much inferior to those available to the white population with whom they must eventually compete. The craft unions continue to exclude them and they are still discriminated against by other unions. The fact that many of the new jobs are in the service area makes it possible for employers to use white women, which adds to the difficulties which Negroes must surmount in finding employment.

The third constellation consists of the urban centers in the North and West. Many Negroes in these areas are recent migrants and because of their inferior education and training they are much less prepared to cope with urban conditions than the local-born. Local-born Negroes and Negro migrants alike tend to be crowded into ghetto-like areas of the large cities where they are exposed to the many disorganizing influences of slum life superimposed on the disorganization which characterizes many Negro families. Negroes have access to public services which are better than those available in the urban South and much better than those in the rural South, but which are still grossly inferior to those available to their white neighbors with whom they must eventually compete. While discrimination in employment is easing, it continues to be widespread. The generally hostile white attitudes that have for so long determined race relations in the United States have left deep scars upon large groups of Negroes with a corresponding undermining of their confidence in themselves and of their desire and willingness to strive to accomplish.

Now that we have delineated the major determinants of Negro poverty and summarized them in terms of three principal constellations, we are in a position to outline a series of policy actions which if undertaken and energetically pursued offer prospects of a significant reduction in, if not the elimination of, this social pathology.

In considering policy directions, it will not be possible to distinguish between the factors contributing to poverty among the population as a whole and those factors which operate differentially in Negro poverty. Much of what is suggested in the following section which has specific relevance for easing the handicapped position of many Negro families would also contribute significantly to reducing poverty among the white population. The general recommendations will be followed by the more specific; suggestions for governmental policies will be followed by suggested policies for other sectors of our society, including the Negro community itself.

Congress must determine whether it will further implement the Employment Act of 1946. It should consider how fast and how far it is willing to go to ensure that individuals able and willing to work who cannot find jobs in the nongovernmental sector could obtain employment on government-supported projects. The magnitude of the challenge is suggested by the following: To the conventional 4 percent or so unemployed should be added the more than a million persons who work part time because they cannot find full-time jobs; the larger number of persons who are underemployed in agriculture, a figure that many experts place in the neighborhood of 2 million; the large number of men with varying handicaps who have dropped out of the labor force because they cannot find work under slack employment conditions; many married women who would like to work if the opportunity were offered; and many young people past school-leaving age who are still in school only because they cannot find a job.

As the U.S. Commissioner of Welfare has pointed out, serious gaps remain in our social security legislation, since, in a considerable number of states, unemployed persons capable of working are not entitled to relief, no matter how desperate their plight. In most localities stringent residency requirements must be met before one is eligible for public assistance. In a $740 billion economy there is no excuse for such regulations, which have the inevitable consequence of spreading demoralization and making it much more difficult for children in many families to acquire the minimum prerequisites for leading effective lives.

In sum, it is not strange that the income earned annually by approximately 2 out of every 3 Negro families in the South and approximately 1 out of every 3 in the North places them within the poverty zone. Against the background which has just been sketched, the more remarkable finding perhaps is the considerable number of Negro families—about half—who have managed to rise out of poverty.

A revision of public assistance should aim at: a reconsideration of appropriate minimum levels of support; a reassessment of the eligibility requirements to ensure that the incentives to work are strengthened; a shift in emphasis from relief to rehabilitation, and the establishment of sufficient administrative controls by the Federal government to ensure that all groups are treated equitably.

The American people are slowly coming to appreciate that the key to economic progress both for the individual and for the nation is the quantity and particularly the quality of the education and training available to present and prospective members of the work force. But we have not yet accepted the fact that the unequal distribution of personal and state income has created an unequal capacity among different localities to raise adequate revenues. A major solution would be for the Federal government to make larger sums available for the support of public education, particularly for those states which are unable to meet a reasonable minimum through their own devices. The Federal government must move more quickly and substantially in this direction—Senator Robert A. Taft recommended this about fifteen years ago. Moreover, it should establish minimum standards to ensure that at least a certain amount is spent—and well spent—for the education of every child. Otherwise, there is a distinct possibility that the poor Negroes, particularly in the rural areas of the Deep South, will benefit very little from an expanded Federal effort.

Inadequate health and medical services for the prevention of illness and for therapy and rehabilitation contribute significantly to the circle of poverty, illness, and inability to work. There is much room for expanded governmental action—Federal, state, and local—to broaden the access of many low-income groups to basic health and medical services. One of the important areas which are now neglected is health education; because of ignorance many children and adults suffer from nutritional deficiencies and other unnecessary defects. No effective program of health control is possible except as part of a much more comprehensive attack on improving the health of low-income families. Once again the Federal government should take the lead in making funds available for such programs; and it must see that the longtime discriminatory patterns which have prevailed, particularly but not exclusively in the Southern states, are broken and that Negroes have an equal opportunity to benefit.

The Federal government has been substantially involved in a wide range of housing and urban-renewal programs both by direct grants and through various credit devices. There is no serious argument among informed persons that despite these public programs—and the tremendous private building boom since the end of World War II— a great many American families, particularly Negro families, live in dilapidated houses and deteriorated neighborhoods. More Federal support will unquestionably be needed if many cities and rural areas are to be effectively rehabilitated in the years ahead. But the problem is complicated; more money alone will not satisfactorily answer the housing needs of the more impoverished members of the community, among whom Negroes loom large. There is an uncomfortable amount of evidence that many of the public programs during the past two decades have yielded little if any direct benefit to the groups, including Negroes, which they were designed to help. New approaches to urban renewal should precede a launching of expanded programs.

New and expanded governmental programs (in which the Federal government must play a key role) on each of these five major fronts —employment, welfare, education, health, and housing—are a necessary but by no means sufficient attack on the problem of poverty in general and Negro poverty in particular. It is difficult to see how significant and speedy progress can be made unless the nation devotes substantially enlarged resources to these ends, and it is difficult to see how these large sums can be secured unless the Federal government takes the lead, especially since the incidence of poverty is generally inversely correlated with the taxable capacity of the states.

One important point should be made explicit about the foregoing recommendations involving expanded Federal effort. The success of such an effort will depend not alone on the Federal government, but on the effectiveness with which state and local governments and the community at large participate in the several programs and strive to realize these national goals.

There are a series of policies involving the design of new programs or the improved administration of existing ones that hold out considerable promise and which should be energetically pursued. The rural regions of the South are one of the principal breeding grounds of Negro poverty. The approaches followed in the recent Appalachian proposals may prove helpful. But we know that the economic rehabilitation of a large area requires not years but decades. In the interim the incomes of many families must be increased to a tolerable minimum at the same time that special efforts are made to improve the preparation of youngsters growing up in those deprived areas so that they eventually can be helped to migrate to an urban center where they will find productive employment. It might be well for the Federal government to consider an adaptation of the principle of Federal action for "impacted areas" to these economically declining communities: It might make special assistance available to prepare the younger generation for migration; it might proffer assistance to the large cities which have been inundated by poorly prepared migrants. The mayors of these cities have repeatedly pointed out that they require assistance if they are to speed the assimilation of those newcomers.

The division of so many metropolitan areas into a declining central city where only the poor live and the suburbs where the middle- and upper-income groups reside has resulted in a serious imbalance between need and revenue. It is time for a thorough reappraisal of state-local taxation with an aim of bringing about a better balance between the two. This is particularly urgent since the government should spend much more per capita for the schools attended by the poor than those attended by the rich. But at the moment, the opposite is true.

There is no way of providing children in broken families with substitute parents. But there are ways whereby the public school, which has served the United States so long and so well, can give children reared in poverty a better start in life. However, such efforts require money; this in turn suggests that we look for some new ways of reuniting suburb and city or at least of enabling the city to share more equitably in available tax sources.

The recommendations advanced so far have stressed government, primarily Federal government, action. Many of these programs aimed at reducing poverty require large expenditures, and therefore can most readily be undertaken by the Federal government. But there are other dimensions to the problem, and we will call attention at least briefly to policies that fall outside the governmental arena and that could prove highly constructive. Let us first consider what businesses can do.

First and foremost, business can adopt a more enlightened attitude toward government and can shift from its classic position of opposition to most social-welfare programs to selective support for those which it feels are sound. Business will have to meet, at least partially, the higher taxes engendered by the passage of these programs. But a sophisticated review of what happens to the tax monies currently collected would show that a great deal of them are not productive—they are used to maintain people on relief rather than to help them become self-sufficient. A successful attack on poverty will be costly, but it should be viewed as an investment. As people leave the public relief rolls, as their crime rate is reduced, as their productivity is enhanced, they and the society of which they are a part will inevitably be richer.

Businessmen are the only ones who can actually eliminate discriminatory practices in employment. They can and should do more than establish a formal equality between Negroes and whites. Many established personnel procedures, such as reliance on tests, are not necessarily colorblind. Insistence on hiring or promoting those who score highest rather than selecting from among those who are qualified—as one large utility company now does—will continue to militate against the Negro's making substantial gains. It is not suggested that business should favor Negroes who cannot perform. But it is suggested that "discretion" should now be used in favor of qualified Negroes, if only to accelerate a more effective integration.

Businessmen can do a great deal in other ways—for instance, by welcoming Negro businessmen into established organizations rather than segregating them in their own employer organizations. In one of the more progressive cities in the South, not even in the Deep South, there are no Negroes in the local chamber of commerce!

Among the most powerful of business groups are local realty interests, which exercise a dominant influence on the shaping of our cities. They have operated in the past to help keep the Negro locked in his ghetto. White buyers and sellers represent the overwhelming bulk of their business, so it is not surprising that these realty interests have been particularly sensitive to the wishes, desires, and even fears of the white community. But they now have an obligation to lead the way in facilitating the Negro's access to whatever housing he can afford to buy or rent. This is a challenge that no responsible group can afford any longer to ignore.

Finally, businessmen can make a significant contribution by participating actively in the formulation and execution of a great variety of programs which can contribute to speeding the integration of minority groups into American society. They have the specialized knowledge and skill that can alone assure that many programs are soundly conceived and effectively carried out. They have a big stake in strengthening the underpinnings of our democratic society, and they can do so by working aggressively to reduce racial strife and by lending their active support to constructive programs that will provide minority members with expanded opportunities.

Many discussions of the race issue are unrealistic because they either assume that all the remedial steps must be taken by the white population or predicate that the future of the Negro rests solely with himself. The foregoing recommendations have been concerned with action which must be taken by the white community; the following outlines what the Negro must do for himself if he is to escape from poverty.

First and foremost, the Negro leadership, which has been remarkably successful in recent years in adding to the reality of Negroes' political rights, must recognize that while this phase of the struggle is nearing success, freedom is only the foundation for equality. It cannot assure it. The leadership has the obligation to call attention to the many steps that the Negro himself must take if he is to transmute his freedom into equality: He must put forth the hard effort required in school and work. He must be helped to shift his time perspective from the near future to more distant goals. He must be encouraged to compete with whites even at the risk of failure. He must venture forth from the pseudosecurity of his segregated world into the larger white world which remains alien and hostile. All these things and many more the leadership must encourage the Negro to do.

In a discussion of Negro poverty, it is important to note that not all Negroes are impoverished and that more and more of them are reaching an income level which will enable them to extend to their less fortunate members a helping hand in consonance with American tradition. Although Negroes have had limited opportunity in the past to develop strong self-help organizations, they can no longer look to the whites exclusively for such help. They have found out what they can do for themselves on the political front. They can undoubtedly do more for each other on the educational, economic, and communal fronts.

Thirdly, there is need for research and objective reporting. Understandably, while they were engaged in the struggle for their political rights, Negroes were acutely sensitive to the release of any information that could be used against them. But with their political and civic rights almost secured—except in the Deep South—they must reconsider this tactic of silence and evasion. The best prospects which Negroes have to help themselves and to get whites to help them depend on the dissemination of the facts about conditions in the Negro community that require corrective action. Glossing over the sources of weakness helps ensure that remedial programs will not be formulated or implemented. The truth, however unpalatable, can make one free because it can be a spur to action.

These, then, are a few of the challenges that the Negro community and particularly its articulate leadership face. They are not easy problems to resolve, but if they are tackled forthrightly, solutions will be found.

To round off the foregoing consideration of Negro poverty and to set it in the larger frame of America's destiny, the following concluding observations are offered.

The Negro revolution is helping to revitalize American democracy by reminding us about the gaps that remain between the promise of our tradition and its fulfilment. It is forcing us to appreciate anew that our democracy is as strong as its weakest link. We cannot continue to prosper as a nation if a significant minority of our population is excluded from the body politic. American democracy cannot be realized as a democracy for whites only.

A blind adherence to the principle of equality in the face of inequality of bargaining power can only perpetuate inequality and can contribute little to the establishment of a more equitable society. After almost 350 years of exploiting the Negro, we cannot merely tell him that he is now free to compete with the white man. He needs help, considerable help, to turn his new freedom into a lever for true equality. A white America that fails to understand these realities will suffer the consequences of thrashing around for bargain answers when only expensive ones have a chance of succeeding.

But it should be added quickly that this approach does not imply support for a Marshall Plan for Negroes. While a strong case can be developed for white America's paying compensation to the Negro for the centuries during which it exploited him, such an approach has serious risks. It is difficult to mix the present belated national effort to free the Negro from second-class citizenship with a new program that would in effect treat him differentially on the score of race. Much more in harmony with our tradition would be a broad program aimed at helping all disadvantaged groups, white and Negro alike. It has always been part of the essence of American democracy that all people are entitled to a more equal start in life's competition.

For many decades after the Civil War America turned its back on the Negro, leaving him to the mercy of the South. Among the important byproducts of the current Negro revolution is a new understanding of the extent to which so many of America's contemporary problems are national rather than regional. State and local governments remain important instrumentalities, but the power of the Federal government must frequently be employed if significant advances are to be made. In view of the scale of resources required, we can no more eliminate poverty than go to the moon unless the Federal government plays the dominant role.

The attack on poverty in general and on Negro poverty in particular helps to highlight another important dimension of contemporary life. We must plan and act on many matters in terms of a time perspective that is quite different from that in which we make annual appropriations. The more intractable the problems, the more farsighted we must be, the more long-range our efforts. But this does not imply that we must have the answers when we start, only that we have the will. Our pragmatic tradition should stand us in good stead. We should not hesitate to experiment and to learn both from our successes and failures!

Finally, poverty is a challenge and a reminder that affluence has value only to the extent that we know what to do with it. A high level of personal and family consumption for the majority is a desirable goal. But it is not sufficient. Only a people with compassion for its poor, irrespective of their color, have a future.

During the past century our young people have spent an increasing number of years in school preparatory to starting work. The patterns of schooling have differed in various regions of the country, and access to and use of the available schooling has differed among various groups in the population. But beneath these diversities have been certain general trends: Children and young people have tended to spend more years in school; the school year has been lengthened; the quality of the staff has been improved; the curriculum has been broadened and deepened to better meet the needs of an increasingly diversified school population; more and more young people have been graduating from high school and going on to college.

Today, more than 4 out of every 6 young people earn a high school diploma, and approximately half of these enter college. Once again, about half who enter college eventually earn their baccalaureate degree—that is, about 1 in every 6 in the age group. Put negatively, 5 out of 6 young people do not graduate from college: 1 leaves at some time in college, 2 stop with a high school diploma, 2 more leave high school.

In comparison, in 1900 only 17 in 100 earned a high school diploma; only 7 in 100 earned a college degree. In 1930, the comparable figures were 35 and 13 in 100. For a great variety of reasons, the American people have been willing to spend increasing sums on education and have been willing to delay the time when young people begin to work. These reasons include the beliefs that education is a good in itself, that it is a mainspring of our democracy because it creates a literate electorate, that it underpins our dynamic economy by helping to develop the potential and skill of future workers, and that it is a cornerstone of a mobile society because it offers the opportunity to youngsters born into low-income families to acquire the prerequisites for moving up the occupational ladder.

Our society has long considered the primary task of the school to be instruction in basic knowledge and reinforcement of basic social values. The school has responsibility only for the second stage of the socialization process—the family has responsibility for the initial effort. The school is the transitional environment between the sheltered family and the competitive workplace, and thus has always served as a training ground for employment.

In addition to instructing children in the use of language and numbers and familiarizing them with certain basic facts about the natural and social worlds, the school provides training in discipline, routines, cooperation, leadership, and the other facets of adult life, particularly those reflected in the world of work.

Whenever a basic social institution such as the public school has multiple functions to perform, it is inevitable that the professional leadership as well as concerned citizens will disagree about the exact emphasis which the institution should place on the accomplishment of one or another objective. No decade has been free of disagreements about the responsibility of the schools for preparing young people for gainful employment, and about the best ways to discharge this responsibility.

Rather than reviewing this never-ending controversy, we will delineate some of the major changes in the relationship between education and employment that have characterized the recent past and those that are likely to be upon us before long. First, with regard to the changes in the economy: The number of jobs which require little more than a strong back and a willingness to work long and hard has been declining rapidly. One generalization that can be safely ventured here is that whenever a machine is invented that is capable of doing the tasks formerly performed by large numbers of persons, it is likely to be installed—even if the machine is costly and even if the workers were paid a low wage. The last several decades have seen more and more routine laboring jobs eliminated in agriculture, mining, construction, and manufacturing and in the service sector of the economy.

At the same time, the economy has created opportunities for an increasing number of persons with professional, technical, or managerial skills—that is, individuals who have completed higher education.

Another development has been the rapid extension of white-collar jobs below the professional and technical level—that is, in clerical and sales occupations. These are the jobs for which a high school diploma or junior college degree has increasingly become prerequisite.

We have noted the steady expansion in higher education reflected in the growing proportion of the population which attends and graduates from college. These are the young people who are filling the rapidly expanding professional and technical occupations. We have also referred to the steady increases in the proportion who complete high school but do not go beyond—the source of supply for the rapidly expanding white-collar sector of the economy. For both of these groups, the schools have done well: They have been able to attract, hold, and educate an increasing proportion of the population for those occupational areas which have been undergoing the most rapid expansion.

But what about the 1 in 3 young persons who leaves high school and then faces a relative and even absolute decline in the number of laboring positions available? The age at which youngsters are permitted to leave school in most states remains sixteen, although a few states require attendance until the age of seventeen or eighteen. In some states young people can get working papers at fourteen. In light of the steady upward drift in the educational and skill requirements for jobs, it must be asked whether the educational authorities have been slow to respond to the changing demands of employers. The answer to this question hinges in considerable measure on the characteristics of the young people who now leave high school as soon as legally possible.

The number of years that a young person must remain in school is determined by law. But the number of years that he is able to profit from education is a function of a great many other variables, including his genetic potential, his developed intelligence, his values, the influences exerted on him by family, community, and peers, and by special circumstances that may dominate his life—such as trouble with the police, early parenthood, emotional instability.

The considerable effort that has been made in recent years to study the school dropout has provided many of the answers to the question of why a significant proportion of young people fail to complete high school. By far the most important reason is that by the time they reach school-leaving age, usually sixteen, many of them are several years behind schedule. Instead of being ready to enter the eleventh grade, they may be in the eighth or ninth grade. This usually reflects an early difficulty in mastering the curriculum, which, in turn, caused the youngster to develop negative attitudes toward school. Classes become uninteresting and the discipline increasingly burdensome. Small wonder that this group takes the first opportunity to escape from these constraints.

Another large group of dropouts are young people who were able to make normal progress in their studies but never became really interested in learning; they do not see much point in prolonging this experience until they acquire a diploma. Many of these young people are growing up in communities which place little importance on educational achievement and which have inadequate school facilities and teaching staffs; often they are not encouraged by family or friends to continue in school. Their early withdrawal usually reflects a pervasive lack of interest.

The third group is a much more heterogeneous assemblage of young people, including some with special talents, who have major problems which make it difficult or impossible for them to continue in school. Some have run afoul of the law and are already in custodial institutions. Others are so disturbed that they cannot meet the minimum requirements of the educational system. A considerable number of girls withdraw because of marriage or pregnancy. Others, usually boys, are determined to get away from home at the earliest possible moment. Some young people from low-income families are under pressure to become wage earners as early as possible. These groups and other distinguishable groups of young people prefer to leave school when given the opportunity.

The term "dropout" has an insidious connotation until one realizes that in earlier generations it could have been applied to youngsters who did not complete elementary school, and that now it is applied to those who enter college but do not stay to earn a degree.

Despite the increasing public clamor for all young people to remain in high school until they graduate, the following realistic factors must be confronted. There is no point in forcing young people to remain in school if they have not acquired the skills with which to learn. And if they cannot relate their school experiences to their present or future life, they do not make any effort to learn.

The ambitious national effort which would be required to ensure that all young people graduate from high school would be justified only if the knowledge and skills they would acquire between their seventeenth and nineteenth years would significantly enhance their opportunities for employment or would add to their individual and social performance as adults. The incremental education—which would be about 20 percent more than they now have—might or might not prove worthwhile.

Moreover, these questions must be faced: Do the knowledge and skills acquired in the last two years of high school add a necessary increment to the young person's personal capital? Or is the present reliance of many employers on a high school diploma as a prerequisite for employment for new workers actually an inexpensive screening device which has the additional effect of reducing the number of potential applicants from minority groups? If underemployment prosperity (which has characterized the American economy since shortly after the end of the Korean War) continues, it is likely that employers who must select new workers from among high school and post-high school graduates will simply raise their criteria, and the young man with only a high school diploma will still be at the end of the queue.

It is not a high school diploma per se that qualifies a young person for work and for responsible citizenship. Rather, it is his value orientation, social competences, intellectual knowledge and skills, and study and work habits that will enable him to find a place within our highly differentiated economy and society. Therefore, to appreciate the challenge to the schools it is necessary to look more closely at emerging social and economic trends.

In a very few years the vast majority of the American people will be living in metropolitan areas. The modern city does not provide the type of protective environment that for a long time was characteristic of rural America, where the uneducated could survive at a modest level. Many of our most acute problems reflect the transfer of the rural population, white and Negro, from the low-income farm areas of the Southeast into the large urban centers. We are suddenly becoming aware of a two-generational gap between the education and skills of the new migrants and those of the settled urban population. It may not be necessary for the urban dweller of the future to be a high school graduate, but it is difficult to see how he will be able to make his way unless he has the equivalent of at least ten years of effective schooling back of him.

The word "automation," like the word "dropout," is highly charged. Some writers proclaim that we are in the early stages of a revolution that will soon result in making work or workers obsolete. The new automated machines, with the help of a few programmers and maintenance workers, they say, will be able to turn out all the goods we need or desire. The critical questions, they claim, will be how to distribute income so that there will be an effective demand for all these goods, and how to turn our new leisure into constructive channels.

Others hold that nothing has changed—that there is no revolution, nor is there likely to be one. They claim that a tremendous gap remains between what we want and need as individuals and as a society and our ability to produce these goods and services. Prophecy is a poor platform for policy. However, the future will certainly be different from the past. No one knows how different, but some clues are emerging.

In the past, the average young person started to work in his early teens; in the future he will probably not start until his early twenties. What will happen to the large numbers of young people who simply cannot master the tools or develop the interests which would enable them to profit from a decade of additional schooling?

What a young person learns at home and at school has always influenced the type of job he can get and the rung he is able to reach on the occupational ladder. But one need only recall the first captains of American industry to realize that in our earlier days a modest amount of schooling did not bar an energetic and talented man from reaching any level of success. Ours was a society in which men competed with one another in the work arena. Increasingly, the competitive struggle has been moved backward, all the way back to the nursery school. What are the implications for a society—especially one committed to providing equality of opportunity—when a man's future is increasingly determined by how well he does in school, which in turn is greatly influenced by the socioeconomic status of his parents? We seem to be galloping toward a new type of society—one in which the good student will land at the top.

At the turn of the century, a young man could come off a farm or disembark from an immigrant ship and get a job in a factory the next day. Moreover, if he performed satisfactorily he could rapidly move up the occupational ladder; his advancement depended primarily on what he was able to learn on the job. If he were really able he could leapfrog out of the laboring ranks into the ranks of management.

The outlook for tomorrow is indeed very different. There are very few entrance jobs in manufacturing, for example, since manufacturing has not grown since World War II and the number of blue-collar jobs in this sector has actually declined. The expansion in employment which the economy has experienced since the war has been primarily in the service sector. A great many service jobs, especially for those persons with little education and skill, pay very little, have very little security, and present few opportunities for advancement. The outlook for the kitchen helper or the hospital orderly is bleak. And there is always the possibility that the machine will lead to the slow erosion of many of these jobs, which will make it even more difficult for the poorly educated and the poorly trained to find a satisfactory niche.

As a result of automation, we can expect a relative, and possibly even an absolute, reduction in unskilled jobs and a relative decline in the proportion of semiskilled jobs. And there is another aspect to automation that should be briefly mentioned. The substantially enlarged resources being devoted to research and development will certainly result in the more rapid obsolescence of knowledge and skill. But this will create a concomitant need for the expansion of educational and training opportunities for adults if the nation is to have a vital work force.

The outlook, then, is for further relative and even absolute declines in the unskilled and semiskilled blue-collar jobs, a probable slowing up in the expansion of white-collar jobs in those sectors where the computer can be installed, a continued growth in professional and technical workers, and a gap—possibly a growing gap—between the total number of jobs available and the total number of younger and older persons available for and interested in working.

Acknowledging that the amount of education an individual has acquired has a significant influence on his prospects for employment, should we assume that all young people coming of working age will be employed if they have earned a high school diploma? If education is only one of the determinants of employability, how much effort should society devote to attempting to keep the dropout in high school, and how much to other approaches aimed at expanding the demand for workers with limited competence?

To what extent can the high school solve the dropout problem, even with substantially enlarged resources? May it not be necessary to seek fundamental improvements much earlier in the schooling process so that all young people acquire the reading and other skills which they will need if they are to make constructive use of four years of secondary education?

Since many high school students with average or even above-average ability drop out because they are not interested in their classes and do not understand the importance of acquiring additional education, could some of this group be encouraged to continue to graduation if more work-study programs were available? Would their exposure to real jobs, their association with adults, their earning of money provide the stimulation and incentive which are now lacking? How practical is it for the schools to seek the cooperation of employers and trade unions in exploring this dimension?

No matter what efforts are made to hold all adolescents in school or in school-connected programs until they earn a high school diploma, some will continue to drop out. To what extent do these young people now have an opportunity to return to school or otherwise acquire a diploma? What steps might be taken to broaden their opportunities for a "second chance?"

Many employers have established the requirement of a high school diploma for all new members of their work force. Is this a reasonable requirement? If not, should efforts be made to encourage them to re-study this requirement in order to increase the opportunities of drop-outs to obtain employment?

In light of the probable speedier obsolescence of knowledge and skills in the years ahead, what actions should be recommended to individuals, employers, and communities so that more adults will have the opportunity to continue their education and training?

The probable increasing proportion of jobs in professional and technical occupations in the future raises the questions of whether there are serious barriers to entrance to college, junior college, or other post-high school educational and training facilities for some qualified young people and what types of action can be recommended to reduce or eliminate these barriers.

Is there any danger that, as a result of the current concern with the future employability of many young people, the high schools will slight or ignore other important goals? What, if anything, can be done to assure that this does not occur?

If more and more adults will need access to educational and training facilities, what steps should be taken by employers, governmental agencies, and other strategic groups in our society to help assure that the required facilities and personnel will be made available?

What actions can narrow the marked differences among regions in their ability and willingness to support education, and the substantial differences between urban and rural communities within the same region as well as between the central cities and the suburban areas of large metropolitan centers? What additional actions are required to assure that each child has a reasonable opportunity to get a solid educational preparation for his later work and life?

The school builds on the foundation that the family lays. What special efforts should be made by the school systems in communities in which large numbers of children and young people are growing up under handicapping circumstances, including the particular handicap of not living with both parents? Should school boards attempt to per-suade the American people that they should spend more money on children from low-income homes than on children from more privileged families? If such a policy is sound, what adjustments are required in our system of taxation to accomplish it? What programs are most likely to prove productive?

If the American people can be persuaded to make additional resources available for education in general and for secondary education in particular, what adjustments are called for in the present variegated patterning of secondary education which includes academic, vocational, and general curricula in comprehensive and specialized high schools?

Many of the issues posed above are of long standing. Some go back to the earliest days of public education. But, as we have noted, there are several new dimensions that should be borne in mind as these problems are studied, for the solutions must be attuned to them.

To summarize: Educational preparation has come to play an increasingly important part in determining the work and careers of the population. This means that any serious deficiencies in the schools will have increasingly serious consequences for the productivity of the economy and the stability of the society. A significant minority of the population grows in a family and community setting which fails to prepare them to profit from what the school has to offer. Therefore, the school faces a special challenge to meet the needs of this disadvantaged minority.

No matter how effectively the schools discharge their responsibilities, not all of their graduates will necessarily secure employment. Full employment will be easier to approach if gross differences in educational background are reduced, but even if these differences are eliminated, to achieve full employment now requires additional changes.

Nevertheless, if the schools are to make an optimal contribution to the preparation of the population for work and life, they must meet the overriding challenge of awakening in all of their pupils an interest in learning and teaching them the basic skill of reading on which a lifetime of continued learning ultimately rests.

The passage of the Employment Act in 1946 by a large Congressional majority underscored the conviction of the American people that the high human and social costs of unemployment require the intercession of the Federal government—first, to prevent depressions with associated loss of jobs and income; and second, if the attempt at prevention fails, to speed recovery and the expansion of employment and income.

During the two decades since the passage of the Employment Act, the Federal government has developed broad monetary and fiscal policy and shaped manpower policy to meet these new goals. Until these goals are fully realized, however, an affluent and humane society is obligated to pursue other policies and programs that reduce involuntary unemployment. The Employment Act allows for continued experimentation aimed at the eradication of all unnecessary unemployment.

The extent to which the public expresses a desire for new legislation and the extent to which Congress responds depend in considerable measure on an estimate of the urgency for action and the prospect that the means exist or can be developed to accomplish the desired ends. Hence, policy is greatly conditioned by the information available to the public concerning the causes and consequences of the malfunctioning of one or another part of the economy. Ideally, decisions on programs should be made in the light of information about their costs relative to the costs of making no changes or to the costs of alternative approaches.

The past several decades have seen substantial advances made in national income accounting procedures which enable economists to assess key changes in the economy in dollar terms. Substantial gains have also been registered in manpower accounting as it bears on employment, underemployment, and unemployment. But neither national income accounting nor manpower accounting provides an adequate basis for an analysis of the full costs of unemployment to the individual or to the community.

This chapter will delineate and assess the many human and social costs that result directly or indirectly from our society's failure to make optimal use of the nation's human resources. Relatively little effort has been directed by academicians toward conceptualizing the complex facets of unemployment and the relationships between unemployment and various forms of social pathology. Moreover, government bureaus and other data-collecting agencies have devoted relatively little effort to developing the relevant data. It must be emphasized that public attention was last focused on unemployment in the 1930s and that from the outbreak of World War II until the last few years it has been at the periphery of the public's concern.

There is a further difficulty in tracing the human and social costs of unemployment. Unemployment is a phenomenon that is closely related to underemployment, delayed entrance into and premature exit from the labor force, inadequate individual and family income, absence of deferred rights and benefits, limited or nonexistent savings, and poverty. The longer a worker is unemployed or the more frequently he is unemployed, the more likely it is that he will early withdraw from the labor force. A full appreciation of the consequences of unemployment must include consideration of these other conditions.

A pervasive impact of unemployment is the barrier that it places in the way of many people looking for work or for better jobs. Three groups in particular are affected: those out of the labor force who want to work, those in the labor force who would prefer to remain at work but are forced out, and those who are underemployed and who want and need a job which will better enable them to support themselves and their dependents.

In the first group were the millions of workers who were not in the labor force in 1940 but who wanted to work and who seized the opportunity to find jobs during World War II. The movement into the labor force was dramatic; the overall participation rate increased from 55.2 percent in 1940 to 62.4 percent by 1944. It was, in fact, this phenomenon that largely accounted for the improvement in the position of nonwhite workers during the 1940s, an improvement that has not been matched in subsequent years.

More recent evidence of the way in which a relatively high level of unemployment is related to labor-force participation was the failure to account for over a quarter of a million male youths who were not in school and not in the labor force in 1964. The calculated unemployment rate of males sixteen to twenty-one was 11.9 percent, but when this group was added the true rate was 19.5 percent.

Many women, particularly older married women, are increasingly interested in holding down a part-time or full-time job for part or all of the year. Whether they are able to work depends largely on the employment situation in their communities. The same general situation holds for handicapped persons and for older persons who, though they have retired, prefer to return to part- or full-time employment. In a study of 100 metropolitan areas, William G. Bowen and T. A. Finegan found that in both 1950 and 1960 the level of unemployment in the community had a significant effect on the labor-force participation rates of five major groups. The "rates of teen-age males and males aged 65 years and older were much the most sensitive to unemployment; married women and teen-age girls constituted a middle group in this regard; and, as we would expect, the participation rates of prime-age males were least influenced by employment conditions." [1]

They noted that the depressive effects of unemployment on labor force participation increased from 1940 to 1960: ". . . whereas in 1940 an unemployment rate 1 percent above average was associated with an overall participation rate about ¼ *of 1 percent* below average, in 1960 an unemployment rate of 1 percent above average was associated with an overall participation rate about ¾ *of 1 percent* below average."

Relatively high levels of unemployment also appear to have had the effect of pushing certain members of vulnerable groups out of the labor force. Although the absolute numbers are small, there has been since the Korean War a 63 percent increase in the proportion of non-white males aged twenty-five to forty-four not in the labor force, and a 58 percent increase in those aged forty-five to fifty-four. Between 1961 and 1965 about 1¼ million men between the ages of sixty-two and sixty-four availed themselves of the new opportunities to qualify for Social Security benefits at age sixty-two at a reduced rate. About three-fifths of those who filed for benefits in 1962 were unemployed. About half had been out of work for more than six months, and a fourth for two years or longer.

Slippage out of the labor force may be considerably greater than the official data reveal. A special study suggests that perhaps as many

[1] "Labor Force Participation and Unemployment," in Arthur M. Ross (ed.), *Employment Policy and the Labor Market,* University of California Press, Berkeley, Calif., 1965.

as 1.8 million single men were not counted in the 1960 Census. About 1 million were nonwhite. The true unemployment rate for single non-white men may in fact have been 50 percent greater than reported.

We see, then, that relatively high levels of unemployment operate to delay the entrance of young persons who are out of school into the labor force and speed the exit from the labor force of men who are still within the conventional or even prime working-age brackets. We see, moreover, the difficulty of collecting reliable information about unemployment because of the slippage out of the labor force.

The third group that is affected by relatively high unemployment is composed of those who are employed part time, but who seek full-time work. In 1964 approximately 3.3 percent of all nonagricultural employees—over 2 million people—and 6.7 percent of hired farm workers—representing approximately 318,000 people—reported a de-sire to work full time but said they could not find such jobs.

Men attached to such industries as construction, lumbering, and agriculture are counted as having a job under certain conditions even though they are not working at the moment and are not being paid. In January, 1964, there were just under 200,000 such workers who could neither work at their own trade nor find alternative em-ployment.

Under the Manpower Development and Training Act, Congress specified that farmers who did not earn more than $1,200 annually were to be counted as unemployed; in this way Congress indicated its desire to help many of the self-employed to obtain training so that they could find jobs that might eventually pay them living wages. There are approximately 900,000 farm owners and managers in the United States whose family income is less than $3,000. Whether these families can escape from underemployment and poverty depends in large measure on job opportunities in urban centers. There are also over 6 million self-employed in the nonagricultural sector, many of whom would welcome an opportunity to change their work. Whether or not they will have this opportunity also depends primarily on a low level of urban unemployment.

The burden of this analysis is clear: Among the most grievous costs of unemployment are the barriers that it places in the path of many outside the labor force who want and need work; many older persons who, though they prefer to remain at work, are pushed out; and still others who want to change jobs in order to be more productive but are unable to do so.

The work that a man does largely determines his income, which in turn largely determines the standard of living of his family. Work also provides individuals with important social and psychological gratifications, considerations that will be explored later. We are concerned here with the relation of work to income, more specifically with the impact of the loss of work and loss of income on the individual and his family.

A study of unemployed workers, carried out by the National Bureau of Economic Research (NBER) in cooperation with the U.S. Department of Labor and entitled *Financial Adjustments to Unemployment,*[2] found that unemployment compensation covered only about 30 percent of the gross reduction of household income of these unemployed families. How did the unemployed cope with the remainder of the reduction? Primarily by reducing their consumption (70 percent), by going into debt (about 10 percent), and by drawing on past savings (20 percent). They economized most on food. The longer they were unemployed, the more they had to rely on cutting consumption, since they had earlier used up their savings and borrowing power.

This study was concerned only with the unemployed who were in covered employment, that is, entitled to unemployment compensation. A recent survey showed that only one-half of all unemployed workers actually receive unemployment compensation. Unemployment compensation replaces only about 15 percent of the total income lost by all unemployed persons (that is, persons with covered and noncovered occupations).

If a worker has been able to accumulate a reasonable amount of savings, and if he receives unemployment compensation amounting to about 50 percent of his normal wages, he should be able to cope with a short period of unemployment. But there are large numbers who are unemployed for a long time, or frequently; who have little or no savings; who are not in covered employment and therefore receive no compensation. Here indeed is a vulnerable group.

Their vulnerability is especially great because, when they do return to work, they are likely to slip down a rung or so on the occupational or income ladder. A 1963 study is suggestive in this regard: It points to the fact that the unemployed who returned to work did not share in the general gains in income achieved by most workers in the early 1960s.

The speed with which unemployment can destroy the economic independence of individuals and families is illuminated by a 1961

[2] The references to the specialized literature cited in this chapter can be traced through item 9 in the Bibliography.

study. Six percent of all families with a worker (not necessarily the head of the family) unemployed between five and twenty-six weeks were forced to seek cash welfare payments, and 9 percent had to seek other types of welfare assistance. Even when unemployment is not prolonged, 1 out of 10 workers loses his independence and becomes a welfare recipient.

Concern with unemployment stems from many sources, but none is more important than the fact that in our society adults capable of working are supposed to support themselves and their dependents by holding a job. The employed can stand on their own feet; the unemployed may become and even remain dependent. But the distinctions between work and independence on the one hand and unemployment and poverty on the other are not clear. Many individuals and families constantly move from one status to another on the broad continuum from a job and adequate income to underemployment or unemployment and poverty. Others fortunately move in the opposite direction.

The following examples are a warning against simplistic categories. There are about 9,000 families in New York City alone which are on welfare even though the head of the household works full time. A low wage and a large number of children will spell poverty even for a man with a full-time job. But unemployment, especially a long spell of unemployment, is more likely to be a major causative factor in propelling a family into poverty.

In 1961, the short-term unemployed family head had a median annual income of slightly over $2,600; those with longer spells of unemployment earned less than $1,500 on the average. In 1962, the loss of earnings of unemployed family heads pushed three-quarters of a million families below the poverty line.

Unemployment contributes to poverty because a loose labor market makes it difficult for the head of the household to find a full-time job and other members to find part-time or full-time jobs. The following figures bear on this point. In 1963, slightly over 3 out of 4 families without any working members had an income of less than $3,000. This was true of only 1 out of 5 families with one wage earner, 1 out of 10 where there were two wage earners, and about 1 out of 15 with three wage earners.

These data suggest that many families are self-supporting because of the contribution of secondary wage earners, although the participation of some of these persons, such as the mothers of young children, is not necessarily a net social gain.

Table 1, which is limited to heads of households and does not differentiate between those who worked less than full time by choice and those who could not find full-time jobs, throws additional light on the close relation among unemployment, underemployment, and poverty. More than half of all families where the head of the family did not work had incomes below the $3,000 level, and half of all families where the head worked only part time were likewise below the $3,000 level.

TABLE 1

Family Income and Work Experience of Head of Family, 1964

Work experience, head of family	Family income, percent		
	Under $3,000	*$3,000 to $5,999*	*$6,000 and over*
All families	17.6	26.9	55.6
Head working	11.8	25.8	62.3
Full time	9.3	25.5	65.1
50–52 weeks	6.7	23.5	69.6
40–49 weeks	11.6	32.1	56.4
27–39 weeks	22.3	35.6	42.0
14–26 weeks	32.1	38.7	29.2
1–13 weeks	52.7	33.0	14.2
Part time	47.5	30.7	21.9
50–52 weeks	44.2	31.0	24.7
40–49 weeks	39.9	37.8	22.5
27–39 weeks	42.5	29.7	27.7
14–26 weeks	49.4	30.1	20.5
1–13 weeks	58.4	27.4	14.4
Head not working	51.8	28.8	19.4

Source: U.S. Bureau of the Census, *Current Population Reports,* ser. P-60, no. 47, table 11, p. 31.

Many workers who become unemployed in one year suffer recurrent spells of unemployment in the same or succeeding years. A 1963 survey found that one-third of those with five or more weeks of unemployment had been unemployed at least a month in each of the three preceding years.

The available data do not permit us to distinguish the impact of unemployment from other economic causes in the tendency of many low-income families to continue from one year to the next to fall below the poverty line or to rise only slightly above it. But it is reasonable to postulate that unemployment and underemployment contribute substantially to this phenomenon of persistently low family income. Of families with incomes below $3,000 in 1962, 70 percent were also below $3,000 in 1963. Of those whose income rose, in more than two-fifths of the group earnings did not exceed $4,000. In many poor families the head has never earned enough to cover the family's needs.

But as James N. Morgan has pointed out, ". . . short-run cash deficiencies and temporary loss of earning power are not the sole explanation for the economic difficulties of poor families; their difficulties also develop from inadequate long-term protection against those contingencies which are likely to curtail further their incomes in the future." [3] In this respect, unemployment is an important determinant, since many rights and benefits accrue only to those who are regularly employed.

Chief among these rights and benefits is social security. Although coverage has been extended and benefits increased, only those who succeed in getting and keeping a job for a reasonable period of time are eligible to receive compensation for unemployment. And they are compensated according to their length of employment and previous earnings. When a worker loses his job, he often loses his rights to a pension, since the vast majority of pension plans have no vesting provisions. Here indeed is a major human and social cost resulting directly from prolonged unemployment. A worker with twenty years of efficient and effective service may lose all the deferred benefits that he has accumulated with his company.

Another frequently serious loss to an unemployed worker is his inability to retain hospitalization insurance, since he is no longer a member of a group plan and he cannot afford an individual policy. If illness strikes when he has no insurance, his savings are likely to evaporate very rapidly. Many families with an unemployed head are precipitated into poverty because of illness. The NBER study referred to above contains suggestive data on this point: Curtailment of hospital insurance is a major method of adjustment to lower income among the unemployed. According to Morgan, poor families generally have little protection against the costs of illness. Three-fifths of the poor families in his study had no insurance whatever; only one-third had hospitalization insurance covering all members of the family, in contrast to 63 percent for the population as a whole.[4]

---

[3] James N. Morgan and others, *Income and Welfare in the United States*, McGraw-Hill Book Company, New York, 1962.
[4] *Ibid.*

Data about the financial circumstances of families as the head of the household approaches the age of retirement are also revealing. The average Social Security benefit for a retired worker and his wife, if she is eligible for a wife's benefit, is $1,565 a year. The Council of Economic Advisors has estimated that a couple would need a capital sum of $19,000 to provide an annuity of $1,500 as a supplement to their Social Security income. This sum would presumably represent life savings; but workers with recurrent unemployment are unlikely to have accumulated any savings, and therefore are much more likely to spend their old age in poverty.

The foregoing data should suffice to make these four points clear: (1) The unemployed and the underemployed are much more likely to fall into poverty than those who are regularly employed. (2) Lack of work disqualifies many persons for many current and prospective rights and benefits provided under collective bargaining agreements and under Social Security. (3) Not having these rights and benefits will further act to trap people in poverty, for they will quickly exhaust whatever savings they have been able to accumulate. (4) When men are repeatedly unemployed or underemployed, they are unable to give their children a start in life which would help them to escape from poverty. Hence unemployment also has an important generational impact.

One consequence of unemployment, of course, is inadequate income and all that this connotes in a society in which money so largely determines the lives that people lead. But work has significance for individuals apart from the important issue of income. A job gives a man the basis for self-respect and a feeling of self-worth. When he loses his job and cannot find another, he must acknowledge that "he has within him no contribution that the economy values," and this in a society where economic evaluations are crucial.

A job also provides a man with a focus for his life. We know about the difficulties which many face in retirement, when they are cut off from the interests and friendships of the workplace. These difficulties are intensified for the unemployed. The humiliation and withdrawal of the long-term unemployed were vividly documented in various studies undertaken during the Great Depression. While the number of these individuals is fortunately much smaller today, the effects may be worse, because unemployment is not currently "legitimized" as it was in the shared misfortunes of the 1930s. Prolonged unemployment may also entail loss of skill, and sometimes it erodes the motivation of a man to become self-supporting once again.

Unemployment destroys the fabric of a man's life. There is no activity to fill his waking hours, no routine to anchor his existence. Day-to-day living is difficult. Time becomes his worst enemy, and the monotony of long hours with nothing to do robs a man of incentive to pursue constructive goals. Idleness is demoralizing; social contacts diminish, self-improvement often appears useless, and the confidence to carry on evaporates. Men without jobs are the failures in a society that traditionally measures success in terms of occupational achievement. But the unemployed do not give up easily, as the continuing search for work, which we will outline below, makes clear.

The tendency of the unemployed man to withdraw from social life affects his civic participation and results in a loosening of his community ties. Wilensky found that people with erratic work histories had much lower social participation than those with orderly work histories.

Although many factors affect whether a man votes or not, it is noteworthy that in the 1964 presidential election 73 percent of the employed voted, 65 percent of those not in the labor force voted, and 58 percent of the unemployed voted.

The consequences of unemployment per se cannot always be distinguished from the consequences of underemployment, low income, and poverty. Therefore, the following assessment of the major correlates of unemployment is frequently more suggestive than definitive. Nevertheless, there is every reason to believe that unemployment, particularly a repeated or prolonged spell of unemployment, is likely to have deleterious consequences such as those we will delineate below.

Migration and Mobility

While mobility is one of the critical adjustment mechanisms which operate to bring workers and work together, much mobility may be uneconomic and a social waste, not a net gain. In 1963, the migration rate for unemployed males was 11 percent, about double that for the employed group.

The amount of effort which the unemployed, the underemployed, and persons of working age outside of the labor force actively make in seeking work in new localities is itself greatly affected by the prevailing level of unemployment. Hathaway has recently reported on a series of studies which point up that in years of high urban unemployment the outflow from the farm to the city is substantially reduced, and many recent migrants who seek places for themselves in the city fail and return to the countryside.

Shuttling between urban and rural areas is probably more common among whites than among Negroes. Because of intense racial discrimination in the rural South, Negroes, once they have migrated into the cities, seldom return to the farm except for an occasional visit. But many who stay in the city do not obtain permanent employment or become effectively socialized in the new urban environment for which they have been ill prepared. The difficulties that confront many cities, such as the deterioration of housing and neighborhoods, rising welfare costs, and unsolved educational problems, are a direct result of their failure to absorb successfully large numbers of migrants.

A closely related phenomenon is the excessive intra-urban movement characteristic of many of the unemployed. Forced to find shelter in the least desirable housing and neighborhoods, they are most likely to be dislocated by urban renewal programs. The New York City Board of Education has reported that in certain schools the turnover of pupils exceeds 100 percent per annum.

Another manifestation of the excessive mobility associated with lack of suitable work opportunities is the plight of migrant farm laborers. Members of this group averaged 155 days' work during 1964, and had an average annual income of $1,581. Farm migrants suffer from unemployment, underemployment, and low income, and their children in turn are seriously handicapped by the frequent disruption or unavailability of schooling.

Family Life

Unemployment is particularly injurious to family life. Until the Social Security Act was amended in 1961, the law operated to speed the breakup of families where the husband was unemployed, since a mother with children was not able to qualify for "aid to dependent children" (ADC) as long as her husband lived at home. A 1960 study of ADC in Cook County (Chicago) found that in 15 percent of the closed cases the father had returned home.

Table 2 presents the relation between the employment status of the father and the circumstances under which children grow up. About 15 percent of all children are growing up in families that are living below the poverty level. Although we cannot assess specifically the respective contributions of unemployment, underemployment, and low wages to poverty, it is reasonable to postulate that unemployment is an important direct cause of depriving children of opportunities for growth and development.

The following data help to point up the substantial gap that continues to exist between the needs of the unemployed and poor and the assistance available to them. Total payments between March, 1964 and March, 1965 under ADC amounted to $1.7 billion. In the latter month, 1.1 million families with 3.4 million children were assisted. Average payments per month, per person, came to slightly more than $34, an amount sufficient to sustain life but little more.

Education and the Young

The linkages between unemployment and poor educational opportunities for the young are easy to delineate, although other factors are likely to be operating at the same time to bring about undesirable school results.

T A B L E   2

Percent of Children Living in Poverty by Labor Force Status of Family Head, March, 1964

Labor force status of family head	Total children Number	Total children Percent	White children Number	White children Percent	Nonwhite children Number	Nonwhite children Percent
Total	68,830	21.9	59,150	15.7	9,680	59.5
Male head	62,160	17.1	55,050	12.8	7,100	50.0
Female head	6,670	66.6	4,100	54.6	2,580	85.7
Employed	59,080	16.3	51,960	11.5	7,120	51.6
Male head	56,290	14.7	50,210	10.8	6,070	47.5
Female head	2,790	48.0	1,750	31.5	1,050	75.6
Unemployed	2,390	47.7	1,900	40.2	490	76.9
Male head	2,090	43.5	1,710	37.2	380	72.3
Female head	300	76.5	190	66.8	110	92.9
Not in labor force	7,360	57.9	5,290	48.3	2,070	82.3
Male head	3,780	36.7	3,130	31.9	650	60.0
Female head	3,580	80.2	2,160	72.1	1,420	92.5

Source: Mollie Orshansky, "Who's Who among the Poor: A Demographic View of Poverty," *Social Security Bulletin,* July, 1965, table E, p. 30.

A Kentucky miner called to court a few years ago by the truant officer said,

> Judge, I'm not the only man in this fix on the creek where I live. They's at least a dozen other men who ain't sent their children to school for the same reason mine ain't a'goin'. They can't send 'em cause they can't get hold of any money to send 'em with. . . . If the county attorney or the truant officer will find me a job where I can work out something for my kids to wear I'll be much obliged to 'em as long as I live.[5]

Even in less distressed areas, families have difficulty meeting the school expenses of children. In New York City, a recent survey of an eighth-grade class showed that in a three month period each child was asked to bring $26.50 in "extra money" to school. In this class, 70 percent of the children came from families on welfare who received 25 cents a month for a junior high school child's extra expenses.

The relationship set out in the following Table 3, which juxtaposes family income and completion of high school, is revealing. The reasons that young people give for dropping out of school are notoriously unreliable because they overlap. Poor academic performance, an adverse social climate in the school, and economic distress—the three major reasons—frequently operate simultaneously. Nevertheless, in a 1963

TABLE 3

Annual Income of Families of 1964 High School Graduates Not Enrolled in College and of Persons Who Dropped Out of School between October, 1963 and October, 1964

Family income	High school graduates	Dropouts *
Total	100.0	100.0
Less than $3,000	12.9	44.6
$3,000–$4,999	23.1	24.8
$5,000–$7,499	31.0	21.9
$7,500 and over	33.0	8.6

* Figures do not add to 100 because of rounding.

Source: Forrest A. Bogan, *Employment of High School Graduates and Dropouts in 1964,* U.S. Bureau of Labor Statistics, Special Labor Force Report 54, 1965, table 2, p. 640.

[5] Harry M. Caudill, *Night Comes to the Cumberlands: A Biography of a Depressed Area,* Little, Brown and Company, Boston, 1963, pp. 360–361.

survey, "economic" reasons were most frequently given by males and second most frequently cited by females (for whom the most frequently cited reason was marriage or pregnancy).

Acceptability for Military Service

The armed services have established physical, mental, emotional, and administrative (moral) criteria which they use in selecting young men for enlistment and induction. In 1963 the Federal government undertook to learn more about those who failed to pass the screening examinations, particularly those who failed the mental test.

Failure on the mental tests means failure to pass the equivalent of eighth grade of school. While some who failed were retarded, the vast majority were educationally deprived. There were many concomitants of unemployment among those rejected. About a fifth came from families which had received public assistance within the five preceding years. About a fifth of the selectees' fathers, or fathers-in-law with whom they were living, were not working. Three out of ten of these rejectees were not working at the time they were examined.

Housing

Unemployment, underemployment, and low income are important determinants of the housing that families are able to obtain. This is suggested by Table 4.

Although during the last two decades Federal, state, and local governments have contributed substantially to the expansion of public housing, in many communities preference for admission to public housing is given to families whose heads have steady jobs. A record of repeated unemployment or casual employment may keep a family out.

Nutrition

As the U.S. Commissioner of Welfare Ellen Winston remarked at the White House Conference on Education in 1965, it is very difficult for hungry—or sleepy—children to profit from instruction. We have noted that economizing in expenditures for food was the most pervasive adjustment made by the unemployed. Yet the lower the family income, the higher the proportion of that income a family must spend on food. The U.S. Department of Agriculture has estimated that while the average family need spend only about a third of its income on food, the low-cost diet developed by the department requires almost half the incomes of poor families.

Health and Medical Care

The medical care received by children and young people is directly related to their family's incomes. The National Health Survey of Health Characteristics of Young People which was conducted from June, 1957, to July, 1958, showed the following: Where family income was $4,000 and over, children up to the age of 4 visited a physician an average of 7.4 times a year, 5- to 14-year-olds made an average of 4.5 visits a year, and 15- to 24-year-olds made an average of 5.3 visits. However, where family income was below $4,000 a year, those younger than 4 saw a physician an average of only 5.0 times a year, 5- to 14-year-olds only 2.9 times a year, and 15- to 24-year-olds 4.8 times a year.

The relationship between dental care and family income is the same. Children 5 to 14 years old whose family income was $4,000 and over

TABLE 4

Condition of Housing by Income Class of Household, 1959, and by Color, 1960

			Percent in:			
	Total number (in thousands)		Standard *		Substandard	
Income class	White	Nonwhite	White	Nonwhite	White	Nonwhite
Total	47,880	5,144	87	56	13	44
Less than $3,000	12,047	2,755	70	39	30	61
$3,000–$4,999	9,536	1,186	85	67	15	33
$5,000–$6,999	10,512	645	93	81	7	20
$7,000 and over	15,786	558	97	89	3	12

* Standard housing, as defined by the Census, has slight or no defects, hot and cold running water, and exclusive use of a flush toilet and bathtub (or shower) within the unit.

Source: U.S. Bureau of the Census, *1960 Census of Housing*, vol. II, *Metropolitan Housing*, part 1, "United States and Divisions," tables A-4, A-13.

visited the dentist on the average three times more frequently than children of the same age whose family income was under $4,000.

Low income also contributes significantly to one of the nation's most costly afflictions—mental retardation.

A major factor in mental retardation is premature birth. Among expectant mothers who do not receive prenatal care, more than 20 percent of all births are premature. This is two or three times the rate of prematurity among those who do receive adequate prenatal care.

Many retarded children, particularly those with mild intellectual defects, are members of ethnic minorities, live under substandard conditions, and lack proper educational and cultural opportunities. An estimated 10 percent of the 423,000 children served by public child-welfare agencies as of March, 1962 were mentally retarded.

Infant and maternal mortality rates are also greatly affected by the amount of prenatal and postnatal care. The amount of care is in turn related to the family's employment and income status. The differentials in maternal and infant mortality rates between whites and non-whites reflect the significant difference in their median incomes. The maternal mortality rate per 100,000 live births in 1963 was 24.0 for white women and 96.9 for nonwhite women. The infant mortality rate per 1,000 live births in 1963 was 22.2 for white infants and 41.5 for nonwhite infants.

Although we know that illness often causes poverty because it makes a man unable to work and to earn, we can also state that illness frequently results from poverty.

We learn from the National Health Survey that in 1959–1960 the rate of days lost from work was significantly higher among persons from families with income below $4,000 than those with higher incomes. In 1961–1962, currently employed persons (persons whose major activity within the past twelve months was work) whose family income was under $2,000 had 17.6 restricted-activity days as compared to 25.4 restricted-activity days for unemployed persons with the same family income. Employed persons with family incomes of $7,000 and above had 10.7 restricted-activity days, and unemployed persons with the same family incomes experienced 21.2 restricted-activity days. In addition, in each age group the unemployed had more restricted-activity days per person than the employed. Also, the unemployed, with few exceptions, had higher rates of disability days than the employed.

In part, the higher disability rates among the unemployed may reflect an injury or disease which prevents a man from working, or working regularly. But the relations between unemployment and illness are more complicated. Many unemployed men prefer to explain their being out of work in medical rather than economic terms: Illness is a more socially acceptable excuse for not working.

Although chronic disease in the adult population is much more income-related than acute disease, there is evidence that in depressed urban areas the incidence of infectious diseases is higher than for the rest of the city. In an intraurban area study of Los Angeles, it was found that the very crowded, low-income, high-unemployment neighborhoods of the city were also the ones with the highest percentage of every major disease reported in 1960. In these neighborhoods, male unemployment rates ranged from 9 percent to almost 30 percent, and 41 percent of the families did not earn enough income in a year to lift them above the "deprivation" level. No other areas in Los Angeles county bear such a burden of concentrated unemployment and poverty. These several neighborhoods contained 17 percent of the Los Angeles population, and the incidence of acute disease was disproportionately high (Table 5).

The relations between unemployment and emotional illness are many. Since most men recognize their responsibility to support themselves and their families, the inability of many unemployed and underemployed persons to find work, or to find jobs which provide them with sufficient income to keep their families out of poverty, is a source of emotional pressure and frustration.

Epidemiological studies of mental illness reflect the uncertainties of diagnosis in the field, as well as the technical problems involved in self-reporting. Several studies, however, have shown a systematic relationship between socioeconomic status and the *treated prevalence* rates.

A series of urban studies point to an association between unemployment, low income, and a higher incidence for psychoses. To the extent that environmental stress contributes to psychoses—and most authorities believe that it does—then loss of work, the inability to find a job, lack of income, and the inability to support one's dependents probably contribute to the incidence of psychosis among the poor, to its prolongation, and to recurrence.

According to an analysis by the Department of Mental Health in California of a sample of patients admitted to state hospitals, 41 percent had had no work history, and 11 percent had had part-time or transient employment during the six months prior to hospitalization.

These transient workers were mostly unskilled, and many had held marginal jobs (shoeshine boy, janitor, etc.). Ninety days after their release from the hospital, 64 percent of those who said they wanted to work were still jobless.

Physicians and social workers often reach a judgment about whether a patient is ready for release from a mental hospital, or whether a person should be admitted or readmitted, on the basis of an estimate about his finding and holding a job. Work is a potent therapeutic agent, and the ability to be self-supporting is often a stabilizing force.

TABLE 5

Index of Incidence of Major Diseases in Selected Areas of Los Angeles, 1960*

Disease	Index of incidence †
Polio, brucellosis, diphtheria ‡	588
Tuberculin reactors and converters	387
Acute conjunctivitis and typhoid fever carrier	294
Amebiases	285
Venereal diseases	271
Whooping cough	264
Dysentery producing shegalla infections	262
Rheumatic fever	252
Food poisoning	248
Epilepsy	231
Viral or aseptic meningitis	214
Tuberculosis (all forms)	167
Meningitis	158
Streptococcal infections	158
Salmonella infections	155
Mumps	154
Measles	152
Hepatitis	148
Parasitic fungus infections (coccoidomycosis)	147
Encephalitis	131

* These areas represent 17 percent of the total population of Los Angeles.
† The base equals 100, which is the expected incidence of diseases in relation to the proportion of the population represented.
‡ Few total cases.

Source: U.S. Department of Commerce, Area Redevelopment Administration, *Hardcore Unemployment and Poverty in Los Angeles*, 1965, p. 33.

Delinquency and Crime

Most studies have found a high correlation between unemployment rates and adult crimes, particularly crimes against property. Although the precise relationships cannot readily be established, we do not suggest that a sizable number of offenses are committed by persons simply because they could not get a job. However, we do know that people who have difficulty with authority, who are alienated in various ways from society, or whose socialization is inadequate are less likely to get or hold a job. Daniel Glaser's study of the inmates of Federal prisons showed that many inmates had been frequently unemployed, and furthermore that prisoners in all types of institutions had been disproportionately employed in low-skill occupations.[6]

As Marcia Guttentag's review of the literature makes clear, there is no simple and clear-cut relationship between unemployment and juvenile delinquency.[7] The condition of the labor market does not appear to have a direct and overriding influence. But unemployment and underemployment certainly contribute to delinquency insofar as they affect the stability of family and neighborhood. B. Lander found that the more mixed the population in a neighborhood, the higher the delinquency rates, and that heterogeneity and instability are often the result of unemployment and the geographic mobility that accompanies it.[8] In Belton M. Fleisher's view, the relationship of unemployment to delinquency is linked to inadequate opportunities for men to support their families and the disorganization which follows.[9]

Because there are other sources of instability in American life that affect high- as well as low-income groups and that affect the employed as well as the unemployed, we would not expect to find unemployment per se the single most important cause of delinquency. It does, however, become more important for older delinquents. Fleisher concludes, for example, that "an examination of delinquency rates and other variables by age and through time suggests that the effect of unemployment on juvenile delinquency is positive and significant [par-

[6] *The Effectiveness of a Prison and Parole System,* The Bobbs-Merrill Company, Inc., Indianapolis, 1964.
[7] "The Relationship of Unemployment to Crime and Delinquency," unpublished manuscript, Yale University (Department of Psychology), New Haven, Conn.
[8] *Towards an Understanding of Juvenile Delinquency,* Columbia University Press, New York, 1954.
[9] "The Effect of Unemployment on Juvenile Delinquency," *Journal of Political Economy,* December, 1963.

ticularly] when it refers to individuals who are over sixteen years of age."

We have noted that three major categories of cost are involved in unemployment. There is, first of all, the economic loss resulting from failure to utilize our working population at an optimal level. The Council of Economic Advisors, *assuming a 4 percent unemployment rate,* has calculated this cost as $27 billion for 1964. Since public policy aims at a lower rate than 4 percent, the dollar losses can be calculated to be many billions of dollars higher. These losses represent the additional amount of national income that would have been produced had the number of unemployed been fewer.

The second category is what we have called the "human costs" to individuals. We have sought to indicate, even though we have not been able to quantify, the costs to the individual adult, child, and family unit that arise directly or indirectly from unemployment and underemployment and which are expressed in disease, emotional disturbance, inadequate schooling, delinquency, and crime.

The third dimension of these costs goes beyond the individual and his family and has a direct social consequence. The community and the nation also incur sizable costs in the form of institutionalization, law enforcement, inadequate development of skills, welfare.

The annual costs to society of three serious types of malfunctioning to which unemployment and poverty contribute have been estimated as follows:

1. The cost of institutional care, facilities construction, and special care in the family home for the mentally retarded amounts to more than $1 billion a year.
2. The direct costs of mental illness to the American economy are over $1.7 billion a year.
3. The cost of maintaining the penal system is between $2 billion and $3 billion a year.

While the social costs of unemployment and underemployment cannot be fully specified, they play an important role in the following five major areas of social pathology:

1. Family disorganization, with the result that large numbers of children are raised in circumstances that deprive them of proper physical, emotional, and social development. Broken families with low income or no earned income find it particularly difficult to provide adequate nurture

for their children, with the result that they may later be economically dependent.

2. The necessary institutionalization of large numbers of children and adults in homes for the retarded, mental hospitals, reformatories, prisons, and Veterans Administration installations. The costs of this are related to the failure of many adults to find employment that would enable them to support themselves and their dependents.

3. Illness, which implies high costs to government and philanthropy for the hospitalization of many unemployed persons and their dependents whose illnesses were neglected because of inadequate income. Other social costs include loss of the economic contribution of persons within the productive age groups because of premature death, and dangers to other citizens from heightened exposure to infectious diseases.

4. Unsuccessful geographical mobility as a result of loose labor markets in urban centers. A large number of pressing urban problems are directly related to the inability of millions of rural people to earn a living on the farm and the difficulties they, together with other disadvantaged people, face in finding employment in urban centers.

5. Rising rates of delinquency and crime. The fact that many citizens in an increasing number of cities cannot safely walk the streets after dark in many areas and that many firms hire private guards to ensure their property's security underscores the major costs to the community when men seek their livelihood from crime rather than from work.

Important social costs that are clearly related to unemployment and underemployment flow from these areas of social malfunctioning. As our understanding of the linkages between unemployment and social pathology is increased, the true costs will be found to be much greater. Nevertheless, even as the record stands, we must make a major effort toward the reduction of unemployment and underemployment:

1. We must expand our present efforts to reduce unemployment and underemployment. Our democracy is committed to offer everybody able and willing to work an opportunity to do so. Further, we must move as rapidly as possible, through legislation and other devices, to assure that the jobs which people hold provide them an income sufficient to support themselves and their families adequately; and social security and welfare measures must assure to those who are unable to support themselves sufficient income to maintain themselves and their dependents at an acceptable level.

2. We must experiment with new policies, programs, and procedures directed toward increasing the reemployment of the unemployed, raising the productivity of the underemployed, and facilitating the return to

employment of those outside the labor force who are willing and able to work. This experimentation depends on increasing the availability of jobs and also on identifying specifically the barriers that now stand in the way of handicapped persons who want to fit themselves into the work environment.

3. Since such a high proportion of underemployed persons grow up and live in rural areas, particularly in the Southeast, and since many of them later migrate to the cities where they become unemployed, special programs should be developed to stimulate the economic development of the areas where they now live. Further, special efforts should be made to increase the probability that migration to the cities will be successful by assuring that people in these areas are better educated and trained before they move and that they receive special services upon their arrival in urban areas to speed their assimilation into the new social and economic environment.

4. Because individual, family, neighborhood, community, and national forces are interrelated with respect to preparing men for work and facilitating or retarding their ability to obtain and hold a job, it is highly desirable that more attention be devoted to mechanisms for coordinating programs at each level of government and among levels of government, as well as between the governmental and the nonprofit and private sectors of the economy. Improved coordination should go far in promoting social efficiency and in ensuring that the dollars spent and the efforts made will have a higher effectiveness in accomplishing desirable social ends.

5. There is clear need for the development of a vastly improved system of social accounting in which the full range of the economic, social and human costs attendant upon a shortfall of jobs and inadequacies in personal and family incomes will be correctly assessed. An improved set of accounts could go far to help guide the public in the choice of appropriate policies and programs to rid our society of the scourge of unemployment, which is still taking a very heavy toll.

Chapter Ten The Social Order and Delinquency

The purpose of this chapter is to delineate and clarify what is known about the pathology of the social environment and about delinquency and crime so that those who have the responsibility for making recommendations about policies and programs will have a better idea of where the ground is firm and where they stand close to quicksand.

We cannot establish clear-cut and unequivocal relations between the pathological conditions and circumstances in a community and delinquency and crime. We cannot point to family disorganization, poverty, racial discrimination, inadequate schooling, or high unemployment alone, or even collectively, as the cause or causes of delinquency and crime. We cannot directly relate poverty with crime. For one thing, young people from middle- and even upper-income families engage in individual or group activities that bring them into conflict with the law. Of course, we recognize that the police are less likely to arrest and charge young people from "respectable" families and more likely to use informal means of adjudication with their parents than when they deal with children from poorer families.

A second reason for caution relates to the type of crime called delinquency. These crimes tend to be public crimes of violence—fist-fights, auto thefts, property destruction. The middle-class child who cheats on a test, steals an exam paper, or seduces a next-door neighbor is equally deviant but less likely to be arrested.

At the same time we must note that a young person living in a high-delinquency area is not necessarily a delinquent. Many if not most of these youngsters grow up without engaging in delinquent activities. We must not oversimplify and say that poverty causes crime. All we can say is that poverty is associated with more delinquencies of the kind likely to show in official statistics than affluence is.

Delinquency is not a clear-cut category, and those who engage in actions defined as delinquent or criminal are not a homogeneous group except for the single characteristic of having a brush with the law.

The more diverse the range of behavior subsumed under the category of delinquency and crime, the greater are the differences among those who are charged and convicted, and the less likely it is that we can establish a simple and clear-cut relationship between their backgrounds and their actions.

There are very few young men who at some time during their adolescence do not engage in one or another kind of delinquent act, usually as a member of a group. If this happens only once and if it does not become part of a pattern of behavior, it is probable that it has little significance either for the individual or the society.

At the opposite extreme are individuals who engage in delinquency and crime for so long that it becomes a way of life for them: They neither know nor seek an alternative adjustment to society.

Between these two extremes are several important subgroups which must be differentiated if effective methods of social control and rehabilitation are to be established. The law recognizes that insane people cannot be held responsible for antisocial actions—but there is considerable evidence to suggest that many who engage in delinquent or criminal actions are not mentally sound, although they are dealt with as if they were. Many in detention homes or in prison might better be in psychiatric facilities, since they do not have the internal stability with which to control their behavior.

Some people respond to temptation or pressure by engaging in a criminal act. They may strike their wives or girl friends, they may steal or embezzle money, they may engage in one or another of a great many crimes against persons or property. But until the time of the crime their behavior has been law-abiding, and usually after their conviction and sentence they again are law-abiding.

The largest group, with whom we will be primarily concerned, are adolescents and young adults who engage in delinquent and/or criminal acts a few times but who do not become criminals. Their deviancy is related to their transition from childhood into adulthood. The fact that their antisocial behavior is linked so closely to this segment of their lives helps to provide a focus for analysis and evaluation. What are the key elements in the growth and development of the individual and what are the key factors in the social environment that might help explain both the prevalence of delinquency during adolescence and its marked recession thereafter?

The human being must learn to behave as a member of society. Primary responsibility for teaching successful behavior is divided among three agents: the family, the school, and the individual himself. If the family is unable or unwilling to discharge its responsibilities effectively, and if no institution is readily available which can step in and take over many of the tasks that are conventionally carried on by the family, the basis will be laid for deviancy in adolescence and adulthood. The young child needs to be helped to control his impulses. The young child needs to discriminate between acceptable and unacceptable behavior. The ability to make this discrimination is not inborn; it must be learned, and the parent is the first and most important teacher. If the parent is too busy, or if he does not care, the child is not likely to learn. He is likely to grow up without knowing or caring about what is right and what is wrong.

By the time the youngster is five or six a part of the socialization process is assumed by the school. The school has three important tasks. First, it must continue the job of helping the child to learn to control his impulses so that he can live at close quarters with other children and with adults without disrupting the larger group. Next, the school must help him to acquire the tools which will enable him to function later in a society that is increasingly dependent on higher orders of literacy, on mastery of numbers, and on a broad range of knowledge about the physical and social environment.

It is during the long years when a young person is in school, responding to what goes on both inside and outside the school, that he slowly decides what kind of a person he wants to be, what goals he wants to realize. The school can assist the young person to develop into an adult whose values and goals are in harmony with the rest of society.

Although parents, teachers, and the individual play the most important roles in the socialization process, other persons are often importantly involved too—especially during the individual's adolescence and young adulthood. One's friends and companions and participation in joint activities are among the most important bonds that condition the life of the adolescent. Somewhat later, the girl one marries and with whom one shares the responsibilities for raising children is likely to exercise a marked influence.

If parents are unable or unwilling to discharge their responsibilities, if the school is incapable of performing its mission, if the individual does not establish acceptable goals, if he begins to run with a group in conflict with the larger society, if he cannot make a satisfying marital choice, then the stage is set for his becoming a deviant. It does not follow that every individual who experiences major difficulty in maturing will necessarily become delinquent, but delinquency is surely a possible outcome. Among the other possible outcomes are mental illness, alcoholism or other types of addiction, suicide, or withdrawal and alienation from the society.

Criminal deviancy implies behavior that is at variance with legal norms. Delinquency and crime describe actions that are prohibited by law; the perpetrator is subject to apprehension and punishment. But the law is what the judges say it is, and arrests and convictions are a function of what the police and the district attorney do.

Not all behavior that is disapproved of is classified as illegal. Moreover, by tradition and convention much that is illegal is not usually subject to repression by the law-enforcing authorities. Charging exorbitant rates of interest, bribing inspectors, failing to protect the rights of clients or the health of patients, using inside information for personal gain, and manipulating prices and markets are illustrations of the wide range of "white-collar" criminal actions that for the most part go unpunished.

Ours is a society that places a high value on the accumulation of wealth. The opinion-forming organs of our society place great stress on personal striving as the key to economic aggrandizement. The poor man is pitied if not despised. Our folklore holds that any man with ambition and desire can rise out of poverty, even though he may not become wealthy.

This orientation to work, wealth, and life is deeply embedded in the American tradition, and poor and rich alike are exposed to them. But we know that the probability that children from middle- and upper-income homes can live in harmony with them is very much greater than for children whose families are unable to smooth their way, which are, in fact, unable to provide them with even those minimum supports which are essential for successful socialization. Thus, the society itself sets up a tension arc between the values and goals which it has established as social desiderata and the barriers that prevent large numbers within the society from succeeding in achieving them through socially approved means. Delinquent or criminal behavior is engaged in by many who seek to achieve what society values highly but who are unable to do so through socially approved routes. Achieving the goal becomes more important to them than following the accepted norms; the risk becomes worth it.

Many young people reach adolescence in a position to continue their education through high school, junior college, and college. During this prolonged period they will acquire a range of attitudes and skills which will assure them of a good starting point for their later struggle for independence and success. But there are many others who do not continue their education; who drop off the preparatory track, or are pushed off as early as the law permits; who have little chance of finding a job; and who then confront with overwhelming urgency the need to do something—to be somebody, to find some place in a society that has little need and less use for them and who therefore resort to delinquent or criminal action. The basic question here is what forms of social pathology contribute to the development of deviant adolescents who later become enmeshed in delinquent and criminal behavior.

An understanding of the socialization process requires the delineation of the conditions that usually play a constructive and supportive part in a child's growth. Among the most important are competent and supportive parents; living in a house or apartment where space is adequate and contributes to health and well-being; a neighborhood which helps to bind families together and which provides wholesome companionship for youngsters; opportunity to join religious, social, and recreational organizations and activities; access to health services for preventive, therapeutic and rehabilitative purposes; adequate space for participation in recreational activities; opportunity to join political clubs and organizations through which the citizenry can make known their needs and desires and can exert pressure to achieve them; opportunity to attend schools which are able to provide learning opportunities for children with differing abilities and interests; and urban planning that is sensitive to the need of relating the several residential areas to the central city through efficient and inexpensive transportation.

The list could be extended, but the strategic elements which have been identified will suffice to provide a background for understanding the ways in which the malfunctioning of the social environment can interfere with the effective socialization of many children.

Family Disorganization

Whether an individual is able to meet the challenges with which society confronts him depends in considerable measure on his experiences during the earliest years of life. The critical issue is whether his parents or parent substitutes were able to provide him with the many types of support which the infant and the child requires to develop his strengths and competences.

There are several possibilities of difficulty arising in this critical area of family support. Because of death, divorce, desertion, illness, or some other reason the child may have no father in the home. Or the father may be unable to earn enough to support his wife and children. In such instances, the young boy may grow up without knowing the model of a man who performs the basic role of successfully caring for his family. Whether the child is severely handicapped by the absence of an effective father depends on whether the lack is characteristic only of his own family or a few families, or whether the situation is found throughout most of the group within which he grows up.

The difficulties that the young child may suffer from such parental deprivation go far beyond the emotional realm, important as that frequently is. It is probable that a family without a competent male wage earner will have an inadequate income. While many mothers without husbands work, they are seldom able to earn enough to support themselves and their children adequately. Moreover, they are seldom able to see that their young children are properly supervised while they themselves are away from home earning a living. Often, therefore, the child without a father is likely to be a child without a mother who can devote adequate time and attention to his needs. He is further likely to grow up in a family where income is insufficient for the essentials for healthy development.

There is no way for a society to protect every family against death, divorce, and disease. There is in fact no way for a society to assume that children will be born and reared only by couples who are married. But a society can avoid contributing to the problem of mothers who face the difficult task of rearing their children without the support and help of a husband. Children who must grow up without an effective father are twice deprived if their mothers must leave them to work for inadequate wages.

Of course, assuring a larger income for these families will not guarantee a secure life for all these children. There are a considerable number of mothers who themselves are so severely handicapped intellectually and emotionally that they cannot effectively discharge their duties and responsibilities as a parent, especially when they must carry the duties of both mother and father. Raising their relief allowance would not necessarily or inevitably redound to their children's benefit. But the number of inadequate mothers would be smaller if the financial pressures on them were less severe. This much is clear: Most mothers can assume the responsibility of raising their own children, and they will be able to do a better job of it if they are not forced to do so with an income that clearly cannot meet their needs. Inadequate income makes it difficult to assure children a balanced healthy diet. Being hungry or ill interferes with effective learning in school. And the child who fails to progress in school will be handicapped.

Secondly, the training and disciplining of a child requires a fine balance between rewards and punishments. In a consumer society, most rewards involve the expenditures of money. Families which live in or close to poverty are frequently unable to find the money to reward good behavior and to encourage it.

Another axis involves the difficulties that poor families experience in obtaining essential health services. Many a child develops a serious physical or emotional illness because of a correctable defect which is ignored because his parents are unable to have the condition diagnosed and treated.

It should also be noted that there is a close link between family income and participation in communal activities. Many children from very poor homes are unable to participate in church affairs or in social and recreational activities sponsored by neighborhood organizations because their parents are not able to provide them with the prerequisites for participation, from appropriate clothes to modest fees. These children are deprived of the opportunity to make friends, to explore interests, and to gain satisfactions from approved activities. They are shut out from much that they would like to participate in, and in the process of rejection they may develop hostile responses to the world which they cannot join.

Finally, the absence of any small amount of "disposable" income above the sums required for sheer existence bodes ill for the *weltanschauung* of the maturing person. He has impressed upon him, not once but continuously, the fact that the world is composed of two groups: those on the inside—that is, those with money; and those on the outside—individuals like himself and his parents in whom society has little interest or concern. He may well feel that if society does not care about him, he need not care about it.

Inadequate Housing

There are few cities in the United States which have experienced a population increase during the past two decades where the supply of living quarters for the poor are adequate to meet the demand. The difficulties facing poor families in obtaining housing are intensified by regulations that limit their access to public housing. Many housing projects will not accept families with a large number of children, or families whose fathers have deserted or which suffer from some other handicap.

The urban poor are likely to spend more than a reasonable proportion of their limited income on housing, even poor housing, and they are forced to do without other essentials such as proper food. Characteristically, they must live in less space than is minimally desirable. Moreover, many live in quarters which are so dilapidated that it is almost impossible to establish and maintain proper standards of cleanliness and responsibility.

The links between poor housing and delinquency are indirect, but they exist. Crowding means that the child is constantly exposed to others, rarely with a chance to be alone to sort out his emotions and experiences. In crowded conditions private emotions become public ones. In addition it is likely that young children become aware of adult sexuality much too early.

Overcrowding also places barriers in the way of school success. A higher incidence of illness, the lack of study space, and often the lack of sleep militate against successful performance in school. Inadequate space also means that children and young people seek to pass the time of day out of the home, in the streets. Under such conditions, it becomes next to impossible even for the deeply concerned parent to exercise effective control.

Peeling paint, broken plumbing, roaches, mice and rats, and other characteristics of dilapidated buildings are not only a menace to health, but they place almost insuperable barriers in the path of a mother who wants to keep her home neat and to instill in her children a pride in their surroundings. After a while, she stops trying. The child who receives little effective training in the care of his own and the family's possessions is likely to grow up without consideration for the property of others.

Slum and Segregated Neighborhoods

During the past several decades, a high proportion of all in-migrants into northern cities have been Negroes from the South and, given the deep-seated prejudice among many white groups against living in the same neighborhood with Negroes, slum areas have developed a second characteristic—they have become racially segregated. Increasingly they have housed the Negro poor—usually the recently arrived Negro poor.

Migrants are particularly handicapped since they tend to come from backgrounds which have not prepared them for the ways of urban life and which have not taught them the knowledge and skills which will enable them to fit into their new environment. They have particular need for a helping hand from those who have migrated before them and from various institutions and organizations which could help them adjust to the new and different. But when, as in recent years, the migrants who preceded them have not had an easy time, they have been hard pressed to lend a helping hand to the next group. And they have not been able to build new social organizations that in turn might provide support to the newcomer.

During the expansion of the Negro ghettos, the white population has left and has often taken its clubs, social service structures, and communal organizations with it. Only in a few instances, and then primarily because church buildings are not easily converted to other purposes, has anything approaching an orderly transfer been made. Even then the earlier residents have often kept their church affiliation and crowded out the newcomers. For these reasons, the migrant poor found little help from voluntary organizations, and government has been slow to develop alternative structures.

A deteriorating neighborhood tends to attract more and more individuals who live marginal or criminal existences. The young people growing up in such an area, even if they belong to a relatively strong family unit, cannot fail to be affected by what they learn about aberrant types of behavior. The amazing fact is not that, given the environment in which they live, so many young people make an easy transition into delinquent and criminal behavior, but that the environment alone does not trap all or even most of them.

Slum neighborhoods, especially racially segregated slums, have additional characteristics that should be noted because they are related in varying degrees to the dynamics of delinquency. Many slum dwellers tend to see themselves as a group apart, in latent or overt conflict with the outside world whose representatives in the area are the police. To "put something over" on the police therefore often becomes a goal or a means of reaching a goal. This too is an experience that many young people early have engraved upon them. The tension between the affluent establishment beyond the slum and the slum dwellers is heightened when racial differences exist; it is frequently a confrontation between poor Negroes and rich whites and the white police who are the representatives of the rich whites.

The neighborhoods in which people live determine also the schools their children attend, the recreational areas they use, the shops and movies they frequent. The larger and more homogeneous the slum area, the smaller the interaction between the slum dweller and the general community. Negro children growing up in a northern slum may reach adolescence without ever having spoken one word to a white child. And except for a few white people who stand in an authoritative relationship to them—such as the school teacher, the policeman on the beat, or the physician in the clinic—they may never have had an effective relationship with any member of the white community.

Living in a segregated neighborhood is a major deterrent to a child's learning about the attitudes and behavior patterns of the dominant culture. Moreover, the distance between the locked-in insiders and the outsiders means that these young people during their formative years do not develop a sense of having a stake in the larger society. They learn to make do with what exists within their ghetto, and since little of this is stimulating or constructive, they soon become either apathetic and indifferent or hostile and aggressive. Segregated slums may not cause delinquency any more than any other single source of social pathology, but they contribute substantially to the development of ineffective human beings.

The School

We have already postulated that the school, together with the family, plays a unique role in transforming individuals from children to mature young people. One of its tasks is to provide its charges with at least that basic body of knowledge and skills which will enable them to find and hold a job. If it fails in this task it fails indeed, since its products will be seriously handicapped when they attempt to meet the demands of an adult world.

There are a great many pitfalls along the road which the school takes in attempting to meet this challenge. Since many of the teachers are new and inexperienced and others are disinterested and hostile, since the facilities are inadequate, and since methods and materials of instruction are often unsuitable, we can be as surprised by what this inadequate educational plant is able to accomplish as by its failures.

But since we are primarily concerned with delinquency and crime and only indirectly concerned with education, we must focus on the school's shortcomings.

First we must remember the linkages between unstable families with inadequate income, poor housing, and slum neighborhoods and the failure of children to learn in school. Compounding this relationship is the fact that the parents—or parent—of these children may not be able to help them see books and learning from books as a desideratum since they themselves are unable to read or can read only haltingly. These parents may have a negative attitude toward the whole school process as a result of their own unhappy experiences some years earlier. In low-income neighborhoods, frequently the doer rather than the thinker becomes the ideal, and so here too the young child receives little reinforcement of the educational process.

As so much of the contemporary literature has made clear, the first task of the teacher is to control the class, for otherwise no effective learning is likely to take place. And so it happens that a great many teachers become preoccupied with discipline. Deleterious consequences flow from this. The rigidity of the classroom creates a degree of tension that makes it much more difficult for the teacher to teach and for the children to learn. More and more, school comes to be a battleground between the constricted child and the anxious or hostile teacher; and more and more the slum child develops a set against doing anything that the teacher suggests. By the time he reaches early adolescence he is likely to read poorly, be far behind in his arithmetic, and generally have little knowledge of his physical and social world. This clearly is not true of all children from the slums; and it is true for some who come from neighborhoods where family incomes are higher. But alienation from school and from learning is all too prevalent a characteristic of many children from low-income homes.

What does this failure along the educational route imply for delinquency and crime? First, many of these children develop a strongly hostile stance toward persons in authority. The teacher belongs to the "others"; the principal is the chief disciplinary officer in the hostile world. It is scarcely surprising that as soon as the law permits, and sometimes even earlier, many adolescent boys, as well as some girls, drop out of school or are forced out. With no place to go, without a job and with no immediate prospect of getting one, with no money and no prospect of getting more than a small amount from their parents or guardians, they fall back on each other. They form cliques or gangs, and they seek for some form of expression—if only to test their wits against society.

The delinquency into which many of them slide is often as much a reflection of the blocking of alternative routes for the purposeful use of their time and energy as it is a deliberate choice to become opponents of the status quo and fight against the values of the society. It would be as wrong to construe their delinquent activities as directed solely or even primarily to the purpose of acquiring money through improper means as it would be to state that their behavior is a protest against the status quo. The constellation of forces that lie back of delinquent behavior encompasses both strands.

The important point, however, is that if large numbers of adolescents drop out or are pushed out of school at fourteen, fifteen, sixteen, or seventeen, after many years of unhappy experience in the classroom, they will find it very difficult to develop an approved method of adjusting to the adult world. They simply lack the knowledge, the tools, and the social conditioning that are required of people who work, even those who are hired for the simplest of tasks. Cut off by the absence of a bridge from school to work, blocked and frustrated at the very time when they should be channeling their energies to build a future for themselves, they start or continue in activities that will sooner or later bring them into conflict with the law. The contribution of the schools to delinquency by failing to prepare young people effectively for the tasks of adulthood cannot be overestimated.

Health and Recreational Services

Reference has been made to the fact that inadequate family income is likely to be reflected in illness and in neglected physical conditions which have an adverse effect on the growth and development of children. But the linkages between health and delinquency go far beyond this simple one. For example, a harelip, eyes that do not focus properly, or any one of many other birth or developmental defects may handicap a child. Since there is no relief from many of these conditions except through surgery, a child whose handicap is ignored may be handicapped all his life.

Medicine and surgery have made great advances. But many parents, especially among the poor who have only recently migrated into a large urban center, do not know of the opportunities for obtaining assistance. If action were taken when the child is young, the cost of successful intervention would frequently be much smaller than later, and the prospects of success much greater.

There is another and perhaps even more important realm where the absence or insufficiency of health services is a liability which will have a delayed though significant bearing on delinquency. There is a great amount of stress and strain in the lives of the poor, particularly in families where a single parent is trying to cope with many children. We know that many of these parents, even if they had a much tougher psyche, would find it difficult to cope with their multiple responsibilities under the trying conditions of their lives. But we also know that many of the adults are emotionally disturbed. It is not surprising that many children whose parents are not able to cope effectively with adversity develop varying degrees of emotional disturbance and disorders that interfere with their psychic development. We further know that many of these youngsters might, with help, be put back on the right track, the causes of their disorders reduced or removed, and their symptoms alleviated.

The best psychiatric services would not put an end to crime and delinquency, but adequate services available in time to those who need them and supplemented by other forms of assistance to the individual and his family might well cut the incidence of later misbehavior by a substantial degree. But it is the rare community that has adequate psychiatric services for those who can pay, much less for those who are unable to pay.

Just as general and specialized health services are important, recreational facilities are important. We noted earlier that people who live in urban slums have a tendency to spend a good part of their lives outside of their homes because their homes are so crowded and otherwise unsatisfactory. But the absence of parks, playgrounds, swimming pools, and gymnasiums means that many young people with animal energy unspent will hang around the doorsteps and the storefronts and pool parlors looking for something to do. This spells trouble.

The growing child, the adolescent, and even the young adult usually has a great amount of physical and psychic energy. He needs an opportunity to discharge it, and games and sports usually provide safe outlets. If lack of space precludes sports and games, the energy will seek another outlet. It does not follow, of course, that those who have an opportunity to play long and hard will not get into trouble with the law. The argument is a looser one. Young people can gain a considerable amount of pleasure and satisfaction from participating in group sports; without this opportunity, they are likely to seek other ways of using their time and energy.

The absence of adequate recreational facilities which is characteristic of almost every large city prevents young people from discharging their energies in safe and social undertakings such as individual and group sports. Dammed up, this energy will escape in channels which involve conflicts with the law. Once again, the promise of adequate recreational facilities would not mean the end to delinquency; but their absence contributes to its increase.

Training and Employment Opportunities

We have noted that a large number of young people seek to escape from school at the earliest possible moment and that others are forced to leave by the authorities. Without salable skills they cannot find jobs, and they do not have ready access to training since they are school dropouts, generally with poor records.

The shortage of part- and full-time jobs for young people, the limited number of training programs for the school dropout, inadequate work-steady programs all contribute substantially to the pressures on the unsuccessful student who leaves school. He is trapped between the two worlds of school and work and anchored in neither. Small wonder that he seeks, with the help of others who are equally rejected, to create a role for himself, often that of engaging in illicit and illegal activities.

The situation of these youngsters has been somewhat eased lately through a series of Federal training and employment programs, but because the scale of these programs has been inadequate to meet the needs of all who qualify, because the administrators of these programs often prefer to select those young people with the most promise of profiting from the opportunities, and because of the formal criteria for selecting from among the applicants, the more handicapped young people—those who have done least well in school and who already have had brushes with the police—are least likely to be accepted into one of them.

These young people most need a new type of learning situation in which they would be able to work along with adults, receive money for their efforts, become experienced in the discipline of the workplace, and develop goals to which they can aspire and which they can reasonably expect to attain. But they are the least likely persons to be afforded such an opportunity. Most employers do not want to hire juvenile workers, especially those with a poor school record. And even though there are more government training programs than there used to be, and even though several of them are aimed directly at the school dropout, it is still quite difficult for many of the youngsters to take advantage of them. Some stay away, believing that these programs are too similar to the school which they disliked and from which they have just escaped. Others, less hostile or alienated, apply to the programs but are rejected because they are adjudged to be unable to profit from them. The most unfortunate are those who try but are repeatedly rejected.

One of the less recognized but still important characteristics of the labor market is the particular handicap that the poor encounter because no one helps to fit them in. People get jobs or training for jobs when they know someone who can tell them that there is an opening and who can vouch for them. But the school dropout from the slum whose father is unemployed or not at home and who knows few men in the labor force does not have this important help.

Furthermore, some of the best opportunities for young people are in the various crafts for which apprenticeship is the way in. But most apprenticeship programs require graduation from high school, and this tends to eliminate most of the youngsters we have been describing; moreover, most apprenticeship programs give preference to the sons or other relatives of the trade-union members. Finally, many crafts have long practiced racial discrimintion. So, on each of these counts, the school dropout, especially if he is Negro, is likely to be blocked.

The Armed Forces

Unlike apprenticeship, selection for the Armed Forces does not require graduation from high school, and color is no longer a bar to many desirable assignments. And yet a great many of the youngsters we have been describing are not currently accepted for military service even when they seek to enlist or when the draft board forwards them for induction. The primary reason for their rejection is that a high proportion fail to pass the Armed Forces Qualification Test, which requires the candidate to demonstrate a degree of knowledge and aptitude usually associated with the completion of the eighth grade. While many young people who drop out of school leave in the ninth or tenth grade, they have not in fact progressed to this level of scholastic achievement.

Others are rejected because they fail the physical examination, and still others because their behavior has been so aberrant that the military believe that they will turn out to be troublemakers. With a manpower pool larger than they need, the Armed Forces are able to pick and choose, and many of these young people are rejected.

Rejection for military service represents still another failure along the road for these young people. They have not succeeded in school; they have been unable to find a place in the civilian world of work; and now they are shunted aside by the military. It would be difficult even for a person with a very strong ego to take these successive rebuffs and absorb them without hitting back. But these are young people whose egos are far from strong and whose reactions to repeated failure are therefore likely to be exaggerated.

Rejection by the military masks a great many lost opportunities. First, the young man would be able to perform many jobs adequately in the Armed Forces. Next, military service would build him up physically. More important, in the Armed Forces he would be exposed to a regulated life, with duties to perform, and his performance would lead to rewards or punishments. He would be exposed to young men from other groups in society. With luck, he would have a sergeant or even a lieutenant who might manifest some special interest in helping him to adjust.

He would be put into a training program, and might move several rungs up the ladder of skill acquisition, conceivably acquiring a competence that would ease his adjustment to civilian life. He would have GI benefits that would help to smooth his transition back to civilian life and facilitate his broadening or deepening his work skills.

Most important of all, if he succeeded in completing his term of service, he would by that fact alone gain a considerable degree of self-confidence, and furthermore he would have an open sesame into many types of civilian employment. There are a great many jobs for which an honorable military discharge is all that the employer requires.

However, we must add that many young people simply cannot cope with the restrictions and demands of military life. If the military had more time and resources to devote to their education and socialization many might be helped over the hurdles, but as it is, many fail.

Social, Religious, and Political Organizations

Our analysis so far has revolved around the fact that home and school have the primary responsibility for nurturing and educating the young so that they can eventually function effectively as adults. We have also called attention to a variety of conditions and circumstances within the larger environment that contribute to making the task of home and school easier or more difficult. In this section, we shall review in particular the role of various voluntary organizations which help to give form and substance to the social, religious, and political life of the individuals and groups in the community.

We noted earlier that as people move out of the central city they tend to take their social organizations with them. The absence of these communal organizations bears particularly heavily on the young, because they are thus deprived of an opportunity to channel their energies in socially approved ways and denied reinforcement for acquiring socially acceptable and approved ways of responding. One major reason why the culture of the slum is different from that of the middle-class suburb is that many of these reinforcing institutions are absent from the slum. The differences that derive from weakened family units and unsatisfactory schools are greatly increased by the weakness or absence of a whole range of social, religious, and political organizations which are the woof and the warp of many well-functioning communities.

We do not have to contend that former Boy Scouts do not become delinquents or criminals in order to point out that the Boy Scouts—and any similar group—provide a structured experience for young people during which they can channel their time and energy into interesting and useful activities, learn to meet responsibilities, and accept a dominant set of socially approved values.

Again, it would be ridiculous not to recognize that many former choir boys eventually get into trouble with the law. But this need not obscure the clear and unequivocal facts that the successful instilling of values is a difficult task and that home and school are more likely to succeed if they have reinforcement from social and religious organizations.

Young people need to identify with models. One of the great tragedies of the slums is the fact that most of the people who live there are by definition failures; the "successes" more often than not are the strong or clever people who have managed despite the oppressive environmental forces. Handicapped children do not have strong models whose modes of behavior follow socially approved rather than deviant patterns. Well-functioning social and religious organizations can help provide these models.

One must not underestimate the importance to a growing child of having an adult at hand who is willing to go to bat for him. If the lower-class child has no father, and if his mother is unable or unwilling because of weakness or apathy to back him up, he needs someone else to cushion him against the larger society. Social, recreational, or religious organizations can often provide such a person, someone to turn to for advice, someone to run to when trouble threatens, or even someone who will come down to the police station to speak on his behalf. Here middle-class children benefit from the network of social relations in which they are entwined.

One consequence of the need for adult support is the feeling of insignificance and helplessness which follows when a youngster comes to believe that the adults he knows are unable to affect the major forces on which the family's well-being depends. This feeling of being a pawn in a vast game is considered by many students of society as the outstanding characteristic of metropolitan man in the second half of the twentieth century. Slum dwellers certainly experience this alienation.

But even those who underwrite this doctrine of alienation recognize that in a democracy there are limits to the erosion of personal influence because the individual citizen does have the opportunity to go to the polls. While the effective exercise of the franchise requires relatively little by way of qualifications and preparation, it does require a little. There are residency requirements and literacy requirements. Moreover, the individual must have that minimum interest and desire to use his franchise. Regrettably, life has been so hard on so many people, people who have for so long felt that they are on the outside looking in, that they see little point in using their political rights even when they are able to.

When adults do not participate in the political process their children are likely to grow up believing that they will not find relief for their personal and communal ills through the ballot box. Feeling left out and shunted aside, perceiving no way of accomplishing constructive ends for themselves, they are more likely than not to disregard and break the law. Many come to believe that the law is an engine of oppression to help the fortunate keep their property.

The terms "Negro" and "race" have been used sparingly so far in this analysis, because what has been said holds for disadvantaged people irrespective of the color of their skin. But we cannot complete the scaffolding without treating race discrimination as a distinctive element.

The last decade has been a tumultuous one with regard to race relations. Great promises were made to the Negro. The walls of segregation began to fall. Many Negroes were able to climb into the ranks of the middle class. But substantial as their progress was, the commitments made to them were not fulfilled.

A great number of Negroes have continued to live on the periphery of American society, unable to find steady employment, unable to earn a decent wage, unable to send their children to well-functioning schools, unable to come within arm's length of the white population. As they approached, the whites fled; if they followed, the whites erected barricades to keep them out.

There is no way of directly assessing the contribution to crime and delinquency of this perverse racial environment, but the linkages between the two are many and strong. Why should a deprived Negro boy, neglected by his family and shunted aside by all with whom he comes into contact, develop strong feelings of identification with the white society?

Most of the good things in this world belong to white people; many poor Negroes have no opportunity to enjoy these good things through their own efforts; many see no reason why they should not attempt to take by force or guile what they can of these desirable things since those are the only ways, they feel, that they are likely to get them. They understand that their actions are wrong and that they will be punished if they are caught and convicted. But there is so much that is wrong with society that they minimize their own deviancy.

Because of the way in which the data of delinquency and crime are collected—and we must never lose sight of the fact that the established methods of collection tend to exaggerate deviancy among the poor compared with the affluent—the proportion of Negroes in many categories, though not in all, are disproportionately higher than among the whites, frequently very much higher. While much of this differential, probably most of it, can be explained by the severe social pathology that afflicts Negroes more than whites (migrancy, poverty, illiteracy, and similar major barriers to adjustment), racial disturbance and dislocation does make a contribution to criminal deviancy. When the depths of racial irrationality are fully probed and understood, we may be amazed not by the extent of the Negro's belligerency against the status quo but by his underlying drives to conformity and acceptance.

Summary

We have set out briefly above the major institutions that play a dominant role in the socialization of the individual, and we have sought
to identify the ways in which their malfunctioning contributes to delinquency and crime. Young people growing up under disadvantageous
circumstances are more likely than others to get into trouble with the
law.

It should be emphasized that all we can say is that it is *more* likely.
We must remember that the majority of young people, even of those
growing up under adverse circumstances, will in one way or another
avoid trouble. And, fortunately, many who get into trouble not only
once but repeatedly will inevitably make a transition onto the path of
conformity with the norms and demands of society. Most delinquents
do not turn into criminals.

Since the linkages between social pathology, delinquency, and
crime are indirect, and in many instances cannot be discovered at all,
caution must be exercised in formulating any generalizations. Nevertheless, we can state that delinquency, and sometimes crime, offers an
outlet for the energies and activities of many disadvantaged young
people who are unable to make an orderly transition from childhood
to adulthood because they have not acquired the competences and
skills which are essential for assuming proper adult roles.

No matter how much the social order is improved—and we have
sought to indicate that there is considerable room for improvement—
a considerable number of children and young people will continue
to get into trouble, and some proportion of them will eventually become delinquents or criminals. We will now indicate very briefly the
places where intervention following evidence of trouble holds promise
of reducing deviancy.

Preschool Children

When voluntary or governmental agencies become aware that children
have emotional or physical handicaps, the quicker remedial action is
taken the more likely it is that these children will be able to develop
normally. To ignore a handicap is likely to result in a chain of aberrant actions and reactions with the probable outcome of later deviancy.

If the child is healthy but the home environment is pathological,
the agency should seek to relocate the child as soon as it is convinced

that the child will suffer if he stays at home. Adequate foster homes and institutional facilities can contribute substantially to the reduction of later deviancy.

The School Child

Properly staffed and well-operating schools are in an excellent position to know when children are in trouble because of personal or family shortcomings. If these children are spotted early and if remedial actions are taken, the children are much less likely to become deviants in the future. It may not be possible to make over every handicapped child, but it should be possible to help him reach a level of development at which he can adjust to his society.

The School Dropout

It is inevitable even in a strong school system that a considerable number of young people, particularly those from low-income homes, will find school oppressive and will drop out. Since the American economy has little or no need for poorly educated, unskilled young people, school dropouts are likely to have nothing to do and therefore to have high potential for getting into trouble. A wise society will structure training and work programs for these youngsters which will provide them with an alternative route for acquiring basic skills and thus preparing for adulthood.

The Delinquent

Even if all of the foregoing steps to strengthen the social order are taken and constructive intervention takes place, some proportion of the youthful population will become delinquent and will be placed in custody. It is urgent that the institutions to which they are confined be run with a strong rehabilitative orientation so that these youthful offenders can be helped to acquire the attitudes and skills that will facilitate their fitting into society once they are released. Counseling, training, job-finding services, and follow-up support are the most important elements in a good rehabilitation program.

The Recidivist

Regardless of efforts to rehabilitate the delinquent and set him on the right path, a proportion of first offenders will become recidivists. But backsliding need not be taken as evidence of permanent failure. While some delinquents will turn into hardened criminals who will never adjust to society, many others, with help and time, will be able to make an adjustment to society. They are more likely to adjust and to adjust sooner if they have a skill with which they can earn a livelihood and if the authorities see that they have an opportunity to obtain employment. They may also require additional supportive services, particularly on their release from confinement.

No society, no matter how affluent and wise, will ever free itself completely from the scourge of delinquency and criminality. These are deeply ingrained in the nature of man and society. But a people that takes its commitments to freedom and equality seriously; a people that is determined to compensate for the ill fortune of history, race, and poverty; a people that is humane in its dealings with those who suffer misfortune—such a people can hope and expect that it will suffer less delinquency and less crime. This will be one of its rewards.

Before adumbrating the relations which exist and those which should exist between work and welfare, we will set out briefly some broad generalizations about the principal dependent groups in the population.

There are four times as many dependent white people in the United States as there are dependent nonwhites. Despite popular assumptions, problems of welfare, relief, delinquency and crime are not primarily Negro problems. The Negro is fortunate in this, since white America has mounted programs to help handicapped white Americans which will also help handicapped Negroes.

Secondly, we must note that it is not only poor youngsters who are neglected and deprived. The problems of delinquency, drugs, suicide, are not confined to youngsters from low-income homes. Consider the other side of the coin: One out of every four Ivy League college freshmen fails to graduate in term. In spite of the careful selection procedures followed by Harvard, Yale, Princeton, and the other Ivy League schools, these delays in course suggest the order of turmoil among the offspring of upper-income families.

Further, many youngsters from high-income groups kill themselves in automobiles every year. These are often masked suicides. We can see, therefore, that the number of disturbed youngsters from affluent families is substantial and indicates that problems of adjustment to work and life are not restricted to the poor.

Prejudice is another aspect. Until after World War II, some leading corporations refused to promote Catholics, and most did not promote Jews to their top ranks. The nation's progress in the reduction of prejudice is reflected in the current struggle over civil rights. There is obviously a close relation between racial prejudice and the large numbers of Negroes who are experiencing difficulties in adjusting to the world of work.

We shall first consider the role of welfare in the nation's major metropolis, New York City, and we shall extrapolate from these data to policy alternatives. There now are about 200,000 cases on the welfare rolls; this means that approximately half a million people in New York City receive public assistance. One out of every fourteen persons in New York City receives public assistance.

Moreover, during the course of a very prosperous year, from November, 1964, to November, 1965, there was an increase of 25,000 cases; 65,000 more people went on the relief rolls. The Welfare Department requested $660 million for 1966. This sum represents about two-thirds of the gross national product of Ethiopia, which has a population of 22 million.

Of the 500,000 people on relief in New York City, approximately 400,000 are mothers and children—families without male heads. Another 17 percent is made up of the aged, the sick, and the disabled. These two groups together take up most of the relief rolls.

When we look at the flow through time, we learn that about 100,000 cases are added to the welfare rolls each year. Fortunately, some persons are able to leave the relief rolls. However, 40 percent of those who ask for relief are rejected, although not necessarily permanently. The city and the state require that the applicant for assistance have used up almost all his assets—his savings, his home, his insurance. It is assumed that this regulation protects the public!

To understand the dynamics of relief, we shall briefly consider the factors that force individuals to request public assistance. Of the 100,000 new relief cases per year, roughly 1 in 4 is precipitated by the loss of employment. A somewhat larger group, about 30 percent of the total, is composed of women with children and no income. These are primarily deserted families, many of which reflect a work-correlated phenomenon. A high proportion of the men who desert their families are unable to get or hold a job. This is not the only reason for desertion, but it is an important one.

The third major precipitating factor is illness. In the United States illness is a more acceptable explanation for failure than unemployment. The 30 percent of the new relief cases in which illness is cited as the major cause probably hides a considerable amount of unemployment and economic failure. Therefore, of all new relief cases, 25 percent are directly attributable to loss of employment; in another 30 percent, unemployment is a significant if indirect factor; and in another 30 percent—those in which illness is claimed—a considerable, if masked, number reflect economic failure. For the sake of completeness, we must note that the only other significant group, amounting to about 10 percent, consists of families whose heads are employed but whose earnings are below relief standards.

The interrelations among unemployment, relief, and illness were dramatically highlighted at the beginning of World War II. Before mobilization, many unemployed were reported as sick. However, with the radical change in the economic environment as a consequence of mobilization, most of the group found full-time jobs!

Nevertheless, the relief rolls in New York City have recently increased in a period of economic expansion. The reason is that the New York economy, like the national economy, increasingly needs workers with skills. There can be, and often is, a mismatching between people and the market, between those seeking work and employers seeking workers. New York City is primarily a white-collar professional and service area, and people on welfare are usually poorly educated and unskilled. Therefore, with a continuing decline in the demand for blue-collar workers because of the gradual exodus of the garment and other manufacturing plants, there is less and less opportunity for poorly prepared, poorly educated, poorly trained, often foreign-speaking persons to find employment.

This of course is an oversimplification, but it does help to explain the apparent anomaly of increasing relief rolls at a time of employment expansion. We next ask: Is this mismatching of men and jobs new? Or, if it is not, why has it only recently come to the fore?

First, these welfare problems are new only in that they are newly visible. Northern cities have such large relief rolls today because Southern misery has been transplanted. The farms of the South used to hold both white and Negro misery. But during the last thirty years, the Southern poor have left their farms and are now found in New York, Chicago, San Francisco, Los Angeles, and Philadelphia. Mismatching between people and jobs, then, is not new. What is new is that the poor now live in the North and the West.

Secondly, we never know the true prevalence of pathology until we decide to do something about it. During the past thirty years, the government has been committed to helping people in need; as a consequence these people have become visible. This phenomenon is well known in the arena of mental illness. Nobody knows how many people in a community are mentally ill until a new hospital is opened. As the beds fill up, a second hospital may be opened, and then a third. We learn about the prevalence and incidence of mental illness by creating treatment capacity. Similarly, when government began to create rights to relief, the nation became aware of the large numbers who required assistance.

A third aspect of change relates to family organization among the poor.

Given the large number of disorganized families, two problems—unwanted children and the deserting male—are especially relevant to a discussion of work and welfare. Until recently there were no effective methods of birth control available to the poor. However, the development of intrauterine devices and pills is a technological turning point. For the first time birth control has become a realistic prospect for a large number of poor, uneducated women.

Next, a willingness to work on the part of young men is a function of family organization, training, and living. A Negro or white youngster growing up in a slum who has never seen a male head of the household go to work in the morning and come home at night grows up with a value system that simply does not incorporate the concept of work as the normal adjustment for an adult male. We learn largely by imitation, and if family life does not present a model of work, an eighteen- or nineteen-year-old young man may not be able to internalize it.

The amazing characteristic of the Negro family today is not its disorganization, but rather the replication of middle-class white values that Negroes who have achieved a modicum of economic stability present. Of course, for the many who live on the fringe of the economy and society, family life remains disorganized, but this is true of white families in similar circumstances.

A fifth new dimension is a function of the failure of the school. Teachers and school administrators—even teachers of education—do not know how to teach the hard-to-educate. The schools are to blame, if at all, only because they have sought to hide this incapacity. Nevertheless, the fact is that we are pouring out into the labor force many who will be permanently handicapped in their efforts to become productive citizens. There was a time, not long ago, when it was not really essential to be literate. The conventional screening device at the factory gate at the turn of the century was a simple one: Applicants were told to roll up their sleeves. Muscle was the basis of employability. This is no longer so.

Next, because of the ignorance and hostility of the citizenry, most welfare systems operate as a disincentive to work. Only recently were the regulations in New York City changed to permit youngsters in families on relief to retain more of their earnings. The old system reduced the relief allowance as the youngster's earnings increased, thereby discouraging him from seeking additional work. The system was particularly pernicious for those at the beginning of their working careers.

Another important point in the relations between work and welfare is Negro hostility to white America, which has reached the point where it interferes with many Negroes' employability. Many ghetto youngsters are so hostile because of the promises which have been made and broken that they refuse to learn in school and refuse to go to work when they are no longer at school. Riots in Watts, Chicago, Hunters Point, and Atlanta are a clue to the depth of this hostility.

We must reconsider the logic of adhering to a system of local responsibility for relief. Such a system has the weight of history on its side, but history alone is an inadequate justification. We must understand that what happens in the backwoods of Mississippi and Alabama is connected with New York City, Chicago, and Philadelphia. We continue to adhere to a system which considers children a state and local responsibility, but this system ignores the fact that children move when they become adults—and sometimes before that. We must begin to ask questions about minimum standards of support, not only in New York but in Mississippi, Alabama, and everywhere else. That we have not done so in the past helps to explain why the major cities of the North and West now have to absorb migrants whose preparation for work and life lags by two generations behind the local population.

Our system of relief is a system of maintenance, whereas what we need is a system of rehabilitation. That we have a system of maintenance instead of rehabilitation reflects the taxpayer's disinclination to underwrite the disadvantaged.

Another point reflects an accepted psychiatric generalization. We believe that it is better for children to be brought up in families, preferably their own families, but if that is not possible, in foster families. However, there are strengths and values to institutional care— good institutional care. In our enthusiasm for a family environment we have forgotten that youngsters often support each other and can learn from each other. Perhaps the pendulum should swing again, this time toward good institutional care.

Another facet of the work-welfare complex is the relation of the central city to its suburbs. Neither New York City nor any other large city in the United States will long remain viable unless a fundamental change occurs in city-county-state relationships. The affluent part of the population cannot continue to come into the city by day, make a good living there, and run away at night to live in secluded suburbs, free and uncontaminated by the problem people that the city creates, attracts, and holds. Neither New York nor any other large city can solve its problems as long as the suburbs continue to stay separate.

We have begun to help the metropolis by a circuitous route—by siphoning a little Federal money directly back into the city. Another way would be to channel additional money from the state. But much more radical reforms are required to enable the city to deal effectively with its serious problems—slum clearance, schools, and welfare.

We also need major educational reforms, not only in the narrow sense of better schools but in terms of new institutions and new school-work relationships which will provide learning opportunities for adolescents who cannot learn in conventional classroom situations. Our economy has little or no use for large numbers of young people, whereas every other economy in the world does make room for young persons of fifteen and sixteen. It may be that as other industrial nations acquire a more sophisticated technology, they too will face problems in the absorption of youth into the labor force.

In any case, young Americans reach adulthood without having had an opportunity to work. Our young people are kept in school because society has no other place for them. During the past few years the expansion of the Armed Forces and the establishment of many new residential and other types of training programs has helped to hold off considerable numbers who would otherwise have been searching for jobs.

Implicit in the foregoing consideration of the relations of work and welfare is the need for improved planning on a community as well as on a regional and national basis. Additional effort must be focused on the local level, for that is where the people are and the jobs are. The only agency of society with the power to plan for the community as a whole and to coordinate independent organizations and agencies is government. It has been argued that, given the inefficiencies of government, it would be preferable to leave the planning and coordinating functions to voluntary groups. But this contention misses two points. First, the very weaknesses in government, weaknesses that stem from bureaucracy, are also endemic in other types of large organizations, profit and nonprofit. They are primarily a reflection of size. Secondly, effective planning and coordination require the exercise of power that government alone possesses. Certainly government cannot and should not do the entire job. But if government fails to plan and coordinate, the neglect of human needs and the waste of tax and philanthropic dollars will be inordinate. The mounting crisis in medical and hospital services in New York City after years of studied neglect is one of many possible illustrations of the consequences that follow government's failure to plan.

One measure of a civilized society is that it gives people a second and a third chance if they need it. To build bridges back to society for people who have failed along the way, especially young people, is exceedingly important. During World War II, in the armed service, we created opportunities for ex-felons and others who had failed in civilian life. It would be unfortunate indeed if we had to wait for another mobilization to repeat that success in creating opportunities for those who most desperately need them. A civilized society should be able to undertake successful social rehabilitation short of war.

Many social scientists approve of the several lines of reform sketched above but believe that they cannot be implemented until the supply of professional manpower is substantially increased. However, their attention is focused solely on the graduates of schools of social work. But there are other sources of an increased supply.

First are graduates of junior colleges. A two-year course after high school is surely long enough to train people at least to handle much of the paper work involved in the administration of relief and rehabilitation. Four years of college is surely long enough to train junior professionals. They would require more guidance and counseling than is now provided, and their needs would also necessitate a redesign of curriculum; but neither task appears overwhelming.

A third important source is the large pool of married women who want to return to work after their children enter school, or even earlier. If schools of social work were to develop more flexibility, and if they could relax their preoccupation with professionalism, they could find many capable persons in this pool. Shorter and more focused training, especially for college graduates, could substantially enlarge the pool. The manpower situation is tight, but with imagination and flexibility it need not remain so tight.

The major thrust of this analysis of work and welfare has been to argue that many people would not have to seek public assistance and that many others would leave the relief rolls if there were more jobs and better jobs available. This does not contend that all problems can be solved via the job market. But it is indeed doubtful whether the causes of indigency and dependency can be successfully attacked without a continuing high level of employment.

Important as a strong demand for labor is, the experience of the last six years has helped to make clear that the reduction of adult dependency requires more than the availability of jobs. It requires workers capable of performing the necessary tasks. If many young people continue to reach working age poorly educated and poorly trained, the nation will have serious problems of dependency. Major reforms must be carried through in the educational-training system.

Employability, however, involves more than effective preparation for jobs. Other considerations, such as access to health services, the availability of day-care centers, and improved public transportation, often prove determining. These several programs must be related in some effective way to the job market if individuals are to have effective access to work.

There is a logic to the concentration of most social welfare programs on children and young people, who still have most of their lives in front of them. But we must not make too sharp a distinction between the generations. Most children are reared by parents or foster parents, and helping parents helps children.

Understanding is a precondition to action, but between understanding and action is commitment. We still lack understanding. We still carry a host of misconceptions about minorities.

And we lack commitment even more than understanding. We must make a commitment to do more, even without certainty of the outcome. Since people act and react as they are treated, we must have faith that if we treat people who need help generously, if we rehabilitate them rather than maintain them, they will respond by seeking to become productive, independent citizens.

The manpower agenda of a modern country is usually composed of items that have forced their way to the forefront. The pressure of events and the values that currently predominate cause these issues to be selected from among a larger number.

Population pressures, together with the long-term upward drift in the proportion of young people who complete high school and enter college, explain the focus of the opening chapter in Part Three. The following chapters on the draft, the shortage of physicians, and paramedical manpower fall within this rubric of compelling issues. A democracy cannot be indifferent to whether or not equity dictates how some young men and not others are selected for military service. Nor can it remain unconcerned about whether physicians and other types of medical personnel will be trained in adequate numbers so that the nation can make full use of the advances of medicine to reduce mortality and morbidity. These are examples of the issues that force their way onto the agenda.

Of a somewhat different stripe are the two chapters on the conservation of talent and on womanpower. These two issues are both more long-range and diffuse. They are not less important, only less insistent and obvious. Of all the nation's resources, talent is the most limited, and only a spendthrift society will neglect to develop and utilize its limited supply effectively. The second issue, womanpower, has increasing significance. Since women make up more than half of the population (they live considerably longer than men), and since more and more women are able and willing to play a role in the world of work, their potential is too valuable to permit to run to waste.

The last chapters can serve as a vantage point from which we can survey the ground that has been covered, and from which we can build a bridge to the Afterword. They place many items on the agenda under the microscope and seek to determine whether and to what extent the actions we have taken and are taking to solve our manpower problems have the sanction of knowledge and politics. Nevertheless, we learn from the Afterword that a democracy, if it is to remain vital, has no option but to experiment even while knowledge is being accumulated and its citizens argue over politics.

Chapter Twelve Manpower Trends at the Colleges

It is venturesome to forecast manpower trends, particularly if one forecasts a trend in order to draw policy implications from it. For example, in 1928, who could have forecast the collapse of the demand for labor which characterized all the early 1930s and much of the latter part of that decade? And in 1938, who would have forecast the expansion of the demand for labor which gained momentum in 1940 and continued until the end of World War II? And who would have argued that most of the married women drawn into the labor market during the war would stay on when peace was reestablished?

Prior to the beginning of the Korean hostilities, who foresaw that scientists and engineers would be in scarce supply throughout most of the decade of the fifties? Who could have known that the resurgence of the economy in 1958–1959 would soon be followed by a 7 percent level of unemployment, and that eight years later there would be mounting evidence of manpower shortages?

Nevertheless, prophecy is a tool with which we must build our plans. We must attempt to delineate the future in order to plan for our institutions. We must take a hard look at the prospective college population in order to plan for our colleges and universities in the future.

What can we say about the college population in the 1970s? A first approximation is easy. Many who today are in the stream of higher education will still be there at the beginning of the new decade, barring only war or nuclear holocaust. Many who today are in the high school stream will be in college by 1970. One of the interesting elements of stability in the American scene is the fact that approximately one-half of all high school graduates enter college. Another is that the proportion of high school students who graduate remains relatively stable. Despite the substantial efforts that are being made by many different leaders and institutions to increase this proportion, the data suggest that the annual gains are modest and that by this decade's end the proportion will still be in the 70-percent range.

These two ratios, when applied to the children already born, provide us with a basis for estimating the prospective supply of college students.

One other aspect of supply is worth noting. Today, about 3.7 million young people reach eighteen each year; this is double the number of young people who became eighteen each year in the early 1950s! The 70 to 75 percent of high school students who graduate and the 50 percent who continue their education must be considered against this vastly enlarged base.

Let us take a closer look at both the numbers in the college stream and the prospective demand for them when they complete their studies. First, will the colleges of the country be able to cope with the vastly enlarged flow of eligible students? There are some straws in the wind which may help us to answer this question. In 1965–1966 a considerable number of major university systems had to turn away large numbers of applicants; the University of Illinois, for instance, had to deny admission to roughly 25,000 applicants. The phenomenon of higher standards for admissions is too well known to require documentation. The most prestigious colleges have no room for many with College Board scores in the 700s!

The counterpart of this situation is the rapid and substantial expansion of many weaker institutions, state and nonprofit, which see a brighter future for themselves and are quick to grasp the opportunity. Political pressures being what they are, the state systems will have to accept most of the students knocking at their doors, with inevitably serious consequences for the quality of instruction they provide. Currently at Michigan State, for instance, many classes are held in dormitories. Often a graduating student is unable to secure a letter of recommendation from a single professor because he never had the opportunity to get to know one well.

Some of the pressure for admission will be released by the rapid expansion of junior and community colleges. What California started a long time ago is now being imitated, if only partially, by an ever larger number of states.

Our concern with facilities for undergraduates is matched by a concern with facilities for professional and graduate instruction. Students who would have been welcomed in graduate departments only a few years ago are being turned away today by graduate faculties in the social sciences as well as in the physical sciences, in law as well as in medicine. And many of those who initially are admitted will be members of a horde; those who are rejected will have to change their occupational choice or settle for an inferior education.

This clamoring for admission to college and graduate school is a function of many factors, of which one is the demand for trained manpower. What can be said about the future shape of this demand?

First, higher education itself will be a major consumer of the trained manpower which it will provide during the years to come. There is no other way for colleges and graduate faculties to expand. In the natural sciences, that is, physics, chemistry, and biology, the key determinant of future demand has been and will doubtless continue to be the scale of the Federal government's expenditures for research and development. We talk a great deal about the dynamics of private enterprise, about the strategic role of the large corporation, but let there be no doubt about it—it is the government's dollars that will largely determine the demand for scientists and research engineers: Two out of three work in the not-for-profit sector.

It is difficult to know what will happen on this front, but it is realistic to point out that our expenditures on space may be leveling off, that we cannot sustain our recent rate of growth in expenditures for medical research, and that the prospects for at least some partial accommodation with the Russians, and conceivably one of these days with the Chinese, is possible. An exacerbation of relations with the East is also possible.

Leaving aside this most important imponderable, it may be worth pointing out that in the last decade or so "research and development" budgets contained a substantial element of the fashionable and that today tough-minded managements are taking a harder look at these budgets. They no longer assume that additional dollars for R&D will necessarily prove more productive than additional dollars spent for advertising or sales. This will have some impact, if only some, on the demand for scientific manpower by the private sector.

In 1965, the Congress passed a new program of technical assistance to American business. It is too early to estimate the additional demands for technical manpower that will be generated from this source, but so far they appear to be modest.

The establishment of a Humanities Foundation may exert some modest counterpulls to the principal incentives which have attracted students to the sciences since sputnik, but it is doubtful that even this foundation will significantly alter the basic contours of the supply of trained manpower, since by far the larger sums of money will be devoted to science. Moreover, to students who choose between science and the humanities, money may be of little importance; interest and aptitude play dominant roles.

Some experts maintain that the establishment of Medicare presages a major increase in the demand for medical manpower. This may happen. But it is more likely that if such a trend develops, it will be reflected at the level of paramedical personnel rather than at the professional level.

The final and most important determinant of the demand for trained manpower between now and the end of the decade will be the trend in the growth of the economy. Some students believe that the economy will continue to grow at an annual rate of 4 percent or more. If it does, the demand for trained manpower is likely to remain strong. But the skeptics do not see a sustained, uninterrupted growth as inevitable. They contemplate the possibility of a leveling off in the growth rate, or even a decline that may extend over a year or two. They do not contemplate a catastrophe, but they see, nevertheless, a break in the expansionary trend. Under these conditions, the demand of the private sector for most, though not all, types of trained manpower could be radically reduced, at least in the short run.

So much for the broad outlines of the future. Let us now take a closer look at some additional dimensions. No economist has as yet provided an adequate explanation for the fact that in the face of a rapidly increasing supply of trained manpower since World War II the relative salary levels of this group have not been adversely affected. At some point, the outpouring of college graduates must act to slow the growth of their earnings. In addition, since the cost of a college education is mounting steadily, the anticipated rapid rise in the number of college entrants and graduates may be slowed. It is likely under these circumstances that the expansion of junior colleges may be even more rapid than is currently anticipated. And industry may soon find that it can make better use of a technician with two years of training than of a four-year liberal arts graduate.

Let us consider the revolution that is taking place with respect to womanpower. About 2 out of every 5 college graduates are women although the proportion of women among those who acquire a master's degree or a doctorate is much smaller. Nevertheless, the more education a woman has, the more likely it is that, other things being equal, she will work. As we recently reported in *Life Styles of Educated Women*,[1] almost all able women who enter graduate school keep an active rela-

[1] Eli Ginzberg and Associates, Columbia University Press, New York, 1966.

tionship to the world of work, marriage and children notwithstanding. More and more educated women are returning to school and to work in their thirties and forties, and higher education is only beginning to adjust to this new development.

Attention should also be directed to assessing another new and important trend—the ever larger number of men who decide, out of desire or necessity, to make an occupational change in mid-career. In a great many instances they represent a new inflow into graduate and professional schools. For example, there are hundreds of thousands of military officers and enlisted men who retire in their early or middle forties at the end of twenty years of service and who must carve out a new career.

After a long period of studied neglect the draft has come to the fore. The public and the Congress are finally aware that the system is awry when in a democracy a high school graduate is 50 percent more likely to serve in the Armed Forces than is a college student. How the problem will be resolved is still unclear, but some of the present inequities will surely be removed. No teacher of graduate students will question that a reform of the draft is likely to reduce by a considerable degree the pressure for admission to various types of graduate and professional schools.

The nub of the racial revolution is that there are insufficient jobs and insufficient income for poorly educated, unskilled Negroes. As far as one can judge, the Negro middle class is in a reasonably good position to take advantage of the broadening educational and occupational opportunities that are becoming available to it. Analyses of the experiences of Negro college youth indicate that most of them are on the way to making it. We must anticipate, however, that both business and government will be under continuing pressure to open more middle- and high-level positions to trained Negroes.

Manufacturing has long been considered the dynamic center of American capitalism. However, total employment in manufacturing is rising very slowly. In forecasting employment, we must not anticipate much of an increase in the manufacturing sector. We may consider it fortunate if manufacturing's relative importance declines only slowly.

Since the end of World War II large corporations have absorbed ever larger numbers of highly trained persons—although the Federal government has been paying for many of those engaged in research and development. Long conditioned to a career system, that is, to hiring a young man out of college and keeping him on the payroll for life, some concerns have begun to question this approach. They still compete aggressively for a share of the new crop, hoping to find some supermen with green thumbs for discovery or moneymaking. But they have caught a glimpse of the fact that the skills of many scientists and engineers become obsolete quickly. They must adjust their long-entrenched career systems to this disturbing new reality.

A little-observed phenomenon is the fact that the less than fully virile trade-union movement, which for so long rested on the shoulders of the skilled blue-collar worker, is undergoing a major metamorphosis. More professionals, particularly in the not-for-profit sector, are joining unions. If, as appears likely in an economy where 2 out of every 3 workers are employed in the service sector, promotions for white-collar workers will come slowly, the growth of trade unions, despite their recent unexciting history, is likely to accelerate.

Recent decisions in Washington point to a deliberate effort to speed the development of graduate education in the lagging South and Southwest. Now that billions of Federal dollars are being spent annually on research and development, our policy makers have belatedly come to the realization that it is a matter of high importance to broaden and deepen our research base. With the aid of Federal money, several third-rate institutions can be turned into second-rate centers; certain second-rate institutions can be helped to achieve first-rate status.

Back of the new awareness of the plight of the large cities and the decline of state power relative to Federal power lies the poor quality of trained manpower in local and state government. Since the public is opposed to the further erosion of state and local government, it must strengthen the personnel in these systems. Therefore, we must anticipate a strong and continuing demand for trained manpower from these sectors.

A few concluding observations. No matter what happens on the political or economic front in the years ahead, colleges and universities will produce very large numbers of graduates. The increased number of graduates of junior colleges will be particularly notable. Included in the increased total will be a great many more women, Negroes, and men who have made mid-career shifts.

Employers will be under increasing pressure to restudy their career systems. They will also spend much more money on the training and retraining of their own professional personnel, for only thus will they slow the heavy costs of obsolescence. With intense competition for the highly talented, many organizations, private, nonprofit, and government, may resort increasingly to new employment patterns which involve part-time rather than full-time work. Again reflecting the continuing competition for the small number of highly qualified persons, employers will not only have to adjust the salaries they offer, but will have to give increasing consideration to other conditions of work. Location will be an ever more important consideration. Men with options will prefer some locations and eschew others.

The next five to ten years will see a large increase in the numbers of young people seeking and obtaining a higher education. Government and philanthropy will have to respond to these pressures, and employers in turn will be affected by the vastly enlarged outflow of college graduates.

However, the number of doctorates which are awarded annually will increase only slowly, particularly in the "tight fields." But there is a risk that the mounting pressures on graduate facilities may result in a decline in the quality of the preparation of young men and women who study for advanced degrees. No manpower policy that sacrifices quality for quantity can succeed. We can avoid this danger if we recognize it in time.

The problem of the draft has surfaced. The President, Congress, and the public now know that the process by which we procure our military manpower is defective. The mounting casualties in Vietnam have unquestionably helped focus attention on this issue: The fact that a high school graduate is 50 percent more likely than a college man to serve in the Army may be glossed over in times of peace, but will not go unnoticed once the number of wounded and dead begins to mount. The act under which young men are drafted is entitled the Universal Military Training and Service Act of 1951, as amended. Today, this "universality" is such that only 46 percent of all men reaching twenty-six have served in the military.

The coincidence of military escalation in Vietnam and the jump in the number of young men reaching eighteen—reflecting the rise in the birth rate after World War II—have precipitated the debate that successive administrations and Congresses have assiduously sought to avoid. Since, under existing arrangements, the Pentagon obtains without difficulty the quantity and quality of manpower it needs, and since the colleges are assured of the student flow which they need to operate optimally, it is understandable that policy makers have avoided disturbing the status quo. But they can avoid doing so no longer.

It is relatively easy to identify what is wrong with the draft as it presently operates. It favors those who have the financial and intellectual resources required for college attendance; until recently, it encouraged young men to marry in order to be deferred; until the recent expansion of the armed services from 2.7 million to 3 million, older men were more likely to be drafted than young men—a double disadvantage since men's lives are more likely to be disrupted at an older age and the military prefer younger men. A less obvious but still clear debit has been the influence of the draft in encouraging many students to enroll in college or graduate school for no reason other than to avoid the draft. Above all, the draft violates the concept of universality, and has helped to make a mockery out of the democratic principle that the responsibility to bear arms rests equitably upon all males.

This list of shortcomings can be enlarged by noting that many presumably eligible men are rejected from military service. The accident of where a man is registered plays an important part in whether or not, and when, he is called up; and there has been no uniformity in the criteria which local boards follow in granting deferments.

The Merits of Selective Service

Nevertheless, there are strengths in this system which help explain why the American people have been willing to accept it for more than a decade.

First of all, the draft has been a highly flexible instrument. During the year when the Korean buildup reached its height, 587,000 men were drafted; a decade later, the annual intake had dropped to 60,000; during a recent twelve months (July 1, 1965—June 30, 1966) 335,000 men were drafted.

Secondly, the draft has contributed markedly to enabling the Air Force, the Navy, and the Marine Corps to rely overwhelmingly on enlistees. Many men volunteer for these services because they know that otherwise they will be drafted. According to a special study of the Department of Defense, 38 percent of the regular enlistees volunteered for this reason, as did 41 percent of the officers and 71 percent of Reserve and National Guard enlistees. To the extent that the armed services gain from having their requirements met by enlistees—they serve longer and they are likely to have better morale than draftees—to that extent much of the credit belongs to the draft.

Finally, the draft has been operated so as to inhibit an inflow of large numbers of men who could not be readily absorbed into a military organization, whether because of lack of aptitude or because of other shortcomings. Not all of the selectivity in "selective service" has been unreasonable.

Lt. Gen. Lewis B. Hershey, the director of the Selective Service System, would call attention to some additional benefits. He believes in citizen responsibility for the operations of the Selective Service System. He sees great merit in a system whereby call-ups and deferments are made by informed persons who live in the same communities as the registrants. The inventory of draft eligibles, maintained by the Selective Service System, is a major support of our mobilization base. In addition, General Hershey would note the remarkable freedom from bribery and other forms of chicanery which characterizes the Selective Service System.

There can be no doubt, then, that the draft has many assets as well as some liabilities. Since no system is perfect, why should we not leave it alone? Besides, there have been recent improvements. Since August, 1965, marriage has not been a ground for deferment, though it still often works out that way; the armed services have revised their criteria for selection, and now accept certain men whom they formerly would have rejected; Congress has recently passed a new GI bill which is at least one step toward greater equity; and the armed services' requirements are such that they now induct men shortly after their twentieth birthday. What more can one system do?

The Demographic Imperative

If the demographic picture were to remain unchanged, *if* the strength of the armed services were to remain at the present ceiling of 3 million, *if* the Department of Defense were to cease its efforts to substitute civilian for military personnel—then there would indeed be a strong case for preserving selective service. However, we face a certain and continuing rise in the number of eighteen-year-olds to a level of over 2.1 million in 1974, which will represent more than a doubling of the number available during the early 1950s and a 40 percent increase over 1964. At pre-Vietnam force levels this would mean that by 1974 only 1 out of every 3 young men reaching twenty-six would have served in the military; and even at the current force level the number would be only slightly more than 2 in 5. And such a surplus of eligible manpower would again threaten to force up the age of induction: Our Selective Service System, operating to catch men before they reach the escape age of twenty-six, takes older men first. The Armed Forces would receive the wrong type of manpower; therefore, before long the present system will have to be changed because the Department of Defense itself will demand a change.

Before discussing desirable changes in the draft, we should explore the alternatives to the draft. Possibly we can get on without it; possibly not. A small number of people, including General Hershey, continue to favor the institution of universal military training (UMT) which was the proposal of the War Department at the end of World War II, but which was ceremoniously buried despite strong support from the Compton Commission and the advocacy of General Marshall. Such a proposal would mean that every young man capable of military service at the age of eighteen would undergo four to six months of military training, and from this total group the armed services would obtain—by enlistment or some form of compulsion—the numbers required to meet their needs. But UMT would meet only part of the equity problem—it is unlikely that there would be enough enlistments to obviate the need for a selective draft; it would be inefficient—the short training would not be of much value; and it would be very costly—perhaps as much as $2 to $3 billion every year.

Another proposal aimed at better matching the large numbers available for service and the limited needs of the armed services is to reduce the required length of service for draftees to below the present two-year minimum. However, even with two years of service for draftees the Army gets limited use out of many men, since so much time must be devoted to processing, training, and traveling. The small gains which would be made in equity by drafting larger numbers for a shorter period of time would be more than counter-balanced by large losses in efficiency and economy.

Can we eliminate the draft completely and have the armed services rely solely on volunteers? The Department of Defense has estimated that even after taking into account the larger pool of eighteen-year-olds who will be available in the early 1970s, the maximum all-volunteer force that could be maintained would be 2 million at the present 4 percent level of unemployment, and 2.2 million at a 5.5 percent unemployment level. This would leave a significant deficit even if force levels returned to their pre-Vietnam figure. An even more serious problem would be how the armed services could attract the specialists who play an ever larger role in the successful operation of modern military organizations. For example, how could the armed services induce 3,000 physicians to volunteer for active duty?

Despite the contentions of some economists, such as Milton Friedman, it is doubtful that the American people would approve of an additional annual expenditure of between $4 and $17 billion for our Armed Forces; this is the sum which the Department of Defense calculates would be necessary to recruit and support an all-volunteer force at the pre-Vietnam level. These sizable additional expenditures have taken into account offsetting savings in training costs and in reduced turnover that a career force would make possible.

A further objection to an all-volunteer force is that it would be exceedingly difficult to man the active reserves. Moreover, the costs of responding to a sudden increase in requirements, such as during the buildup in Vietnam, could be horrendous if we had to rely on monetary incentives to attract quickly several hundred thousand additional men.

A third approach would be to develop, under universal "military" training, a system of civilian assignments which would be considered the equivalent of a term of duty in the armed services. Currently, two years in the Peace Corps is treated in this way by most draft boards. Can we designate a large number of such positions—teaching or social work in depressed rural and urban areas, scientific or technical work in specified fields, and civilian jobs in U.S. overseas operations other than the Peace Corps? The list of high-priority useful jobs can be readily enlarged.

However, there are many objections to this proposal, too. Among the most important are the clear advantages that this would give to young people from middle- and upper-income homes who attend or graduate from college. In addition, the problem which would result from paying these young people at the prevailing rate of civilian wages would be enormous—as would be the problem which would result from paying them less! Furthermore, the availability of alternatives to military duty might have a serious effect on the inflow of trained manpower into the armed services; any other assumption would not be realistic. Finally, our liberal-democratic traditions cause us to view with strong distaste the kind of large-scale and permanent governmental direction of civilian labor that such a program would entail.

These arguments against the suspension or abolition of the draft hold for now and for the proximate future. If the fighting in Vietnam were to come to a halt; if no other front were to become active; if the size of the Armed Forces could be reduced from the present 3 million to closer to 2 million; if energetic efforts were made to replace several hundred thousand men in uniform (in clerical positions, in base maintenance, in hospitals) with civilians; if the reserve structure could be further reduced—then in fact it might be worthwhile to see whether the conditions of military service could be improved to a point where the armed services might obtain the military manpower they need solely through enlistments. But this is clearly something for the distant future, not for tomorrow.

The Lottery as a Workable Alternative

The real challenge is to design an alternative that will result in a more universal sharing of the risk of service while providing the armed services, at a reasonable cost, with the numbers and quality of manpower they require. Many observers believe that a lottery can substantially meet the test for equity. If all young men are not needed by the armed services, a lottery is the fairest method of determining on whom the obligation should fall. However, even a lottery should not mandate the induction of all those selected at one specific age, such as nineteen. It is clearly advantageous for the armed services if certain young men complete college or even go further in their education before they are called upon to serve. Those who receive a deferment to continue their education, however, must take their chances when they complete their schooling. They would enter the lottery at that point. Since more than 70 percent of all young men complete high school, and since half go on to junior or four-year college, it is reasonable to suppose that approximately one-third would enter the lottery at an age older than nineteen.

The key element of a national lottery for military service is an annual list of all young men liable for military service. The requirements of the armed services would determine the proportion of the group to be called. Those not called in any one year could make their plans with reasonable assurance that they would not be called at all, except in an emergency. Such a system could be put in effect just as soon as the international situation begins to stabilize. Unless the Vietnam war accelerates far beyond our worst fears, the number of young men available for service will grow steadily larger than the number required.

General Hershey has long opposed the lottery. He argues that it has not worked satisfactorily in the past and that it would be unsatisfactory again. He states that the American people would object if such fundamental decisions as who should serve and who should be deferred were to hang on the turn of a wheel. He believes that reliance on the decisions of local citizens is much to be preferred.

Now, it is quite true that no system can be perfect and that the most carefully constructed lottery will have its faults. Thus, if the requirements of the armed services fluctuate, the risk for men entering the lottery in one year instead of another will not be the same. This kind of multiple chanciness can be nerve-racking for those who are involved. But the fact remains that the present system cannot be continued and will not be continued once the Congress and the Presidential Commission highlight its gross inequities. Given that fact, a lottery would appear to be the most sensible and least problematic of all alternatives to selective service.

A lottery can be reinforced with "fringe benefits" to make the incidence of luck less brutal. Since there would still be gross differences in sacrifices between those who serve and those who do not, the gap could be reduced by raising the level of military pay and by providing educational and training benefits for the inductee and enlistee. For instance, it would be desirable if the armed services were to provide educational and training benefits, prior to their entering upon a term of active duty, for young men who join the enlisted reserve. Such a system would prove both efficient and economic, since it would reduce the amount of time and resources that the armed services have to devote to training their own specialists. The GI bill, which was recently passed, also makes a contribution to greater equity. Transitional education and training benefits for career men—men who, at the end of twenty years' service, must fit themselves into the civilian economy —would also be desirable.

One other point: Present standards for military service lead to the rejection of large numbers of young men of limited aptitude and education—roughly one-third of the age class. The manpower pool is sufficiently large that the armed services do not have to induct the hard-to-train and hard-to-discipline. From the vantage point of the armed services, such a policy is easy to appreciate. But if the frame of reference is broadened from the military to the national scene, this policy is not the only possible—or the only correct—one. Under recent Federal legislation, we have been spending over 2 billion dollars annually in training and retraining young people without jobs, and we shall probably soon spend much more. In World War II, the armed services, particularly the Army, did an outstanding job in providing special training opportunities for a half million illiterates.

The establishment of the Job Corps, the Neighborhood Youth Corps, and other training and training-related efforts under civilian auspices appears to have decided the issue in favor of the civilian sector.

Yet the commitment of Secretary of Defense Robert S. McNamara that the armed services will induct annually about 100,000 men with low aptitude scores suggests that some policy ambivalence exists about the preferred manner of dealing with disadvantaged youth.

This move by the Department of Defense may provide the opportunity for a good experimental study of the relative effectiveness of military versus civilian efforts at socialization of, and skill acquisition by, disadvantaged youth. It is by no means clear that private corporations, nonprofit organizations, or civilian governmental departments will be able to do as good a job as the armed services.

This much is clear: Military manpower policy can never be effectively separated from national manpower policy. And national manpower policy must always be the concern of the entire citizenry.

Chapter Fourteen Physician Shortage Reconsidered

The concern with the present and prospective shortages of physicians has been of long standing. Already eight years ago one was out of step if he questioned whether in point of fact a shortage either existed or threatened.

Now with the Bayne-Jones and Bain reports, the National Institutes of Health Report on Manpower for Medical Research, the Recommendations of the Subcommittee on Manpower of the Commission on Heart Disease, Stroke and Cancer, the *Health Manpower Source Book* (section 18), and still other analyses as reference sources available, it may be well to return to this theme. A 1966 week-long *ad hoc* conference on medical education, attended by leaders in the field and a few outsiders, has provided the stimulus.

With only a ripple of dissent, the conference concluded that it was not only desirable but essential that the supply of physicians be increased by at least 4 percent per annum over the next decade or so.

One should consider what an increase of 4 percent per annum means. Instead of slightly less than 7,900 graduates from medical schools, which is the current annual figure, 11,700 would graduate in one year a decade hence. However, the last governmental estimate, in 1964 (*Health Manpower Source Book*), was that the new supply of American doctors in 1975 would be slightly less than 9,200. This estimate contemplated an additional 1,600 licensed physicians from Canadian and foreign schools. The combined total would lead to a modest increase in the rate of physicians per 100,000 population— from 150 to 154.

The conference recommended an increase of almost 30 percent more than the government's estimate of the number of physicians in 1975. Why did it recommend such a radical increase? The principal reasons adduced were as follows:

The rate of population increase, the loss of physicians by retirement or death, the increased demand for physicians' services resulting from higher consumer income and new governmental programs such as

Medicare, the increasing time that physicians must spend per patient as a result of new medical and surgical procedures, and the following desiderata: To improve the quality of medical care by increasing the number of younger, better trained physicians, to emancipate the country from reliance on foreign-trained physicians, to enable the United States to contribute more readily to assisting developing nations, to establish better medical care for many disadvantaged groups, and to reduce the average hours of work of physicians.

How can any reasonable man be unpersuaded by such weighty claims? Here are some of the reasons that at least this participant continued to voice his skepticism, not about the need to increase the supply of physicians, but at defining the situation as a crisis and at calling for an increase of that magnitude:

The conference assumed that the population is increasing at the rate of 2 percent per annum. In point of fact, the current rate of increase is about 1.3 percent. To postulate a 2 percent rate of increase means an error of 50 percent in the projected increase.

Next, the *Health Manpower Source Book* estimated that up to 4,900 physicians would die each year.

Rising income at home is not new. The per capita income of the United States has increased about threefold since the turn of this century, and the number of physicians did not even double between 1900 and 1960. Clearly, real per capita income and the number of physicians do not have to increase in tandem. Medicare can certainly be expected to lead to an increased demand for physicians' services, but its greatest impact is likely to be on the demand for additional nursing services.

Again, it is expected that certain new medical and surgical procedures will require a large amount of physicians' time, but it is hard to believe, as some contended, that all the "slack" in the utilization of physicians' time has been squeezed out of the system. One participant called attention to a forthcoming report by the Medical School, University of Washington, which will show that 50 percent of a pediatrician's time in his office is devoted to procedures that paramedical personnel can equally well perform. Clearly, one can still look for gains in productivity.

One can accept the conclusion that physicians trained after World War II are better prepared than the older members of the profession —a conclusion that was forcefully advanced; however, the overwhelming proportion of all physicians in active practice in 1975 will belong to this group.

Some foreign-trained physicians are Americans. But the majority are foreigners who cannot return home or who do not want to after completing their training. An arbitrary refusal to license them would simply force many to move to another country.

The President has announced a program for expanding the role of the United States in helping to raise the health standards of developing nations. But the numbers of physicians likely to be involved will not be large. More than physicians, Asia and Africa need sanitarians, veterinarians and public-health nurses.

It can readily be stipulated that disadvantaged populations in rural and urban areas need more and better health services, but the critical question is whether the graduation annually of an additional 1,000 physicians in the Northeast would, in fact, assure such services either for the slum population in New York or for poor whites and Negroes in low-income rural areas of Mississippi. Moreover, although the poor undoubtedly need more good medical care, they need, even more, jobs and income.

Everyone knows that many physicians work too many hours for too many years. But this is not primarily because there is no one to take their place. Most independent professionals work hard because they want to. Moreover, most independent professionals work beyond their sixty-fifth year because they want to.

There is no scientific way of determining the relative strengths of the several suggestions advanced to support the need for a vast acceleration in the training of physicians and the countervailing arguments that have just been sketched. But the issue can be further explored. Here are some of the statements made in passing at the recent conference that went more or less unchallenged:

Many general surgeons are not very busy and therefore a great amount of unnecessary surgery is performed. The situation is particularly shocking when hysterectomies are considered. We were told that many women undergo mastectomies when a less radical procedure would do. Many thyroidectomies are performed when psychotherapy would be preferred.

There is substantial overdoctoring for a host of diseases, including in particular infections of the upper respiratory tract.

The major proponent of annual physical examinations was unable to convince his colleagues of its virtues. With the possible exception of the Papanicolaou test, screening devices, including even mass x-ray surveys of the chest, were questioned. Without good follow-up procedures, screening appears to have limited value.

Although the potentialities of rehabilitation were not denied, we were reminded that only modest improvement could be expected from major efforts to help any large group of seriously stricken patients such as victims of strokes.

The conference certainly agreed that excessive surgery, overdoctoring, and limitations in preventive medicine and rehabilitation are characteristic of the present state of medical practice. And there was further agreement. It was recognized that the amount of medical services that a specific population group wants or needs depends, among other things, on its cultural background, education, and other characteristics. Hence, the desired ratio of physicians to population in Boston or New York cannot be applied to the South—surely not to the rural South.

The point was made that unsupervised residents and other less than fully qualified personnel are responsible for most of the physicians' services rendered in many large municipal and county hospitals in metropolitan centers. No one believed that this defect could be eradicated simply by enlargement of the output of medical schools.

No one questioned the contention that the principal gains in health that the country has sustained have been due more to the rising standards of living and to advances in public health than to curative medicine. But this conclusion was not linked to discussions of future requirements for physicians.

Again, it was generally recognized that the control of cigarette smoking, of diet, of sexual promiscuity, and of reckless driving offers potentially large gains in the public's health; no connection was made between this fact and the limited role of physicians in achieving these objectives.

Similarly, there was a discrepancy between the recognition of the desirability of rationalizing the delivery of medical services through the training and more effective use of paramedical personnel and the impact of this on the requirements for physicians. The marked gains in the medical-service industry over the past half century were predicated not as much on the expansion of the number of physicians as on the improvement in their training and on the increase in paramedical personnel.

Much of the discussion was directed to ways in which the path through medical school and postgraduate medical education could be improved and shortened. Admission of selected students to medical school after two years of college, a three-year medical school, eliminating the internship, and reducing various residencies from five to two years—all this and more was advanced and responded to favorably. It was clear that such reforms, if they are adopted, would add significantly to the potential supply of physicians. However, whereas each of these possibilities was noted and approved, it was not believed that, either individually or in total, they would significantly affect the output of physicians.

There is one additional circumstance that must be considered in determining the scale of medical education. In a democracy, well-qualified persons should not be arbitrarily barred from pursuing a career of their choosing. This appears to be a strong argument for expanding training facilities. The pressure to enter medical schools will inevitably mount in a period of sharply rising undergraduate enrollments. To balance freedom of occupational choice, social investment in medical education, and the requirements for an efficient system of medical services will not come easily.

What more can be added?

Physicians are in a position to create their own demand. They often have wide margins of discretion about whether to ask a patient to return to the office for one or more follow-up visits.

The per diem cost of hospitalization, and of medical costs as a whole, is mounting alarmingly. One sure way to accelerate this rise is to increase the number of physicians in the total personnel supply. The effective use of physician manpower depends in the first instance on a taut supply of physicians.

Most economists believe that the public good would be served by a vast increase in the number of physicians, which would, through competition, reduce their average earnings and eliminate the excessive gains from their restricting the supply. Although no economist can look with equanimity on monopoly, in this instance the cure may be worse than the disease. If it is true that physicians can create their own demand, only a vast "oversupply" would bring average earnings down, and then only at the individual and social cost of overdoctoring. Given the alternatives of high average earnings for a taut supply of physicians and a loose supply, lower earnings, and overdoctoring, one might opt for the first.

One thing appears clear. No arbitrary figure, whether it is 4 percent per annum or any other homemade statistic, is a proper guide for determining the rate of expansion of the supply of physicians.

Chapter Fifteen Paramedical Manpower

In recent years, much has been made of the "shortage" of medical manpower, of a "crisis" in the medical field. But in this country, the word "crisis" is used too freely. The United States is rich; we are rich in money, people, skills, and goods. But those who have only a little want more, and those who have a great deal want even more. Therefore we are always short of good things.

The dynamic nature of our economy and society helps to create the very shortages about which we complain. We are now spending much more money in the health field than we used to spend. The assumption is that we now are receiving more and better health services than a few years ago. However, since prices are rising very rapidly, the additional dollars may reflect primarily higher payments to the participating factors of production. But if the perspective is broadened to include a broader sweep of time, we know this is not the whole or even the largest part of the story, because there has been a marked increase in the manpower and other resources devoted to health and medical services.

The health-services industry has in fact been remarkably responsive to market changes; productive resources measured in manpower terms increased by over 50 percent between 1950 and 1960. During this decade, it was one of the fastest-growing industries in the country. There is basis for concern in the present and persistent imbalances in the demand and supply in certain categories of scarce manpower, but the field as a whole has demonstrated a high order of flexibility.

In 1940 medical personnel represented 3 percent of total nonagricultural employment; in 1960 the proportion was 5 percent. The absolute figures in 1940 and in 1960 indicate even more dramatically the response of the health-services field to the rapidly increasing demand.

Before considering the specific characteristics of the health-services field, let us review the broad dimensions of the service sector of the economy, of which health services are one important part. We have seen that 2 out of every 3 workers in the United States are employed in the services sector, and only one in the goods-producing sector. We have seen further that the services tend to use a greater proportion of highly trained persons than does the goods-producing sector. Since more and more of total employment and a much higher proportion of scientific and technical manpower are centered in the services, the future of the economy is increasingly wrapped up with the education and training of the labor force. A man requires a solid educational foundation in order to acquire a high order of skill. Moreover, he must have access to continuing education and training if he is to avoid obsolescence of the skills he has acquired. Therefore critical linkages have come to exist among the growth of the services, educational and training opportunities, and a trained manpower supply.

A further reason that the health-services industry should be particularly sensitive to matters of education and training is its requirement for very large numbers to meet both its replacement demands and the demands reflecting growth. In addition, the more specialized education a person acquires, the more likely he is to remain attached to the field which he enters. Although this proposition must be applied with caution to certain types of professionals, such as engineers and lawyers, since many of them do not remain in their profession, it has general validity.

The service field is characterized by a high proportion of women workers. Among the most important of the special characteristics of women workers are: They tend to acquire, on the average, less education and training than do men; many of those who work prefer to work part time or only part of the year; and their pattern of entering, leaving, and returning to the labor force varies from that of men. There are many other ways in which women differ from men with respect to their preparation for and participation in the labor force, including the time they study, the fields they enter, and their attachment to their occupation. No employer can afford to ignore these important differences, particularly if he is highly dependent on women for his labor force.

Until recently, trade unions were underrepresented in the service sectors of the economy. A shift is now under way. Nevertheless, unions are still underrepresented when the employer is a nonprofit and/or governmental agency. However, changes lie ahead. Perhaps the trade unions' strengths in the future will be centered in the not-for-profit sector. Today, more and more governmental agencies find it necessary to permit their employees to join unions, although most have a no-strike clause in their agreements. However, if collective bargaining breaks down, if serious disagreements cannot be resolved, no-strike clauses tend to be ignored. New York State has long had a law on its books which precludes public employees from striking and which punishes a violation with dismissal. But there has been a series of strikes by public employees in New York in which, after settlements were reached, the penalty was waived. The simple fact is that in most instances the penalty of dismissal would not provide the relief that the governmental employer needs or desires.

In many service fields, nonprofessional workers tend to have low wages, poor working conditions, and a limited range of fringe benefits. This reflects a great many different forces, especially the small extent of unionization in the nonprofit sector. An additional reason for the low wages and the unattractive working conditions in many parts of the service sector is that economies of scale, which make it possible to pay people more, are difficult to introduce. The effective management of service operations is much more difficult than the effective management of a manufacturing plant.

We have noted that the services tend to make use of a high proportion of professional workers. It is in the nature of professional work that it is difficult to set output norms and even more difficult to establish and control the processes of the work flow. Moreover, professionals balk at close supervision. The scope for managerial initiative is constricted. It is next to impossible, for instance, for a university president or a dean to introduce a series of organizational changes that will lead to greater utilization of academic resources, particularly faculty time and effort.

Against these general characteristics of the service sector, we can consider the health-services industry from the viewpoint of its manpower requirements and the problems that it faces in meeting them.

First, the manpower required to provide services must usually be located close to the place where the services are to be used. Thus, while certain members of the health-services industry are mobile, most of the workers must be recruited from the locale where the physician's office, the public health clinic, or the hospital is located. In addition a high proportion of all health workers cannot be effectively utilized until they have had some period of specialized education and training. This in turn means that training structures must be so distributed throughout the country that potential workers have access to them. Otherwise those who are able and willing to enter the field will find other work, and those who require trained and competent workers will not find them.

Whether the health-services industry can fill its jobs will depend on more than the availability of adequate local training facilities, crucial as these are. At the same time that health clinics and hospitals are looking for workers to hire and train, so are a great many competing employers. The prospective employee considers not only the time and other costs required to obtain training, but also the wages and working conditions that he can look forward to. For a great many different reasons, the wage structures in health services, particularly on the subprofessional levels, have tended to lag behind other fields. The health-services industry is still locked in an uphill struggle to make its wages more competitive.

Another reason that it finds it so difficult to maintain an adequate supply of trained manpower is its heavy dependence on female labor, particularly young women, who have a relatively high rate of withdrawal from the labor force. In addition, many workers leave for other types of employment where the wages and working conditions are more attractive. As a consequence the health services have long had a very heavy replacement demand.

These difficulties are compounded by the fact that so many workers in this field see so little opportunity ahead. Many workers are willing to put up with initially low wages or adverse working conditions if the future looks bright. This is, in fact, the situation of the young physician during his year of internship. He is willing to accept a modest stipend and to adjust to an arduous working schedule because he can look ahead to much higher earnings and improved conditions in the near future. But such favorable prospects are not part of the career expectations of the nurse, the medical technician, the aide. In practically no other field are the ceilings for most beginning workers so low. The ambitious and talented person has little room for advancement through performance on the job. If he wants to improve his position, he must return to school and start off on a different track which will land him at a higher point in the hierarchy. But this is much too costly in terms of time and money for most.

An effective training system can, however, be a major asset in personnel procurement and retention, particularly if it is closely aligned to both the wage structure and the promotion ladder. The armed services have discovered that they can alleviate the skilled manpower shortages which they confront because of high rates of turnover by establishing more attractive career opportunities. They now encourage men to remain in the service for many years by providing successive levels of training which qualify them for higher-paying and more prestigious positions. But the health-services industry has not yet succeeded in doing this, partly because it is difficult to encourage the many independent professional and technical organizations to engage in the necessary joint planning.

The Federal government has undertaken to help alleviate health-manpower shortages through liberal grant programs to trainees and educational institutions. However, its ability to offset the many negative factors outlined above should not be overestimated. For example, the Nurse Training Act of 1964 committed the Federal government to spend large sums for the training of nurses. However, one careful student of the subject, after reviewing early experience under the act, suggested that the net result of the efforts of the Federal government might actually reduce the supply if the small diploma schools are inhibited from expanding and since no operating subsidies are provided the degree programs.

The hospital has always played a crucial role in the training of health personnel. Nevertheless, hospitals have never been able to perform an effective educational and training mission. They have been neither properly financed nor staffed. In fact, they have been able to carry the costs of training only by extracting a large amount of free labor from physicians, nurses, technicians, and others. Recently, they have sought to recapture some of their training costs from Blue Cross and other third parties, but they have met substantial and probably growing resistance. The patients and the insurance companies do not want to underwrite the costs involved in training medical manpower, and maintain that these costs should be assessed against the community at large.

The fact that most other types of specialized education and training have been brought under the rubric of the formal school system adds to the tension of medical education and training being so heavily centered in the hospital. The hospital is less able to provide free tuition than is the vocational high school, the junior college, the state university. Nevertheless, while there has been some shift as more medical and health education has been brought under the rubric of the state educational structure, the hospital continues to be a major educational center.

The hospital, both as a training institution and as an employing institution, together with the other major agencies in the health-services field, has made an imperfect adjustment to the revolution in manpower that has been under way in this country since the onset of World War II. During the last quarter century more and more married women have become interested in working outside the home. But if they are to do so, especially at a high level, adjustments both in the educational-training structure and in employment must be made. We are such a youth-centered country that we have been slow to make adjustments which would enable women, especially mothers, to work part time. Resistance has been even greater where the control of a profession has been in the hands of single women who have had no interests or concerns other than their work. Many of the leaders of the nursing profession have not encouraged the types of adjustment that would ease the recruiting and retraining of married women.

Another factor that has been added to the manpower difficulties in the health field grows out of the underinvestment of capital. Manpower utilization is a function of the demands of the job in relation to the skills of the worker, the quality of the supervision which he receives, and the capital that has been invested. There is considerable evidence to suggest that the hospital and other health agencies do not efficiently utilize their personnel. Poor supervision and inadequate capital investment tend to encourage health agencies to use more people than necessary. The dollars at their disposal must be spread thinner, and each worker is paid less. If the hospital is forced to function with antiquated plant and equipment because the public is underinvesting, this makes for poor manpower utilization.

A central challenge to every service field is that of providing not only an adequate quantity of services but also services of high quality. It is clear that we want teachers, ministers, physicians, and nurses who are competent. But every field must establish realistic standards. For example, nursing leaders have been seeking to attract more persons with baccalaureate and master's and even doctor's degrees into nursing. Yet hospital administrators have been looking in the market for a different type of personnel. They have been more interested in obtaining two practical nurses than one nurse with a master's degree.

While quality is a consideration of importance, it can be an umbrella for many different kinds of machinations. Some years ago psychiatrists at the Menninger Foundation outlined the qualifications of a good ward attendant. They said that a man with an eighth-grade education, with a friendly personality, and with a willingness to work with sick people would be a better attendant than a college graduate. Emotional characteristics may be and often are much more important than intellectual qualifications. A man who finds it satisfying to work in an environment made up of people who are mentally ill may well be better qualified than a highly educated person.

A serious barrier to effective manpower utilization in the health field is the continuing struggle among the many professional and semi-professional groups. Each group has a role to play; yet each devotes an inordinate amount of time and energy to improving its position on the hierarchical ladder and seeking to prevent others from impinging on its rights and prerogatives. The struggle for economic power and social prestige between physicians and nurses, between nurses and technicians, and between technicians and aides makes the design of rational, long-term policy for manpower utilization next to impossible.

Now, the health-service field alone does not have sufficient leverage to remedy this chronic infighting. The people at the top do not want to change the system; the people at the bottom are too weak to change the system; those in between cannot agree on what should be changed —and if they could, they would not be able to change it.

But our society does have a way of resolving what might appear to be unresolvable. The market is a potent mechanism. If the supply of registered nurses proves inadequate, somehow a new source is opened up. Practical nurses' training programs were established over the opposition of the leaders of the nursing profession, and middle-aged women with limited education were attracted into the field. If they are able to earn 80 percent of what a registered nurse can earn, at the end of one year instead of three years of training, the likelihood is that there will be a long-term shift toward a higher proportion of practical nurses.

Similarly, if the leaders of psychiatry continue to insist that psychiatrists must get their medical degrees before they can practice psychoanalysis, other disciplines may intrude on this preserve. Before long, psychologists, social workers, ministers, counselors and others will be practicing psychotherapy.

The problem of an adequate number of properly qualified medical manpower will probably never be solved, because the level of demand for medical services is in considerable measure determined by the supply. Whatever the supply, the demand will always rise to a point beyond it. We have lived, and we will have to continue to live, with manpower shortages. There are, of course, some ways that are better than others to cope with shortages. We must use what some have called the "crisis" in medical manpower, or what could be better defined as a "chronic condition," to learn (1) more about the people who can be recruited and trained, (2) more about preferred methods of training, (3) more about the relationships of training to the wage and career structures, (4) more about the balancing of professional and group conflicts, and (5) more about effective management.

There is a danger in establishing requirements for training that are unrealistic, requirements that prevent the market from attracting the numbers needed to provide society with the services it requires. It is the responsibility of the leadership of the several professional organizations to strive for standards that they consider essential for the provision of services of high quality. But quality can never be a sole preoccupation. Quantity is also a legitimate requirement. The balancing of the two is the real challenge to professional leadership.

Chapter Sixteen The Conservation of Talent

This chapter will consider the talented individual and his search for a place in the world of work. Our concern here will be with how the individual seeks to shape his career in the external world which provides both opportunities and barriers.

We shall consider the impact of three dimensions of this external world on career development. The first is the current educational and guidance structure as it facilitates or retards the optimal development of talent. Second, we shall review the manner in which specific work environments in corporate enterprise, academic institutions, and government influence the utilization of talent. Finally, we shall review certain broad social policies such as compulsory military service, the maintenance of high-level employment, and the pattern of social expectations as they affect the conservation of talent.

Our society has become increasingly dependent on people whose talents, skills, and competences have been developed to a high order. And our society has become so structured as to enable people with talent to make effective use of their specialized abilities. Many changes have been made in the society that the Founding Fathers envisioned and planned for, one which was primarily composed of yeomen, small numbers of craftsmen, and still smaller numbers of merchants and professional people.

Today there are more men and women employed in professional, technical, and managerial positions than there are farm workers and craftsmen. And this group is growing more rapidly than any other sector.

Although earlier societies did recognize the importance of talent, only a very few individuals actually reached high orders of excellence in religion, statecraft, military affairs, humanities, or the arts. These earlier societies reached their highest levels of accomplishment through the contributions of the talented few, but the work of the philosophers, writers, and artists was only peripherally related to the everyday tasks performed by the majority of the population. The essential difference between these earlier societies and our own is that they were sensitive and responsive to the one man in a million, while we must be concerned with the education and training of multiple millions of professional and technical persons. Other societies have been responsive to genius, but since genius is unique, it can be recognized and honored but cannot be produced. Talent, however, is much more widely distributed among the population, and the conditions that govern its development and utilization can have a much more direct and specific effect on the progress and welfare of these societies.

A society that recognizes its dependence on the many who are talented and trained rather than the very few whose genius develops idiosyncratically must pay particular attention to the process which determines the way people acquire competence and skills, for a professional or mechanical training takes twenty or more years and increasingly requires continuing efforts to maintain competence throughout the whole of a man's career. The educational process, then, stands in a crucial relationship to an advanced industrialized society. The quality and number of persons who acquire competence depends on how effectively the schools perform their mission. It is therefore appropriate to begin a discussion of a policy for the conservation of talent by considering those findings that bear specifically on education and guidance.

Let us look at the financial outlay involved in this education for the professions, for academic work, and for the higher positions in business, government, and nonprofit organizations. For many years local and state governments have assumed the burden of financing elementary and secondary schooling; they have also underwritten, but much more selectively, the costs of college and graduate instruction. Since the end of World War II, the Federal government has developed a multiplicity of programs aimed at covering the direct costs incurred by many who pursue advanced studies. In addition, colleges and universities have broadened the amount of scholarship and fellowship aid —and loans—that they have been able to extend.

But certain untoward developments must be set against these favorable trends in financing education. In many urban communities the elementary and secondary school systems are so mediocre that a small but increasing proportion of parents feel obliged to enroll their children in private schools. This means that the financial burden of education is very substantial even before a young person enters college. Moreover, the rise in tuition and in the costs of room and board has been very rapid during the postwar years. The elongation of the educational process has added to the costs. Two or three years in military service further delays the completion of a young man's developmental cycle and postpones the day when he can become fully self-supporting.

There is no need to elaborate the foregoing. While those who successfully complete advanced education and training are eventually in a better position to earn higher incomes, the hard truth remains that many are unable to finance such a long and costly preparation or can do so only by deflecting valuable time and energy away from their studies to earn money to help defray their expenses. Many college and graduate students must devote much time to odd jobs to pay for their education. And many are able to continue their education only through the aid extended by the GI bill.

From the point of view of policy, there still are a large number of financial barriers to the fuller development of the nation's talent. Many able young people, especially from homes where college has been beyond the family purview, early make decisions about their educational and occupational future that preclude college. Some make this decision on the basis of incorrect information; they could, in fact, secure the necessary financing. Others are probably correct in estimating that the financial burden, even if they could have it underwritten, would be more than they are willing to shoulder. Although financial barriers interfere less with the continuity of education of able people at the higher ranges of the educational hierarchy, losses are substantial, especially among the large numbers who have interests in the arts, humanities, medicine, and many of the social sciences, where governmental and other fellowship funds for advanced study remain relatively small.

There is much to be said in favor of the argument that tax dollars should be used to make educational opportunities available for each individual to develop his competences to the optimum. But important as education is, there are other basic individual and social needs, including health, defense, social welfare, and research, which require government funds. Available government funds have not been adequate to cover these priorities. Although, as we have seen, government has historically met a substantial part of the direct costs of elementary and secondary education in the United States, students and their families and philanthropy have covered much of the costs of higher education. Since those who acquire a higher education are likely to have substantially higher earnings, the pressure on them to cover part if not all of the direct costs of their education is not contra public policy.

The crucial point here is that no individual who has the capacity and desire to proceed with his education should be blocked by lack of funds. Those without financial resources should have access to educational opportunities through free tuition, scholarship aid, or loan funds. Even then, these students would have financial problems. Tuition is but one part of the cost of education. Living expenses are a second major component. Earnings foregone are a third. Many students are handicapped in the pursuit of their doctorates because they have to support themselves and their families. With the constant elongation of education, and with compulsory military service, many able young people must delay marriage, and particularly having children, until they are in their thirties—or they must find other means of support. A realistic policy must bring these additional dimensions within its purview.

More money can help, but other adjustments are also required. It would be highly desirable to explore the possibility of collapsing the time required to earn a doctorate. Some significant experiments are under way—from advanced college placement to dovetailing undergraduate and graduate programs more effectively. But two barriers stand athwart those experiments. Many educators still believe that young people should move in chronological lockstep in order to assure their emotional stability. They see a danger in mixing sixteen- and nineteen-year-olds in the same college freshman class. Moreover, the American public seems to refuse to consider individuals under twenty-one and often even under twenty-five as fully responsible adults. There has been a marked tendency toward the "infantilization" of American youth—a tendency which contributes to the unnecessary prolongation with corresponding excessive costs of higher education.

The current attitudes help to explain why educational and occupational guidance places so little emphasis on the expeditious completion of one's studies and the early assumption of a responsible role in the world of work. While the years of college and graduate study should be a period when the individual has an opportunity to explore and deepen his interests and competences, the protection of these important personal goals need not necessarily be in conflict with other desiderata, which include bringing one's formal education to an early successful conclusion and starting of one's career. There is ample room for a restructuring of curricula and promotion procedures and for more and better guidance aimed at the conservation of time.

There is another aspect related to the conservation of time. Many a young man, even one able to earn his doctorate expeditiously and get an early start on his career, is still likely to be plagued by financial responsibilities. Let us consider the young man who marries and is in academic life, particularly one in a field where the opportunities for outside income are relatively limited—as in the humanities. While he is in the lower ranks, his academic salary is too small to support a growing family even at a modest level. He will be strongly tempted to seek assignments which yield a little extra income. He will often turn the "free" hours that he should be devoting to further study and research into extra teaching or other routine assignments that have no value to his career other than providing him with some additional income. Much valuable talent is eroded by the struggle for existence that many face in the early years of their academic career. Since government and foundations are making ever larger sums available for research, the allocation of some part of these monies to young academicians under terms of maximum freedom to pursue their careers as *they* see fit would probably prove to be an important measure. If more young people can broaden and deepen themselves during the early years of their career, if they can assume responsibility for their own intellectual progress, it is more likely that they will be productive.

In earlier generations relatively few people acquired a doctorate. The degree was of importance primarily to those who were set on an academic career and those who planned to practice medicine or dentistry. The last several decades have witnessed a substantial broadening of this group, so that today it includes a significant proportion of those who look forward to a career in the natural or social sciences or in research in industry or government as well as those who aspire to higher positions in many other fields such as education, business, social work, or library service.

The universities have begun to make some adjustments to these new facts of life. These include the establishing of new doctoral degrees in professional fields. But it is questionable whether they have faced the full ramifications of the vast extension that is under way. Individuals today are pursuing their education up to the doctorate, not with the aim of devoting their lives to research, but simply in order to serve in a staff or administrative capacity in profit or non-profit organizations or in government service. Even after they have been modified, the requirements for the doctorate of philosophy do not fit the needs of most of these new professionals. And if the modification proceeds too far, the new professional degree may have little in common with the essentials of a true doctorate.

This question must be faced. Soon the major universities will not be in a position to cope with the vastly enlarged numbers who will be seeking a doctorate. While the number of institutions competent to provide instruction at the doctoral level can and should be increased, this may not be sufficient to meet the increased demand—especially if standards are to be safeguarded. The range of possible alternatives— which include the possibility of reestablishing the importance of the master of arts and science degrees—should be carefully explored. These degrees can meet the needs of many who desire to pursue their studies beyond the baccalaureate level, but who do not necessarily have to acquire all of the competences now demanded of those who secure the doctorate.

There is scope for adjustment both upward and downward. Many who pursue the doctorate might sensibly stop short (at least initially) at the master's level, while many who acquire the doctorate should look for broadened opportunities to continue their studies after they begin to work.

Although individuals with doctorates were once employed almost exclusively by the universities and the independent professions, an increasing proportion now earn their livelihood by working for large companies. Universities have long known and acted upon the principle that members of their faculties can stay abreast of progress in their own and related disciplines only if they have considerable "free" time for continuing study and research. This explains the sabbatical and particularly the nine-month academic year. However, most other employers of professional personnel do not understand the necessity for balancing routine work with opportunities for self-development. A very few corporations have introduced modifications in the time demands they make on their professional employees, but most companies continue to treat professionals as other salaried personnel. The same is true of the several levels of government and most nonprofit organizations. The outstanding exception is the Armed Forces, which have long provided excellent opportunities for the further education of their personnel—especially those who have been marked for advancement.

The failure to broaden and deepen one's knowledge on a continuing basis will inevitably speed one's decline into professional obsolescence. It is therefore essential to the more effective utilization of talent in the United States that nonacademic employers provide adequate opportunities for the further education and training of their professional staffs. Admittedly the provision of such opportunities is difficult to arrange in a competitive environment and costly to carry out. But nothing is more costly for society as a whole than toleration of the accelerated obsolescence that results from the failure to provide these opportunities.

It makes no sense to strive to find the scarce resources required to expand the universities so that they can turn out more qualified persons if a high proportion of those who graduate will be employed under conditions that ensure that their skills will soon become obsolescent and that their potential will atrophy. The barriers that now block business, government, and nonprofit organizations other than universities from making adequate investments in the further education and training of their professional personnel should be carefully studied with an aim to finding effective remedies.

We cannot, of course, assume that all the causes of skill obsolescence lie outside the academic realm and that all is in order in colleges and universities. Many in academic life find that the environment exercises a deterrent influence on the further growth and development of their potential. The inadequacy of university financing is reflected in the great amount of time spent by the faculty in routine tasks that could be better performed by others, from secretaries to research assistants, but there is no money available to hire the others. Lack of finances also results frequently in shortages of essential resources, from adequate libraries to adequate laboratories. Few academic institutions are able to help defray even the traveling costs which would enable many of the faculty to pursue their research away from home.

Money is not the only deficiency in the academic environment. Insensitive administrators who are more concerned with procedures and controls than the advancement of knowledge and cantankerous colleagues who find their satisfactions in infighting rather than in productive scholarship also detract substantially from an optimum environment. The absence of a stimulating intellectual environment, which can be established and maintained only through the joint efforts of a sympathetic administration, congenial colleagues, and good students, probably is responsible for the greatest toll. It is hard for a man to run against his environment, especially if he has much to lose and the prospect of gain is slight. Even a man with considerable inner direction and strong work motivation will slacken his efforts to keep himself intellectually vital if he finds little support and encouragement in his environment. The location of academic institutions in out-of-the-way places is a further deterrent. Lively minds need a lively environment.

It seems clear that today much intellectual potential goes to waste as a result of the many weaknesses in our institutions of higher learning. This waste is compounded because, as the faculty spends too many hours teaching or in committee work and too few on study and research, students will be less well trained and motivated. Here is a sector where major efforts at conservation are called for.

There are other deterrents to the effective utilization of specialized knowledge and skill that warrant consideration. There is considerable mobility of highly educated persons among the different sectors of the economy—academic, corporate, nonprofit, government, and self-employment—as well as considerable mobility within the same sector. In some instances useful mobility is facilitated by an industry-wide pension and retirement system such as that among a large number of academic institutions and among most of the agencies of the Federal government. In many other instances, inability to transfer pension and retirement rights undoubtedly acts as a deterrent to a man's finding the type of employment in which he can make the optimum use of his education and skills.

A more subtle but still very important deterrent to the effective utilization of persons with special knowledge and skills in corporate enterprise is the heavy weighting of the promotion and reward structures of most organizations in favor of those in line management, to the neglect of those who continue to pursue their specialized interests in the laboratory or in other professional work. Many men who would prefer to pursue work within the area of their professional training find that they cannot reach even a reasonable level of monetary reward and prestige unless they shift into general management or sales. Although several large companies have sought to provide two routes of advancement—one for those in general management and another for those in technical work—these efforts so far do not seem to provide real options for many able people. Corporate enterprise is still so structured that it pulls the abler technical people out of the fields of their specialization into general management. While this does not mean that every man with a Ph.D. in chemistry or biology who enters corporate employment should remain in the laboratory throughout his working life, the fact that many who would prefer to do so are substantially blocked from participating in the rewards that industry offers its successful employees is an impediment to the more effective utilization of talent. Further efforts to provide truly effective career opportunities for technical personnel in industry would contribute to the conservation of talent.

The hierarchical structure of industry appears to present more barriers to the effective utilization of talent than the hierarchy found in academic life. The essential difference appears to be that the scientist in industry operates largely in a closed world. His immediate circumstances and, even more, his future prospects are very much a function of his relationships to his superiors. If he runs into serious conflict with them, his only option is to leave and find employment elsewhere; but such a move may be very costly if he has accumulated valuable deferred benefits. An academic is in a considerably better position. A young professor can make a name outside his own institution. If his papers are published in established journals, he will soon build a reputation that his superiors must recognize; if they do not, he will have relatively little difficulty in moving to another institution. Once he has acquired tenure, he can afford to go his own way, even to the extent of risking conflict with his superiors, without fear of serious reprisals. Most able academics sooner or later become largely independent of their superiors. This is not to say that the university is free of backbiting, bickering, politics, and jealousy; it states only that the constraints under which most people in the academic world operate are considerably less than those found in industry.

In corporate structure the route into middle management—and especially the route from middle into higher management—is rocky. One characteristic of this path is that most corporate supervisors tend to control the flow of ideas up and down; this makes it difficult for able young people to make their capacity known. Moreover, those who advance up the supervisory hierarchy are frequently more skillful in politics than in the technical aspects of their work, with the result that those below them frequently do not receive the professional guidance they need. Industry must reconcile its need to control its programs, funds, and personnel with the necessity of providing competent professional leadership for its scientific and research personnel.

The foregoing difficulties are not limited to profit-making organizations. They also exist, sometimes to an exaggerated degree, in government and nonprofit organizations. Particularly when an organization is engaged in the accomplishment of a broad program, such as the development of a new weapons system by the Armed Forces, the likelihood of serious conflicts between line and technical personnel is heightened.

Tightly structured and controlled organizations present one other important deterrent to the effective utilization of talent. Many men must broaden and deepen their competences by engaging in work-related activities off the job. But many business organizations as well as departments of government and groups in the nonprofit sector of our society do not want their personnel to engage in these activities; they are certainly disinclined to make any adjustments in time to facilitate their doing so. They try to restrict the activities of their personnel to the organization, and in so doing they interfere with their continuing growth.

This brings us to the third set of relationships which we want to explore—namely, how broad public policy can better contribute to the conservation of talent. For example, military service can exercise a positive, negative, or neutral influence on the career development of young men. Some young men mature rapidly while in the service; others waste two to three years; and still others come off more or less even. For these reasons it is well to keep in purview at all times the impact of military service on the development of talent.

Another dimension of the interplay between broad social forces and the development of talent is illuminated by considerations of marriage patterns. The actions of young men are determined in no small measure by the actions of the young women whom they marry. During the past several decades the age at which young people marry has been dropping, and so have the ages at which couples start and complete their families. As we pointed out above, these developments put an added strain on the financial resources of young people, especially those who plan for an elongated period of education. The willingness of young wives to work and the willingness of parents who are in a position to do so to assist young couples has helped to ease some of these financial pressures. But many parents are in no position to help, and most wives are unable to keep working after they have children.

The reasons for early marriage are easy to understand, but the forces which encourage young couples—especially those couples who have not finished their college or graduate educations—to have their children early are less evident. Unless there is a markedly adverse turn in employment conditions, there is little prospect that the age of marriage will rise appreciably. But perhaps we can look forward to a postponement of the time when young couples start a family. The pressure for delay may come from the distaff side as women (as well as their husbands) recognize that they owe it to themselves not to terminate their education prematurely. Their adjustment later on, within the family and outside, will depend to a marked degree on their educational achievements.

One other facet of career development has to do with discrimination during the course of a man's education, military service, or employment. In general, the more intelligent group is not seriously handicapped because of religious or ethnic background. However, this does not deny the cumulative consequences of the centuries during which widespread racial discrimination has existed throughout American society. Negro children have frequently been forced to attend schools where the staff and facilities are grossly inadequate; the financial and other pressures under which they live are often so severe that they find it much more difficult than others to continue with advanced education; and when they acquire skills and competences, they find barriers to employment.

Negroes represent about 10 percent of our population. Yet they account for probably less than 1 percent of the fellowship winners in the graduate and professional schools and our major universities. This is at least a rough first measure of the challenge that this country faces as it comes to grips with the eradication of all forms of racial discrimination. Political freedom for the Negro is a necessary but by no means a sufficient step to assure his full participation in American society.

There are several other groups that are also handicapped in the development and utilization of their talent. These include the 5 million Spanish-speaking people in the Northeast and the Southwest and West, and the much larger numbers of low-income white families heavily concentrated in the Southeast but present on farms, in small communities, and in urban centers in every section of the country. A great amount of valuable potential runs to waste because millions of young people are born to parents who do not have the wherewithal to give them a proper start in life, and because community resources fail to provide them with an adequate range and quality of opportunities. The "war on poverty," like the "war on segregation," has been too long delayed.

Another shortcoming in our society is the absence of a strong demand for the work of painters, sculptors, musicians, actors, poets, and other artists, which means that many with talent in these fields either face a life of insecurity or even penury or must change their career objectives. Only a very few can look forward to the large rewards that are often showered on the exceptional man. Artists have never been able to rely on the competitive market for their living. Yet there are relatively few institutionalized devices to assist them. The amount of money that philanthropy and government have donated to underwrite the work of artists has been very litle compared to the vast sums donated toward other social ends. A society that is continually enjoying an increase in real income should give early and serious consideration to the additional steps it might take to provide greater incentives for the development of artistic potential and for the support of those who want to devote their lives to artistic endeavor.

There are many disparities between the support and encouragement given the natural and social sciences and that provided the humanities. The power of money is such that those in a position of authority and influence should see that the imbalances prevailing among the major fields of intellectual work are not permitted to widen further and, indeed, that efforts be made to narrow the discrepancies now existing. No society can gain in the long run from tempting men away from the type of work they are inclined to follow and where their talents lead them.

A period of sustained high-level employment makes a significant contribution to the development and utilization of talent. A strong job market encourages many to pursue their education to the doctorate and facilitates their or their wives' earning the necessary funds for such a pursuit. Moreover, a strong demand for their skills means that few are ever without work. A tight labor market gives them an opportunity to move readily from one job to another either within the same organization or in different organizations, and their mobility frequently helps them acquire additional skills. Moreover, those who find that they have made the wrong occupational choice do not face insurmountable hurdles when they contemplate a radical change. In these and still other ways a strong demand for professional, managerial, and technical personnel is a major contribution to the more effective utilization of talent.

There are, however, a few drawbacks incident to the strong market. For instance, the market encourages excessive changing of jobs, and this has negative rather than positive results. There may be some "spoiling" of young men by the inflated rewards which they are able to earn. But on balance the positive effects far outweigh the negative ones.

The conservation of talent truly depends upon minimum unemployment. For many young people will not develop the momentum and many will not put forth the effort required to overcome the multiple barriers that they will encounter along the preparatory route unless they see some reasonable prospects ahead. A continuing high level of employment is essential for a democratic society which has always placed and must continue to place the highest value on the freedom of the individual to choose his own career and to pursue it as he sees fit.

The solutions will not come easily, but they will come to the extent that the American people appreciate the challenge which they face and the rewards that they can gain from meeting it successfully. We dare not fail to conserve our most precious resource.

Chapter Seventeen Womanpower

In the heyday of liberalism and *laissez faire,* it was assumed by both political scientists and economists that the individual held the key to his own future. If he had drive, direction, and discipline, they contended, he could pull himself up by his own bootstraps and rise to the top of the social and economic ladder. Some social scientists considered that this newly acquired scope for self-development and upward mobility was the result of giving the offspring of the poor access to public education, but others glossed over or ignored the role of social institutions, even the school, in the structuring of a free society.

To hold that what happens to an individual is primarily the result of his own actions is still an important theorem to some people, although today the followers of this nineteenth-century doctrine of extreme individualism are very few in number. A more recent and sophisticated view of the development and utilization of human potential starts from a different premise. It assumes that the models upon which young people pattern their future roles, their educational preparation, their occupational choices, the distribution of energy between their work and the other facets of their lives—all of these critically important decisions and actions reflect in large measure the families and society into which they were born and reared, the quality and quantity of the educational institutions to which they have access, and the economic and social forces that shape and give content to life in contemporary America.

Although the exceptional person is able to swim against the stream and to construct a successful life for himself markedly different from the pattern followed by his relatives and friends, there is no general or universal process whereby the individual, self-propelled, determines his own course and future against only a few constraints in the social setting. This heroic theory has limited relevance for the contemporary United States.

Since external forces do play major roles in individual development, we shall call attention in this chapter to the range of policy actions that suggest themselves with regard to the life-styles of educated women. We believe that these recommendations hold promise of contributing to the more effective development and utilization of the knowledge and skills of the most highly trained sector of the female population. We shall consider guidance and counseling, education, the job market, and the community and governmental arena.

With respect to guidance and counseling, the first recommendation relates to the desirability of providing more knowledge to parents about the opportunities that are available to their daughters in their efforts to become well educated and to make effective use of their education and skill without necessarily foregoing marriage and children. Many women are able to combine meaningful work with marriage and the raising of a family. Consequently, parents who want their daughters' primary responsibilities to involve homemaking and child rearing can safely encourage them to pursue their education through college and beyond, and thus prepare for a career without seriously jeopardizing their chances of marrying.

Moreover, parents of the new generation of teen-agers should know that their daughters will not experience much discrimination either in pursuing a higher education or in finding suitable employment. While their daughters may encounter some barriers because of their sex, it is unlikely that these obstacles will prove more than a minor hindrance in the pursuit of their plans. Proper guidance therefore requires that parents become more knowledgeable and more objective about the vastly broadened opportunities that are now open to young women both in pursuing their education and in making use of it.

Although these first recommendations are directed toward parents, they have equal validity for all who are in a position to influence the values and goals of girls and young women—teachers, counselors, and others in leadership positions.

Next, major adjustments are called for on the educational front. Some school systems still steer able girls away from a college preparatory course on the ground that they will be able to do just as well if they take a commercial or general program. Furthermore, those who do follow the academic curriculum are less likely to be encouraged to study mathematics and the physical sciences than are boys. This may reflect differential aptitudes and interests of boys and girls with regard to these subjects, but there is no objective basis for such a high percentage of able girl students to eschew these fields. Of course, another factor that has reenforced this pattern has been the correct perception that, until recently, the barriers to further educational preparation and to employment for women with those competences were substantial. But times have changed. First, the barriers have been radically lowered. Second, total employment opportunities in engineering and the physical sciences have expanded very rapidly. And third, mathematics has assumed increased importance in many of the social sciences —surely in economics, psychology, and sociology.

It is urgently necessary, therefore, that those who are in a position to influence the curiculum choices of young women be alert to these changes and that they incorporate them into educational and occupational counseling.

The challenges to the college authorities with respect to young women are manifold. First, they should attempt to provide educational and occupational guidance to freshman and sophomore students which would alert them to the expanding role that work has come to play in the lives of women. Second, they should attempt to stimulate them to crystallize occupational objectives within larger life plans. Third, they should help these young women to consider course alternatives from the vantage point of advanced studies or future employment. Furthermore, if the guidance and counseling which young college women receive are to be helpful, special stress must be placed upon the development of an awareness of both the opportunities and the difficulties of combining family and career.

Additional institutional reforms are required to enable women to develop their full potentialities. Women in search of college and graduate education have long been handicapped by a shortage of campus housing. In the past, legislators and private donors have shown a preference for expanding facilities available to male students. More campus housing should be made available for women students.

The lack of adequate scholarship and fellowship funds is another barrier. It is frequently more difficult for a young woman to earn part or all of her expenses than it is for a young man. Next, government support for graduate education, which in the past has been weighted in favor of fields that women have generally avoided, should be granted for the humanities and the social sciences as well as for the natural sciences. Finally, it should be recognized that refusal to make scholarship and fellowship funds available to young women on the ground that they will leave their fields when they marry is no longer justified. Women who acquire graduate degrees do not become lost to their fields. While they may interrupt their careers for periods of time, the overwhelming majority continues to have an active relationship to the world of work. However, because of these interruptions certain adjustments will be necessary to enable these young women to stay abreast of developments in their field and to have opportunities to complete their education or continue their careers at a later time. Among the approaches that have been tried are systematic correspondence courses, refresher conferences, special sessions at professional association meetings, and the opening of regular university classes to part-time students.

There are still other adjustments which will be required to enable married women to return to school or work, part time or full time. If they have been at home for a considerable period of time, they need educational and occupational guidance. While pioneering efforts to help such prospective returnees have been made, there is a deficiency of these services in the community at large. Few colleges or universities, fewer professional societies, and still fewer conventional counseling and placement agencies have demonstrated an interest in and a capacity to assist these educated women.

Moreover, most educational institutions, as well as most licensing bodies, have shown remarkably little flexibility in adjusting their qualifications for admission, graduation, or professional certification to take into account the increasing maturity and experience that many of these women have acquired since they last attended school or worked. The number of able women who have been denied admission to graduate schools of social work because they lacked certain kinds of undergraduate preparation, the number who have been refused licenses to teach because they lacked "education credits," and the number of nurses and other types of medical personnel who are not permitted to work in their specialty because their prior experience in a different state was disregarded by the licensing board, constitute a significant waste of potential and skill. While remedial action has been under way for some time, reforms have been too few and too slow. The simple fact is that the basic education, training, and related institutions in our society are geared to the prototype of a man moving along steadily from one stage to the next except for a possible interruption for military service. But this prototype is no longer valid even for men. Every year a larger number of men in their thirties, forties, and even fifties return to graduate or professional schools to refurbish their knowledge, to broaden their careers, or, increasingly, to prepare for radical shifts in their careers. In a few areas—such as graduate education in business—academic institutions have demonstrated some flexibility with regard to student selection, curriculum, and related matters. But in general, most academic institutions remain hidebound and do not make the major modifications required to meet the special needs of adults with interrupted education or careers, among whom women predominate.

Much more needs to be done to facilitate the refurbishing of the knowledge and skills of women who have interrupted their education or careers. In addition to the few colleges and universities which are currently experimenting with new programs, every responsible institution involved in the education of women must evaluate its resources to learn how to assist this large and potentially valuable group of mature women.

In the third major arena, employment, adjustments are also urgently required if educated women are to make fuller use of their education and skills, and if society is to make use of these women in areas where their skills are greatly needed. In many fields of employment there has been a long and persistent bias against the hiring of women, no matter how well qualified. This has been true in varying degrees in such diverse sectors of the economy as business management, engineering, college teaching, and nonprofit administration. World War II marked the watershed between strongly exclusionist policies and more tolerant if still discriminatory attitudes in many of these areas. It is generally agreed that government, particularly the Federal government, has provided one of the more hospitable environments for the employment of women in general and educated women in particular. Nevertheless, the efforts of the present administration to increase the number of women in policy-making positions underscore the relatively small numbers who have succeeded in moving up the executive ladder.

Since most organizations promote heavily from within their own ranks, women will be unable to compete for preferred positions unless they are hired in the first instance for entrance jobs. While many opening jobs which were previously closed to them are now available, many employers continue to avoid hiring women. They are not prejudiced against women; they simply do not want to lose a good employee after a few years. But these employers do not know the new characteristics of women at work today. First, there are a considerable number of educated women who want and are able to have continuous work experience. Second, of the many who drop out, a significant proportion are likely to return after a short interval. Moreover, many women are undecided about whether to remain at work or to withdraw for a period of time from the labor force. Their decision often hinges on whether they feel that they are engaged in important work, whether they see prospects for promotion, and whether their earnings are sufficient to enable them to make arrangements which will facilitate their continuing to work. The arrangements which employers make with their qualified women employees often determine the response of many of them to the counterpulls of the job and home.

More employers today are willing to hire educated women. But this is only a first step. An immediate second challenge to employers is to change from restricting their assignments of women to a few conventional staff positions to place them where their skills and competences can best be used. It can be stated unequivocably that at present more employers are willing to hire women than to assign them without reference to their sex.

A third challenge relates to the willingness of employers to open their intramural and extramural training programs to able women employees. With the exception of a few fields, such as retailing, where women have long been part of the executive structure, access to training opportunities has been very limited. Many employers see little point in making expensive investments in their women employees since they do not believe the women will remain long enough to justify the cost. Cutting able women off from training opportunities is a sure way to speed their withdrawal from the labor force. The employer, by acting on his doubts and denying women the opportunity for training, helps to assure that they will in fact act in accordance with his expectations.

Many employers are reluctant to promote even well-qualified women to higher positions. Their rationalizations cover a wide range: Women make poor supervisors; many men resent having to report to a woman; in case of stress women are likely to become emotional; in many situations it is difficult to transact important business if a woman is a participant; women are often unable to be absent from home. While there may be an element of fact in each of these attitudes, and while every one of these conditions may operate to reduce the effectiveness of a particular woman in a position of responsibility, this line of argument misses the crucial point.

The issue should be formulated in a different way. Is it desirable to pass over a better-educated, more experienced woman with more intelligence and potential in favor of a less qualified man, even if one or another, or even several, of these characteristics may have an adverse effect on her performance? Is it not true that the male competitor may also have some potential disabilities? He may drink; he may be involved with women; he may have reached a point in his life where he does not want to work hard.

Although discrimination against educated women in employment is constantly being reduced, the fact remains that with respect to initial appointment, assignment, training, and promotion, they continue to face many specific barriers. Employers have a responsibility to examine critically their personnel policies as they affect women and move speedily to remove obstacles and barriers that rest on subjective impressions and preferences and that are not substantiated by a hard look at the evidence. They should consider the indirect benefits of a shift in their policies which would give women broadened opportunities to compete for preferred positions in the organization. There is little doubt that such a change in the organizational atmosphere will itself affect the way in which many women think about and act with respect to their work. More and more of them will shift from a short-range job to a long-range interest in a career. And their employers will have greatly strengthened their scarce manpower resources.

In addition to the adjustments which will be required if employers want to utilize the potential of able women, other factors must be taken into consideration. Many able women cannot work full time at their jobs. They do have important responsibilities at home. However, many women with family responsibilities are able and willing to work part time or part of the year. While some employers have made adjustments in working hours, in location, in scheduling of vacations, and in other regards, and are thus able to draw upon a large pool of able women workers, most employers have remained rigid in these areas.

It is easiest to introduce one of these adjustments—part-time work —when the individual is able to carry through his assignment on his own and where there is little necessity for interaction with other members of the organization. Part-time work is particularly appropriate for such positions as college teacher, research worker, and editor. But the opportunities for drawing on the rich manpower reserve represented by women who can only work part time have not been fully tapped even in areas which have been characterized by continuing shortages. The senior administrators in many organizations are loath to deviate from the conventional pattern. Often, this is because they believe that part-time women workers loosen discipline and otherwise weaken the dedication of the full-time staff. Over the years, personnel officials have seen substantial advantages in having a single set of rules and regulations for the entire work force. But this overlooks the high "hidden" cost of cutting off potentially valuable workers because of the rigidity of the rules.

There is also a need for employers to be more receptive to the educated woman who, having been out of the labor force for some years, is ready to return to work, frequently on a full-time basis. Such women, after a little orientation, are likely to be highly responsible and steady—more so than the younger members of their sex.

Two additional dimensions of the changing employment scene should be at least briefly noted. The first is the frequent rule against nepotism. Young women tend to marry young men with the same background. Graduate students tend to marry other graduate students working in the same or allied fields. Many of these women look forward to a career in much the same way as do their husbands. But many find that they face hurdles in addition to that of the necessity to devote time and energy to their homes and families. Many colleges and similar institutions still have rules which prohibit the hiring of the members of the same family. Sometimes these prohibitions are broad and apply to every position in the institution; sometimes the limitation is more restricted—husband and wife cannot be appointed to the same department. And in some cases, there is only the interdiction that an individual cannot serve under the direct administrative supervision of a spouse.

However, good personnel practice dictates that the fact that occasional difficulties may arise when a man and wife work in the same department or division should not obscure the benefits that can accrue from competent husband-wife teams especially in a period of continuing shortages of academic persons.

Old policies do not fit the new situation. In place of nepotism restrictions, employers should explore the desirability of offering employment on a family basis. More and more, educated men will weigh the offer of new positions in terms of the family's net advantage. Will he *and* his wife gain if they move? If his wife is working, and especially if she has a good job, the answer will often hinge on the prospects of her doing as well or better in the new environment. The farsighted employer of professional and managerial personnel must be increasingly alert to these family aspects of employment if he hopes to attract the best people. He must make an attractive offer to a prospective employee, and offer suitable employment for the wife as well.

The growing role that educated women are playing in the world of work and will increasingly play as employers shed their prejudices, as the hours of work decline, and as increasing numbers of the oncoming generation prepare for a life within which work will have a permanent place, will certainly have an impact on the significance of volunteer activities for women. Some women will continue to engage in volunteer activities, but their numbers will be fewer and they will be more selective.

Volunteer organizations have come more and more under the control and direction of full-time paid professional staffs. While there is still a place for the volunteer either as a board member or as a worker, the scope for her participation in many organizations has been substantially reduced. While some women find no difficulty in fitting into this constricted role, many others, especially those with considerable professional education, are loath to limit themselves to money-raising activities or to routine chores. They find little satisfaction in either role.

If volunteer organizations are to retain their corps of workers in the face of the increasing attraction of paid employment, they will have to devote more consideration to the utilization of volunteers in responsible, meaningful, and efficiently scheduled work. Volunteer organizations can make a contribution to the preservation of the skills of educated women during the years they are out of the labor market by drawing on this valuable pool for their own ends. But to do this will require major reforms.

Governments also have roles to play in facilitating the development and utilization of the talents of educated women. The broadening of higher educational opportunities for women—including such steps as building additional dormitories for college and graduate students, increasing scholarship and fellowship assistance, designing new curricula for married women who want to continue their education—will require a substantially enlarged investment in higher education. Much of the additional funds will have to come from government—Federal, state, and even local. In addition, however, philanthropic agencies must understand and act on the fact that if valuable national potential is to be saved, nongovernmental monies must also be made available for encouraging more able young women to pursue higher education and more older women to return for it.

A further need is to expand counseling and placement services to assist mature women as they are ready to return to school or work. Part of this challenge must be met by the educational institutions, and part by government agencies, professional societies, and profit and nonprofit organizations. There is a wide gap between the need of many educated women for advice and the number of reliable organizations that are in a position to counsel and guide them.

Remedial public action is also called for to remove the unnecessary hurdles that the established leadership of various professions, working through licensing boards, place in the way of mature women when they seek to reestablish their careers. The various professional societies have an obligation to review their panoply of restrictive policies and procedures in light of the best interest of the public. If professional groups continue to avoid this challenge in the future as they have in the past, it will become the responsibility of the public licensing boards and officials. Their elaborate rules and regulations must be scrutinized and adjusted in order to encourage the return to work of highly educated and qualified women.

Since many married women can return to work only if they have household help, current tax legislation should be revised in order to temper this problem. In a one-parent home, child care is presently deductible as a business expense in an amount up to $900, and a married couple is permitted to deduct up to this amount if their combined annual income does not exceed $6,000. These restrictions on the size of the deduction and the maximum family income reflect the disinclination of Congress both to erode the income-tax base and to encourage mothers to seek employment outside the home. But since the principle of allowing deductions for child care has been accepted, it appears that it would be reasonable to raise the amount of the allowable deductions and the ceiling on the size of combined family income to bring both in closer alignment with present levels of family income, with costs of household help, and above all with the changing attitude of American society toward working mothers.

Many families who can afford full-time or part-time help still find it very difficult to find qualified persons. There may be an opportunity for profit-seeking enterprises which have experience with similar types of labor to formalize this casual labor market by taking responsibility for recruiting, screening, hiring, supervising, and paying household help. The domestics would become employees of the "labor contractors." Such an approach might lead to a larger, more qualified, and more satisfied supply of domestic workers.

There are other ways in which married women with children could be assisted. The present structure of child-care centers under government and nongovernment aegis should be expanded and improved so that they serve not only low-income families but middle-income families as well. The latent demand for such services is probably considerable. More imaginative financial arrangements involving government, non-profit organizations, and the consumer might contribute substantially to meeting this social need through partial government subsidies, tax exemptions for nonprofit organizations, and primary reliance on consumers to pay the rest of the cost. It is an area worth exploring.

This brings us to the last recommendation, which relates to the desirability of greater public investment in basic and applied research on the development and utilization of the potential, education, skills, and competences of the female portion of the population. While we favor more research on the development of talent in general, the environment in which girls and young women develop differs from that in which men develop and therefore demands specifically directed attention. As a research area, the socialization process in childhood, adolescence, and young adulthood should therefore have high priority.

The time has come for our society to realize that women have half of the nation's most valuable resource—human talent. But they must be afforded the opportunity to develop it and to utilize it. A democratic society that places barriers in the way of the full utilization of the potential of half of its citizenry is violating its commitment to basic traditions of freedom and equality of opportunity, and this violation slows its progress.

This argues strongly for the removal of barriers inherited from the past that have led to the continuing waste of resources and to the underutilization of skill. The elimination of these barriers will enhance the scope for self-determination for women. And the enlargement of freedom for all members of a democracy is the best assurance for its continuing prosperity and well-being.

The major thrust of this chapter will be to make explicit the psychological theories that today underpin and guide public and private policies with respect to the development and utilization of our human resources. After delineating these theories, questions will be raised about their validity. Finally, some suggestions will be made about future directions for both research and policy. To give body to this discussion, reference will be made to major manpower problems that are high on the public's agenda.

We shall begin with education and review briefly three major programs: those aimed at assisting preschool children to adjust to school (Operation Head Start), efforts to reduce the rate of dropouts, and special methods of encouraging talented youngsters.

With respect to the Head Start program (which the administration has indicated is no longer experimental, but has become a permanent part of the attack on poverty), the basic psychological assumption is that the learning potential of children from deprived homes becomes atrophied before they are six and that special efforts aimed at children at the age of three are therefore required. Three questions are immediately suggested. How was it possible in times past that many children from severely deprived homes entered school at the age of six and made normal or even accelerated progress? What experimental or other evidence is there that atrophy actually sets in at so early an age? In light of the difficulties of transporting children as young as three to and from school and of holding them in school for more than a few hours a day, might it not be more advisable to concentrate on the expansion of kindergartens for four- and five-year-olds? Or even to put more resources at the disposal of the school authorities for the instruction of six- to nine-year-olds?

Certainly, there is a tactical political advantage in the Head Start program. The public and Congress have always been attracted to the new and the spectacular. Our questions relate more narrowly to the validity of the psychological assumptions underlying this new effort.

During the past several years, almost all the leaders of opinion in this country have told young people to remain in school until they are eighteen or, preferably, until they acquire a high school diploma. Since many private and public employers will not consider hiring anybody without a high school diploma, we do not need to be persuaded that a diploma is a useful and often a necessary first step to employment.

Still, there are serious questions about most of the efforts that are being made to hold young people in school. A high proportion of dropouts stop learning several years before they leave school. Does it make sense to seek to persuade youngsters to stay in school if they cannot profit from their classes?

The limitations of a situation in which women must try to teach young men during their tumultuous adolescence are worth exploring. This may be a significant reason that a large number of boys drop out of school. Moreover, there is no psychological theory which would support the infantilization that is characteristic of our ever more elongated educational cycle. If Pitt could be Prime Minister of Great Britain in his early twenties an able student should be able to acquire a doctorate by the same age. But very few do under our slow-paced, lockstep system.

Basic to the dropout problem is that many young people never learn to read effectively. What do we know, even at this relatively late date, about the psychology of learning? The barriers to reading have still not been thoroughly investigated and the remedies are still being formulated.

Let us make a radical shift—from the dropout to the talented youngster. American education has always been concerned with children with high IQs. In light of the amount of time and effort that psychologists have devoted to intelligence testing, this concern is scarcely surprising. Still, an economist concerned with marginal analysis must ask whether some redirection of effort in favor of the exploration of other manifestations of high potential might not yield more significant returns. We know next to nothing about talent in the arts, about social talents involved in the leadership of people and groups, and about many other scarce and valuable attributes. Even in the professions and in science and research, we are only beginning to understand the importance of a high IQ relative to other qualities involved in superior performance.

Preoccupation with IQ scores has led school authorities to favor placing bright children with their peers and adjusting the curriculum to their superior capacity to learn. This is a reasonable approach, but we do know much about the disadvantages that may accrue from keeping all the bright students together, both the excessive pressure on many of them as well as a failure to use them as a spur to those who are less bright. Is it really bad for bright students to be bored occasionally and be forced to fall back on themselves? And may there not be some long-run gain if able young people are exposed early in life to others who are less bright? After all, they will eventually have to live with them.

In addition to questioning the strict segregation of students according to IQ, there are questions about the approach, long entrenched though recently less popular, of insisting that young people proceed through school with others of the same age. Is there any validity to the contention that a sixteen-year-old or even a seventeen-year-old is too young to be admitted to college? Probably not, especially if allowance is made for the costs of preventing properly prepared young students from moving ahead. It seems particularly dangerous to single out one or another aspect of human development and formulate policy with respect to it without regard to the other forces at work and without weighing carefully the consequences of alternative decisions.

Before leaving the subject of individual development, let us consider certain widespread assumptions which characterize our society. Once again, we will focus on the psychological assumptions underlying established approaches.

The first and possibly the most pervasive assumption is the belief that a weak family structure and particularly emotional instability manifested in relations between parents or between parents and children foreshadow pathology later in the lives of children. The extreme formulation of this position sees all adult malperformance as a direct consequence of family pathology. Some years ago, in tracing 1,000 failures in Massachusetts, Warren Stearns was unable to identify the environment as the causative agent.[1]

Several questions suggest themselves. First, the phenomenological one: How much disturbance falls within the range of the tolerable, and how much is predictive of later pathology?

In our studies of the ineffective soldier [2] we attacked this problem

[1] "1000 Unsuccessful Careers," *American Journal of Psychiatry*, 1949, vol. 105, pp. 801–808.
[2] Eli Ginzberg and Associates, *The Ineffective Soldier: Lessons for Management and the Nation*, 3 vols., Columbia University Press, New York, 1959.

in a slightly different way. We found it necessary to broaden the concept of emotional instability as an explanatory principle to one of "adjustment potential," thus including not only emotional but also intellectual, maturational, and other aspects of personality as partial determinants of behavior. And we made room also for the structure and functioning of the organizations within which men work, as well as the supports and barriers in the larger environment that affect their level of accomplishment. We found that the simple and direct links between family pathology, emotional instability of children, and adult malperformance were much too telescoped; too many important variables were omitted from the equation.

Another concern is guidance and counseling. We start by acknowledging that many people, especially young people, cannot easily find their own way in a rapidly changing and increasingly complex economy and society. And yet what is the *real* evidence that justifies the major efforts now under way to expand substantially the number of counselors at many different points in our society—in school, in the employment service, and in social welfare agencies? In fact, the Federal government has a major program known as Youth Opportunity Centers where guidance and counseling are the primary and sometimes the sole service.

What do we really know of the therapeutic effect for disturbed people of "talk," and of the practical uses to which "listening" can be put by those who are floundering? Eysenck [3] and others have raised serious questions about these processes. Even assuming that the processes have intrinsic value, what do we know about the quality of the advice that is provided? How many psychotherapists have affected the values of their patients, not necessarily for the better? How many school counselors have given young people advice such as the students in San Francisco schools received in the early 1950s when they were told not to pursue science and engineering because these fields had a surplus of manpower—a statement that may have been correct in the 1930s when the counselors were trained, but was patently wrong during the Korean War?

We can adapt the famous remark of the biochemist Lawrence J. Henderson that in the first decade of this century a patient with an uncertain condition who selected a physician at random had only a 50–50 chance of profiting from the encounter, and say the same today about vocational and most other types of counseling. With regard to

[3] H. J. Eysenck, *Uses and Abuses of Psychology*, Penguin Books, Inc., Baltimore, 1953.

minority youth, for example, until recently the advice that was proffered Negroes by white counselors in positions of influence and authority was more often bad than good and was not infrequently malicious and exploitative. E. Frederic Morrow's *Black Man in the White House* [4] is a good illustration of this.

Let us now briefly review what we can describe as "special services to disadvantaged people." We shall single out a few programs. The first relates to expenditures for mental health. In 1959 the Federal government spent approximately $50 million in this area; four years later the figure was about $180 million; and in 1965, it spent over $280 million! Congress made these much larger sums available on the grounds that the costs of mental illness are horrendous—and they are —and that the National Institute of Mental Health was getting results—which is the point that still warrants careful appraisal. Many witnesses pointed out to congressional committees that the patient census in state mental institutions, after rising for many years, had not only leveled off but had actually declined. But they failed to add that changes in patterns of hospitalization had resulted in considerable numbers being treated elsewhere; in addition, they neglected to state that the readmission rate was continuing to rise. In any case, we have no basis for assessing whether the new drugs and other therapeutic approaches based on research were responsible for the decline in the patient-census figure, or whether such mundane considerations as better diet, better-trained attendants, and a generally more humane system of hospital administration were largely responsible. Few leaders in the field of psychiatry claim that during the past decade there have been steady gains in knowledge that have led to successful new therapeutic approaches in the treatment of psychotic patients. They are much more cautious.

The next area of greatly expanded interest is mental retardation. Certainly many of the mentally retarded have been seriously neglected in the past. Certainly more can be done for many of them than has been done in the past. Moreover, we have had a few spectacular successes in preventing retardation by righting chemical imbalances in early infancy. But looking ahead, the prospect is still bleak. Even under the optimistic assumption that research will open up additional new avenues for prevention, rehabilitation will probably continue to present great difficulties. The major challange which we shall confront, and one that we have not even begun to face, is the provision of opportunities for large numbers of the mentally retarded to work in a

[4] Macfadden Publications, Inc., New York, 1963.

society that does not really need their labor. We can do this—and most other things that need doing—if we understand the problems which we face, and if we have the will to put forth the effort required. Large expenditures for research are often a relatively inexpensive evasion for coming to grips with major social challenges.

Now to our second major axis, which is the utilization of manpower resources. Since the contacts between psychology and manpower have been most intimate with respect to testing, let us start here. Most tests have not been validated against the work that potential employees will be required to perform; the higher the level of skill required, the more inadequate are the available tests; and the use of Rorschach and Thematic Apperception tests for assessing the "leadership potential" of businessmen and others seeking executive positions or advancement is an insult to intelligence and an invasion of the rights of privacy. We are in a quagmire with respect to culture-free tests, since life is not free of cultural determinants. Furthermore, the spokesmen for minority groups are correct in contending that most testing instruments yield results that have some hidden "culture-bound" bias. Moreover, we know too little about the extent to which experience in a new environment is likely to be reflected in much higher scores on retests. Obviously, there is a place for testing both in schools and in industry, but the proliferation of testing in the industrial arena probably bespeaks the business competence of the sellers of tests rather than that of the buyers. American corporations waste tens of millions of dollars on tests that are not sound, that are not relevant, that are not necessary!

Let us look more carefully at one manpower group—the Negro. The first question that arises is whether it is correct or useful to think about Negroes as a homogeneous group. The answer is no, especially in relation to their employability. An illiterate Negro on a marginal farm in the South has little in common with a Negro high school graduate working in the post office in Atlanta or a Negro lawyer in New York City. To consider 20 million Negroes as a single group is an invitation to poor thinking and worse policy.

A more complicated question is how to most effectively eliminate the barriers to employment based on race—an elimination now called for by the law of the land. Some say that employers should be color-blind. However, after 350 years of segregation and exploitation, the Negro will not profit significantly from this kind of belated equality. He needs more consideration than that. While it makes no sense to tell employers to hire unqualified Negroes, it does make sense to tell them to modify their often arbitrary selection and promotion devices and thus ensure that when qualified Negroes appear, they are placed at the head of the queue at least for some time to come. Unless all sectors of American society act to show some modest "favoritism" toward Negroes, most of them will remain outside the gates. Equality of treatment implies a basic equality of bargaining position. As a result of history, the Negro carries gross handicaps that place him in a particularly weak bargaining position.

To shift from the economic to the political realm—conditions for the Negro are improving; yet his frustration mounts. What should the white community do? A small minority wants to do nothing, on the assumption that this will be better than to venture along untried and dangerous paths. Although most Americans want conditions to improve for the Negro, they are startled by Watts and other manifestations of riot and violence. However, the better his circumstances, the higher the Negro's demands. Many whites are perplexed; others are hostile. But Pettigrew has warned us that we are dealing with three variables, not two—the conditions that Negroes confront, their broadening opportunities, and their rising expectations.[5] And the last may be the most important of the three. The white community has to assume that Negroes will want more and more, sooner rather than later.

Of course, this generalization does not apply to all Negroes. Some, having had so little personal freedom or worldly goods, never developed a sense of responsibility. And now that they do have options, they may decide that circumstances weigh too heavily against them. They may prefer to avoid responsibility, paying the price of continuing in a marginal existence. They know what poverty is, and they may prefer it to work and struggle.

Although we do not fully understand what is happening in the Negro community at large during these tumultuous days, or among significant subsections of it, it is startling to find a considerable proportion of Negro college youths, both in the South and the North, who view the civil rights movement as something "out there," apart from themselves.[6] The forces affecting the utilization of Negro manpower and broadly altering the relationship of Negroes to American society are so complex and dynamic that so far we must treat all generalizations as tentative.

Now to some questions about programs that are tangential to our

[5] T. Pettigrew, "White-Negro Confrontations," in E. Ginzberg (ed.), *The Negro Challenge to the Business Community*, McGraw-Hill Book Company, New York, 1964.
[6] E. Ginzberg and Associates, *The Middle Class Negro in a White Man's World*, Columbia University Press, New York, 1967.

primary concern. For a long time, the American people have invested considerable sums in public housing on the premise that improvement in a family's physical environment will be reflected in improvement in its social and personal behavior and performance. The record is now in, and the evidence gives little support to the theory.

We are now entering upon a more elaborate economic development program which aims to keep various stranded populations at home in the hope that the local economy can be turned around. This is the nub of the efforts in Appalachia and elsewhere. However, there are dangers to government's interfering with the individual's taking the initiative in moving, unless government is willing and able to back up its promises to reverse the local economy. Our new efforts may mean promises that will discourage out-migration.

One of the most interesting aspects of the new programs to reduce poverty is the plan to use the "indigenous poor" to help themselves. While the first assumption is sound—namely, that many middle-class people have little understanding of the way in which the poor think and act—can the indigenous poor really help themselves? A few may, but in an open, free society that has been enjoying substantial prosperity, it is hard to believe that there is a great amount of leadership talent ready to be tapped among the poor.

The foregoing illustrations and evaluations might suggest that psychology has made only a modest contribution to manpower policy. This conclusion would be wrong. It has made at least five major contributions. First, the public has been encouraged to adopt a more humane attitude toward people who are ineffective. We do not shoot soldiers who break down in battle; we treat them for emotional illness. Second, the public has acquired a positive stance toward the amelioration of social and human ills, particularly through reliance on education, but also through other approaches, including supportive services. Third, psychology's study of the distribution of human attributes has contributed substantially to the decline in discrimination toward women, Negroes, and others who were formerly beyond the pale. Fourth, psychology has led to more constructive views and behavior with regard to the rearing of children and the development of young people. We accept strife and crisis as part of normal development, and love and sympathetic understanding as more useful than repression and punishment. Finally, psychology has thrown a searchlight on the critical importance of work for individual and social integration. These are contributions that we do not ignore or minimize. They are major and command respect and approbation.

At the same time, however, some difficult questions remain open in the area of our special concern in the relations between psychology and manpower policy. Following are some of the more important ones: What kinds of family environment can best assure growth and development without emotional pathology? What are the key psychological barriers which prevent children from being able to learn? How does society effectively distinguish between the ineffective performer who needs rehabilitation and the "deviant" who must be confined? Are there any psychological clues which would indicate what actions would reduce the potential explosiveness of the Negro community in the United States? How useful is the prospect of work as an integrative force for people who have lived on the periphery of society for years, who have held the least desirable jobs? How can we find the balance between helping people and assuring that they will continue to help themselves? And finally, how much effort should be devoted to assisting individuals directly, as distinct from improving social institutions that have an influence on large groups of people? These are difficult questions, but there are a few to which we can point directions.

First, no single discipline—whether it be psychology, economics, sociology or politics—should be relied upon to shape and design policy.

Second, although manpower policy starts and ends with the individual, it always involves a wide variety of social and economic institutions—particularly the home, school, private or nonprofit enterprise, and government. Therefore, the tools that are used for analysis and evaluation must encompass not only the individual but these institutions as well.

Third, it follows that the contribution that psychology can make to manpower policy will be greater if more psychologists become literate and perhaps competent in the allied disciplines, for no scholar in the realm of policy can afford to isolate himself. As psychologists move out of the confines of their discipline, they will contribute more to manpower policy and manpower policy will in turn redound to the benefit of psychology. The moral is clear. Disciplines develop by interacting both with other disciplines and with the society at large. Both psychology and the nation stand to gain as psychologists move beyond their conventional boundaries. Psychology has contributed so much that we can look forward with eagerness to its greater contributions in the future.

Chapter Nineteen New Manpower Programs

Every individual and many groups play a part in the formulation and implementation of manpower policy in a democracy. Parents who save part of their income to send their children to college, the young man who enters an apprenticeship program, the trade union that negotiates wages and working conditions for its members, the employer who establishes an on-the-job training program, the professional association which studies the short- and long-run outlook for the demand and supply of specialists, the local government that raises its tax rate to improve the quality of its schools, the state government that establishes a development council, and the Federal government whose several policies impinge directly and indirectly on the nation's work force and the effectiveness with which it is utilized—all these individuals and groups play a part in the shaping of manpower policy.

In our pluralistic society the weight of decision making with respect to manpower, as well as most other facets of our social and economic life, has traditionally rested with the individual and his family and with the private economy. Local government has played only a modest role; the role of the Federal government has been even more restricted. Congress has acted only on a few critical manpower questions: slavery, immigration, and higher education. The Federal government's economic policies, particularly concerning tariffs, transportation, and taxes, have had some spillover effects on manpower, but its total involvement has been modest.

Despite our democratic tradition and our laissez-faire economic policy, the weight of events in the last quarter century has put manpower on the national agenda.

The malfunctioning of the economy during the 1930s, when as many as 1 out of every 4 workers was unemployed; war mobilization in the forties and early fifties, when the combined military and civilian demand for labor expanded rapidly; the sputnik challenge of 1957, which aroused concern about the adequacy of our scientifically trained manpower; the upward drift of unemployment after the end of the Korean hostilities to a level above 6 percent; the awakening national conscience about the more than 30 million Americans living in poverty in the midst of plenty; the doubling since the early 1950s of the number of young people reaching working age; the racial revolution which could no longer be contained—these are the factors that, singly and cumulatively, have been responsible for the emergence of a manpower policy and its current position of national priority.

Although President Theodore Roosevelt had coupled the term human resources with natural resources in his conservation program, the concept of a national human-resources, or manpower, policy dates from the end of World War II.

The Employment Act of 1946, promulgated because of the high level of unemployment in the 1930s, stipulates that "it is the continuing policy and responsibility of the Federal Government . . . to foster and promote conditions under which there will be afforded useful employment opportunities—for those able, willing and seeking to work . . . and to promote maximum employment, production, and purchasing power."

But it was a long time—from 1946 to 1964, when President Johnson signed the bill which cut taxes substantially—before the American people were willing to permit the Federal government to experiment with using the full range of its broad fiscal and monetary powers to help establish and maintain a high level of demand for goods and services. The subsequent decline in unemployment to the lowest levels in a decade is a favorable omen.

Two years before this important breakthrough in fiscal policy, Congress experimented along another axis in partial implementation of the 1946 Employment Act. The unemployment rate, which had been above 5 percent for several years, approached 7 percent in 1961, and this forced Congress to act. In passing the Manpower Development and Training Act in 1962, it took three important steps: It established a national training and retraining program for unemployed and underemployed persons; it provided for an annual assessment and report by the President on the state of the nation's manpower resources; and it granted authority to the Department of Labor to undertake contract research in the manpower field. Congress thus indicated its awareness that new approaches, new programs, and new mechanisms were required to assure all who were able and willing to work an opportunity to do so. In the opinion of the large majority of both political parties who supported this legislation, the free market required assistance and support in order to expand employment at a sufficiently rapid rate to meet the nation's needs.

There was some legislation prior, congruent, and subsequent to this major act which had a direct bearing on manpower policy. The National Defense Education Act of 1958 provides support for training in occupations which are in short supply. The simultaneous increasing scale of Federal support for research and development also had important manpower consequences by assisting in the training and employment of many types of specialists, from space technologists to biologists working on cancer research.

The Area Redevelopment Act of 1961 established the principle of Federal assistance for the rejuvenation of economically stricken areas. In passing the Accelerated Public Works Act in 1962, Congress underscored its concern with the shortage of jobs and sought to stimulate directly the expansion of employment. The Vocational Education Act and the Higher Education Facilities Act, both passed in 1963, were further expressions of congressional concern with the deficiencies in both programs and facilities available for the preparation of young Americans for work and life.

Our economy and society are subject to a high order of change. The approaches and solutions that serve the nation well in an early period often become inadequate. Moreover, we tend to exaggerate the success of earlier resolutions. Finally, the steady rise in national expectations forces us to seek better solutions.

It can no longer be assumed that the economy will grow at a rate sufficiently rapid to provide jobs for all who are able and willing to work.

It is no longer certain, nor even probable, that there will be an automatic matching between the skills that employers require and the capabilities of those seeking employment.

We can no longer rely on the more or less haphazard expansion of institutions of higher learning to provide the number of educated and trained men and women that the nation requires to meet the threats from without and to respond to the opportunities within.

We can no longer assume that the benefits of technological progress, particularly in the guise of automation, will be automatically diffused throughout the population, improving the jobs and income of all.

An affluent society with more and more disposable income can no longer ignore the widespread poverty in its midst.

It is imprudent for the nation to permit its irreplaceable resource—the potential of its people—to remain underdeveloped.

The American people cannot continue to permit economic and educational discrimination against various minorities, particularly against 20 million Negroes, without placing its conscience and its security in jeopardy.

Certain regions of the country are being bypassed by progress. The waste of human and other resources in these declining and depressed areas can be reduced and eliminated only through broad communal action.

It is no longer realistic to assume that every individual will be able to find his own niche in the increasingly complex technological society which ours has become.

It is irrational for the nation to devote so much talent and money to research and development in the physical and biological realms while ignoring the need for new knowledge as a guide to action in the human and social realms.

The following ten goals stand high on America's agenda.

The rapid growth of employment
The matching of men and skills
The expansion of the supply of trained manpower
The diffusion of the benefits of automation
The reduction and elimination of poverty
The full development of human potential
The elimination of discrimination
The rehabilitation of depressed areas
The improvement of labor-market institutions
The broadening and deepening of manpower research

The first and the most ambitious effort so far of the Federal government to fashion a manpower policy apposite to the times was the passage in 1962 and later modifications of the Manpower Development and Training Act (MDTA). In its first four years expenditures under this act have totaled almost $900 million, and approximately 700,000 persons have completed training or are in the pipeline. The initial concern of MDTA was to retrain skilled workers who had lost their jobs because of automation or a decline in economic activity. Because the economy began to expand in 1962, and the fear of automation was found to have been vastly exaggerated, the focus of MDTA shifted to helping marginal workers increase their employability. Follow-up studies suggest that the new and more difficult objective was achieved reasonably well—approximately 3 out of 4 workers who completed institutional training were placed in jobs. For the small but growing numbers who were trained on the job, the record showed that 9 out of every 10 were placed in jobs.

The question which remains unanswered is whether many or most of those who undertook training would have been swept into employment by the strong economic recovery which characterized the United States in the period 1962–1966. Unquestionably many would have found jobs on their own; it is equally certain that training enabled many to get jobs or to find better ones.

In the first three years after the 1963 reform of vocational education, the level of Federal support for vocational education was increased approximately fourfold, from about $55 million to $250 million annually. This growth was paralleled by substantial increases in state and local expenditures. Total reported expenditures for vocational education by all levels of government exceeded $800 million in 1966, an increase of almost half a billion dollars in three years.

The new Federal legislation also introduced more flexibility in expenditure patterns. No longer was it necessary to concentrate most of the Federal funds on agriculture and home economics; support was authorized for a new field—office occupations; and Federal monies were made available for the first time for construction of new facilities.

Too little time has passed to permit a definitive assessment of the full impact of the Vocational Education Act of 1963. Enrollments are up, programs are being strengthened, and research—a long neglected dimension—has been stimulated. A great deal more needs to be done in the structuring of curricula and the strengthening of teaching methods; in finding the proper balance between general and vocational education; in determining whether vocational education can be centered most effectively in the high school, junior college, area vocational school, or in some other institutional structure; in deciding what the school should do, what should be left to the employer, and what should be joint responsibility. All these basic questions remain open. Yet for the first time in the country's history the problem of designing an effective system of vocational education is on the nation's agenda.

With the passage of the National Defense Education Act in 1958, the Federal government substantially increased its support for higher education. Recently, it has increased its support for elementary and secondary education. In 1966 its combined grants for education totaled $4.3 billion, compared with less than $1.8 billion in 1960. In addition, the Federal government has substantially expanded its loan program so that its total impact on education has been that much greater.

But substantial as this effort of the Federal government has been, it must be placed in perspective. Total annual expenditures for education at all levels, public and private, are now (1966–1967) in excess of $40 billion. This means that the direct Federal contribution is little more than 10 percent.

It is significant that a breakthrough finally occurred which made it possible for Federal monies to flow into elementary and secondary education, but the significance of the breakthrough is still to be demonstrated. With defense, space, welfare, highways, and housing competing for funds, it is too early to assess whether the Federal government will be able to provide all children with access to adequate elementary education and secondly to provide those with both the desire and the competence opportunity to continue their education irrespective of the financial ability of their parents.

Training and education, both vocational and general, are two of the major cornerstones of the emerging manpower structure. A third important dimension is the attack on poverty. Since its inception in 1964 the Office of Economic Opportunity has supported a great many different programs aimed at alleviating the circumstances of the poor, some of which are directly or closely related to manpower objectives. Among these is the Neighborhood Youth Corps, which provides part-time employment—and income—to 350,000 youngsters in school, a smaller number of out-of-school youths, and 150,000 young persons during summer vacations. The Corps has met its objective of encouraging young people from low-income homes to remain in school better than its objective of providing meaningful work experience and training for those who have already dropped out of school.

Another program is the Job Corps, which provides training generally limited to one year for deprived young men and women in rural settings and in camps adjacent to urban communities. The Job Corps offers a second chance to those who never had a real first chance, but it has experienced a great many difficulties—from the high per capita cost of the program through community hostility to a high dropout rate. But, although the early evidence was read by Congress as a go-slow sign, it should not be interpreted too bleakly. The program continues, and it will be some time before the definitive evidence needed to permit a balanced judgment is available.

The Office of Economic Opportunity also supported a work-study program at the college level, which was later transferred to the Office of Education in the Department of Health, Education, and Welfare (HEW). This program is aimed at easing the financial strain that young people from low-income homes face in this day of high tuition and rising living costs. The program has been successful; the need exists, the part-time jobs are found, and the funds are administered by each college.

At the heart of the poverty program lies the Community Action Program (CAP) through which the Office of Economic Opportunity has sought to involve the poor directly in planning for their own improvement and in the process to provide employment for many. No comprehensive estimate has been made of the number of positions created by this programming, and the balance sheet may never reflect those who obtain employment, especially full time.

The Office of Economic Opportunity has also financed some work-experience projects for those who have had no training at all. A similar program has been financed by HEW.

By 1966 Congress had concluded that it was necessary to do more than establish these programs in order to create employment opportunities for those most in need of them. It therefore passed the Nelson-Scheuer and the Kennedy-Javits amendments to the Economic Opportunity Act, which are expected to expand jobs for the hard-to-employ in government and in nonprofit institutions, primarily in urban centers and secondarily in rural beautification efforts. The combined sums appropriated under these amendments are less than a quarter of a billion dollars annually, but these amendments are a major breakthrough in the design of a more comprehensive Federal manpower policy. They take cognizance of the fact that neither the stimulation of employment through fiscal and monetary policy nor the emphasis on training can individually or jointly accomplish the basic aims of the Employment Act of 1946.

The effectiveness of the emerging manpower structure is difficult to assess because of the need to differentiate among the legislation, the scale of funding, and the efficiency with which the entire effort is being implemented. As in all social matters, time is a critical dimension.

However, in reviewing the attack on poverty, the following points can be singled out. The potentialities of a concerted attack on the eradication of poverty—including the return of an optimum number of persons to profitable employment—have not been tested; so far the country has been willing to make only a foray or two, not a full-scale attack.

Poverty is a multifaceted phenomenon which is found in every section of the country. If we use the common dividing line to denote poverty—a family income of less than $3,000—over 9 million of the 47 million families in the country, more than 30 million persons, need assistance. Over 11 million are children; they represent one-sixth of all our youth. The heads of poor families are likely to be sixty-five or older, to have had less than an eighth-grade education, to be female, to be nonwhite, to be unemployed, and to live on a farm.

The Economic Opportunity Act of 1964, which provided for expenditures of about $900 million in 1965 and an approximate doubling for 1966, is directed toward helping the poorly educated, the unemployed members of minority groups, the rural farm family—in short, all sections of the population, adults and children alike, who live in poverty. It is estimated that during the first year of operation 1.2 million people were helped by this act; the goal for 1965–1966 was 3 million.

In the shaping and reshaping of manpower programs Congress and the Administration have attempted to assist the many disadvantaged members of the Negro minority to find a niche in American economy and society. In 1962, the Council of Economic Advisers calculated the economic costs of discrimination at $17 billion annually. The human costs cannot be assessed: The life of every Negro citizen in the land is burdened by the virulence of racial prejudice—and the white community has been trapped by the oppressive environment which it has created to keep the Negro in his place. Lyndon Baines Johnson is the first President to insist that the Negro must be fully integrated into every sector of American life. He has maintained that nothing less than first-class citizenship with all the rights and privileges that attach thereto can be offered to the Negro and that nothing less will be acceptable to him. Each title of the monumental Civil Rights Act of 1964 (particularly Title VII, which deals with equal employment opportunity), reenforced by the Voting Rights Act of 1965, represents a major step forward in the struggle that is now joined and that can be resolved only by eliminating all discrimination in American life. The President stated in his address at Howard University in June, 1965, that "the next and more profound stage of the battle for civil rights . . . is to give twenty million Negroes the same chance as every other American to learn and grow, to work and share in society, to develop their abilities. . . ."

Legislation has helped to establish a new deal for the Negro in American life. But there are limits to what can be accomplished by legislation. The extent to which disadvantaged Negroes on Southern farms and in urban centers can transmute their new legal rights into social and economic realities will depend on the extent to which leadership groups, particularly those in business, labor, education, and community planning, recognize their obligation to help and in fact do so.

There are two new Cabinet departments: Housing and Urban Development, and Transportation. The policies of the Federal government which are aimed at helping the Negro minority have little prospect of success unless these two new Federal agencies enable Negroes to buy or rent housing which they can afford and unless they develop an effective system of inter- and intraurban transportation so that those living in the central cities will have access to jobs which are expanding on the periphery.

Brief reference should be made to certain additional Federal legislation which has important manpower dimensions for the long run. In March, 1965, the President signed the Appalachian Regional Development Act, which establishes the Appalachian Regional Commission consisting of one Federal co-chairman and one member from each of the eleven cooperating states. The bulk of the $1.1 billion authorization is to assist in the construction of the Appalachian highway system, which will provide jobs for the inhabitants of the area during the period of construction and which, it is hoped, will eventually serve as a magnet to attract new enterprises to the area. The other provisions of the act aim at research and demonstration projects to improve the quality of the region's human and natural resources. Congress drafted the act to encourage the maximum of local and regional participation. The Federal government took the initiative, but the act looks to a partnership between the several levels of government, private enterprise, and nonprofit institutions.

Related to the foregoing in philosophy and based on the four years of experience with the Area Redevelopment Act is the Public Works and Economic Development Act of 1965, passed by substantial majorities in both Senate and House. This act seeks to extend broad Federal assistance—grants, loans, and technical aid—to areas which are lagging behind the general economic growth of the nation. It is an act to create new economic activity, new jobs. The bill authorizes expenditures of $3.3 billion to rehabilitate the economies of the underdeveloped areas in this country by stimulating new business enterprises and creating permanent employment opportunities. Here is a further piece of evidence of the growing belief of Congress that private enterprise needs assistance in expanding employment—assistance from government and nonprofit institutions.

American agriculture has long been plagued by chronic underemployment and unemployment. In 1965, Secretary of Labor W. Willard Wirtz, in the face of strong employer opposition, decided that the time had come to put an end to the foreign labor force that many farm owners had relied upon, primarily Mexican nationals. By a series of administrative actions and interpretations the Secretary established a new minimum wage of between $1.15 and $1.40 an hour and prohibited the hiring of Mexicans as long as Americans are willing to work for such a wage. Until this determined action, which led to a cutback in foreign laborers to only a few thousand, the American public had demonstrated an appalling lack of interest in and concern with this most depressed sector of the work force. Now a better future lies ahead for farm workers and particularly for their children. Farm owners will get an adequate labor supply only by paying satisfactory wages, establishing satisfactory working conditions, and offering work for longer periods of the year.

Congress has also acted to raise minimum wages, generally to broaden coverage under Social Security, to expand counseling, to bond trainees with prison records, and to provide mobility allowances. Its major omission in the arena of manpower has been its failure to strengthen significantly the Federal-state Employment Service.

An active labor-market policy cannot be effectively shaped and implemented unless the 2,000 offices of the Employment Service are substantially strengthened and subsequently assume a key role in providing the range of services that job seekers, especially the hard-to-employ, urgently require. Many employers fear Federal control over the supply of labor. It is hoped that safeguards against such Federal control will be established when the Federal government makes another effort to pass this much-needed legislation.

Because the manpower problems facing the nation are exceedingly complex and since many of the solutions are not at hand, Congress has taken a positive view toward experimentation and research. Until the last few years the Federal agencies were not able to support research in education, manpower, and employment. But Congress has been increasingly liberal in its support of research, experimentation, and demonstrations. Congress has thus underscored its hope and expectations that new knowledge will lead to significant gains in manpower utilization.

American democracy is pragmatic and therefore experimental. But it has ideals and principles which give shape and direction to its actions. Current manpower programming is guided by three principles:

1. Every American has a right to the opportunity to develop his potential to the full. Color, lack of income, or any other handicap that has previously blocked the path of many citizens will no longer preclude educational achievement or occupational advancement.
2. Investment in human beings can yield a high rate of return. To find a job for a man who has been on the relief rolls, to give the underemployed farmer additional skills, and to help the physically handicapped find a part-time job—all result in a benefit to the country far above the cost. In addition, these investments will enable individuals to shake off despair and despondency and develop self-respect and contentment.
3. The Federal government has a responsibility to take the lead in shaping a national manpower policy. But it can succeed in designing it and especially in carrying it out only with the wholehearted support of all sectors of the public: business, labor, universities, churches, community action groups, and private citizens. Each has a crucial role to play. In a free society, manpower policy is—and must be—the concern of every citizen.

Recent legislation represents a significant first contribution to the fashioning of an effective national manpower policy. But much, very much, still must be done before the nation's human resources can be effectively developed and productively utilized.

American democracy has not yet succeeded in creating a true equality of opportunity for all. Therefore, we must rectify past omissions today while we cope with the challenges of the present and the potentialities of the future. These are the directions in which we must go:

1. We must implement the Employment Act of 1946. There are millions of unemployed and more millions outside the labor force who want to work but are unable to find jobs.
2. The substantially enlarged Federal expenditures for education and training in recent years are a significant step forward. But the creation of an adequate structure to furnish the range and depth of opportunity for every child and adult to develop his full potential will require very much larger expenditures—tens of billions of dollars.
3. To make optimal use of the potentialities of automation will require much more planning at every level, from the Federal government to the plant site. America can be made a better land in which to live and work.

Machines can help accomplish this, but only if we learn to use the machines for our purposes.

4. Federal expenditures for the eradication of poverty are helping only a small minority of poor persons. The atrophy of competence and the erosion of the human spirit which result from generations of poverty is not easily reversed. One must include more groups within the poverty program.

5. As the nation becomes more urbanized, we shall no longer be able to hide our uneducated and underemployed on marginal farms. As these people move into the cities, they need a great amount of help to adjust to urban living. We have only begun to recognize this challenge. Urban riots in the North and West are a warning.

6. Two out of every three American workers today are employed in the service sector of the economy, and as time goes on, the ratio is likely to increase. However, many service jobs demand little, pay little, and offer little prospect for advancement. American entrepreneurship faces a challenge to improve the quality of jobs and careers in the service sector.

7. The recruitment, testing, placement, training, upgrading, transfer, and retirement of a labor force consisting of 80 million persons requires the effective cooperation and coordination of a great many different government, nonprofit, and private agencies. While labor market institutions have been strengthened under the stimulus of an active manpower policy, we must devote sustained effort to making these institutions fully responsive to the tasks which they face.

8. In periods of war and cold war, such as have characterized the last quarter century and which may continue, new policies must be fashioned to reduce radical fluctuations in defense employment and to establish equity for all those liable for military service.

9. The Federal government directly employs over 5 million persons in its civilian and military agencies, and through its expenditures it directly affects the employment of another 6 to 7 million. In addition, its major programs in education, science, and research have a pronounced effect on the numbers and distribution of the nation's trained manpower. Through a variety of administrative devices, including the President's Committee on Manpower, the administration is striving to bring about a higher degree of efficiency in the utilization of these large numbers of persons, together with an improved coordination of Federal programs that have a pronounced manpower impact. But here, too, we have only started to design and use these basic planning and control mechanisms.

10. More and more responsibility attaches to the Federal government. It must strengthen existing programs and launch new ones. And it must coordinate and integrate those already in existence; its efforts with respect to education, training, poverty, depressed areas, housing, health,

and welfare need to be fitted together so that each reinforces the other. But if the Federal government is to succeed, it needs the wholehearted cooperation of state and local government and community leaders. For the implementation of manpower policy must always be local.

It will require unflinching faith and sustained effort for the American people to support the type of manpower policy that can provide the quality of people capable of building a great society and which can assure a better life to all Americans, to all men.

Afterword Manpower Policy in a Democracy

We pointed out in the Foreword that, while the United States has had a manpower policy since its inception as a nation —one might add that its emergence as a nation was speeded by the wrong manpower policies pursued by the British, such as the quartering of troops among the colonists—our early manpower policies were both implicit and limited and dealt primarily with education and immigration. However, as we have seen, during the past several decades manpower policy has been vastly broadened in scope and has become an explicit dimension of national policy.

Americans respond energetically to problems and often act without reference to antecedent principles or subsequent implications. It might be well, therefore, to consider briefly the points of congruence and dissonance between the new manpower policies that we have begun to pursue and our basic democratic commitments, as well as some of the latent tensions which may arise as the new policies are implemented.

One could begin by stating that manpower planning and democratic values are in fundamental opposition to one another and that it is likely that the more a nation becomes involved in planning, the greater the danger to its values. There is an inherent antagonism between placing high value on the freedom of the individual to choose his work and to select his employer and the thrust of manpower planning which aims at influencing, even directing, the choices that people make about their future occupations and the decisions they reach about current employment. We recognize the right—even the duty— of government to control, in varying degrees, the supply of manpower during the course of national mobilization, but this one exception apart, the burden of our democratic tradition dictates noninterference.

But we know that one man's freedom may be another's fetters. We have seen that most of the young people growing up on farms today have no prospect of supporting themselves as farmers. This is clear to the government officials and the academicians who have studied the transformation of American agriculture. But it is not nearly so clear to many of the poorly educated, isolated parents of these children. A policy of public silence or noninterference in the arena of agriculture could worsen substantially the prospects of millions of these young-sters. It can be argued persuasively that the Federal government should interfere more in order to alter the powerful forces that are steadily eroding the employment prospects in many rural areas—either by seeking to counter the trends by broadening the economic base or by doing something special and extra to facilitate the eventual relocation of most of the younger generation when it reaches working age. There are a number of other areas in economic decline where the same chal-lenge exists—where, if nothing is done to help the young, freedom may prove to be, as in Anatole France's parable, only the freedom to go hungry.

The President and the Secretary of Defense have recently raised another issue which involves the conflict between manpower planning and individual freedom. They have sent up trial balloons in favor of national service for young men who do not serve in the military forces. Their proposal seeks to make the requirement for a period of national service, military or otherwise, more nearly universal; it rec-ognizes the difficulty of obtaining through market mechanisms the manpower required to perform high-priority missions in the civilian sector; and it postulates that a period of national service would be beneficial to the young people involved. However, the proposal has not yet been reconciled with the serious questions that must be raised about the legitimacy of a democracy's using compulsion in the absence of a clear and overriding threat to national security, the dangers of relying on labor obtained through compulsion when the market is unable to attract and retain workers in certain fields, and the validity of the presumption that compulsory service would be beneficial.

We have adumbrated the reasons why the draft is inequitable and must be changed. But it surely does not follow that it is sound policy to broaden compulsion to achieve a higher degree of equity. Unless the gains from additional compulsion can be demonstrated to be very substantial, the whole weight of American history and experience dic-tates that we must balk at more compulsion. Freedom for the indi-vidual must never be reduced unless it can be clearly demonstrated that more opportunities for others have been created thereby; and even then caution is in order.

Related to the issue of individual freedom is the potential conflict between manpower policy and equity. Current efforts at both governmental and nongovernmental levels to speed the employment and promotion of Negroes have brought this issue to the fore. This new aspect of our manpower policy starts from the recognition that employment opportunities have long been characterized by discrimination against Negroes and that new employment policies directed toward increasing equality of opportunity may do very little to right distortions of such long standing. As a consequence of this realization, employers have been encouraged, sometimes forced, to take positive steps to improve the position of the Negro. Some employers have, of course, voluntarily moved in this direction. However, a policy which mandates the hiring of any qualified Negro instead of the best-qualified white applicant or a promotion policy which follows the same procedure is a violation of the principle of equity with respect to the white man who is left at the hiring gate or who is not promoted despite his superior qualifications. The critical question here is whether, without employer actions to increase the proportion of Negro employees in general and particularly in preferred positions, adherence to rigid policies of objective evaluation—which of course were not followed in an earlier day—might not perpetuate the lack of opportunity and consequently the depressed condition of the Negro. This, then, would be a new manpower policy introducing major changes in employment and promotion patterns whose aim is to establish equity for the Negro, an approach that can succeed only if it ignores, for the time being at least, the question of equitable treatment of white workers.

This approach to facilitating the integration of the Negro into the economy and society has been decried by many who have never raised their voices in protest against the policy long established in law and administration in most governmental agencies which allows a certain number of preference points to veterans in their competition for employment or promotion. The balancing of equity for the individual against equity for the group is never easy to accomplish and can never be automatic. One thing is clear: The adoption of manpower policies that militate against equitable treatment of the individual should be approved only in the face of overriding pressures.

A critical objective of manpower policy, particularly for the individual employer, is efficiency in the use of available manpower resources. But a great range of manpower policies in use today are in direct conflict with this criterion of efficiency. Through legislation, collective bargaining, and company policies, employers frequently must follow selection, promotion, and discharge procedures which redound to the benefit of the less capable—with consequent adverse effects on efficiency. But it is the judgment of society that important as efficiency is in the utilization of manpower resources, it cannot be exalted above all other goals and objectives.

Democracy maintains that employers should not be free to turn away all applicants above a certain age. Nor should they be permitted to disregard the claims to special consideration which an employee has earned through twenty or more years of faithful service. Nor should they be able to follow their own preferences when it comes to promotion or discharge. Even on the ground of efficiency itself and without consideration of other values, a manpower policy that in a particular instance results in the hiring, promotion, or retention of the less capable may still contribute to the efficiency of the system as a whole. Work in a democratic society cannot be commandeered; it must be elicited. And the employer's preoccupation with efficiency will founder unless he has the tolerance, if not the active support, of his work force for the personnel practices which he seeks to establish and follow. In complex systems, the optimization of a particular move may not yield the best overall results, and short-run efficiency must frequently give way to long-run morale objectives.

There is an interesting paradox about manpower planning which conditions greatly what is ventured and what can be successfully implemented. Manpower policies introduced by the Federal government are likely to have the biggest thrust, both in terms of money and other dimensions of power. But the objective of manpower policy is the individual, who is very far removed from the center of government power and who is influenced by a great many other forces in his immediate environment. With the single exception of the operations of the Selective Service System, it is doubtful whether the Federal government, even with its overriding power, can exercise directly through its manpower policies more than a modest influence on individuals in communities throughout the country. Yet it is the Federal government that has taken the initiative during the past years to underwrite a great amount of new legislation with specific manpower content. The new legislation includes making available opportunities of employment to people in depressed areas, making training and retraining opportunities available to the unemployed and the underemployed, facilitating the relocation of certain groups of stranded workers, establishing new criteria for the support of vocational education, and making a large number of fellowships, scholarships, and loans available to those who are willing to pursue their studies in selected "shortage" occupations. In some instances, the Federal government has sought to operate directly. In most cases, however, it has sought to implement its several programs through state and local governmental agencies and various nongovernmental institutions.

Complex problems have arisen in connection with determining the proper role of the Federal government in a Federal-state pattern. The original Manpower Development and Training Act contemplated the speedy assumption by the states of a considerable part of the financing of the new development and training mission; the drafters of the legislation believed that the equality of the program would be considerably enhanced if the states which had a major role in carrying out the provisions of the act had to invest their own money. But it soon became clear that Congress would have to cover almost all the costs or permit the legislation to die. Only a few states were willing or able to carry their share. In this, as in many other recent instances, the costs of new manpower programs have been carried almost entirely by the Federal government.

It is not easy to obtain the full benefits of a Federal-state system if the Federal government is the banker and the states the beneficiaries. Such a system can work, but the odds are against it. As we have indicated, to be effective, manpower programming must eventually be made at the local level—where the people live and work or are looking for work. This means that in addition to Federal and state government, local government must play a role, frequently a dominant role, and this exacerbates difficulties of coordination.

So far we have dealt with the three levels of government as if each were a unified organ, which of course it is not. Nevertheless, to launch and implement a successful manpower program requires integration at each of the three levels of government, as well as integration among them. There is mounting evidence of discontent and frustration among legislators and administrators at Federal, state, and local levels because the barriers to effective coordination are being removed so slowly.

When we seek to identify the major challenges, several stand out. We have already mentioned the role of the Federal government as the predominant source of funds. In addition there is the absence of appropriate governmental machinery for the administration of manpower programs at each level, particularly at the state and local levels, which historically have lagged behind the Federal government in both organization and personnel. The new manpower programs can operate effectively only if the long-established departments of education, labor, and welfare are reorganized so that they can respond to new problems in new ways. The existing machinery and procedures were designed long ago to cope with other problems. The rigidity and inflexibility of our governmental structures present an analogy with the situation in developing countries—the inadequacy of established governmental institutions to cope effectively with the new opportunities that have become available through foreign aid in the form of grants and loans. In many of the new countries the existing organizational structure is inadequate, and the key personnel are frequently unable to recognize the new opportunities and to respond to them.

It would be fortunate if there were some simple, or even complex, formula which would point the way to necessary and desirable reforms. But of course no such formula exists. Without it, we need analyses in depth to help delineate the major barriers that stand in the way of efficient implementation together with an experimental stance which will permit us to remodel and redesign existing structures and to create new ones more appropriate to the tasks at hand. We need political leaders and administrators with strength and integrity who will devote their energies and abilities to these tasks rather than to protecting their positions or attacking their opponents. We need a press and, in turn, a public with more appreciation of the difficulties of the task and more interest in constructive reforms than in exposure and vilification.

So far we have been concerned with the role of government in manpower policy and programming. This emphasis reflects the primary role of government in this area. But ours is a pluralistic economy and society, and voluntary groups frequently play major roles in the design and implementation of manpower policies. We need only recall the influence of the American Medical Association on health-manpower legislation, the National Association of Manufacturers on unemployment compensation, the American Federation of Labor on the administration of joint apprenticeship, the various academic pressure groups on the scale and control of scientific research and training programs, the various veterans' organizations on military manpower policies, and the Catholic Church on welfare and population programs and policies.

Voluntary organizations play strategic roles in establishing education and training policies in many fields; moreover, their members account for the overwhelming number of jobs in these fields. Therefore, their actions and attitudes have a major impact on the development and utilization of manpower. The complexity of designing and implementing manpower policy in a democracy is illustrated by the fact that the coordination that must be achieved among governmental agencies is only the first of a three-stage process. The second stage involves effective interchange between government and voluntary organizations. And the third—and from many points of view the most essential—is the collection of information, its dissemination to the individual, the way in which he evaluates it, and the actions which he takes or fails to take with respect to it.

In addition, information can, or should, enable a man to make a sensible decision about the choice of a career or location. But the collection and dissemination of information are necessarily neutral. In the 1930s, the American Medical Association sought to persuade the medical schools of the country to reduce their admissions because it was concerned about underemployment of physicians. In the late 1940s an engineering society, in collaboration with the U.S. Department of Labor, warned about a prospective oversupply of engineers. In the middle 1950s a subsidiary of the Ford Foundation warned about a critical shortage of teachers. There have been repeated inquiries into and reports about the "nurse crisis." After sputnik, various governmental and nongovernmental bodies, after determining that a gap existed between our scientific and technical manpower resources and our requirements, sought to alert the nation to the danger which it faced.

However, despite the fact that many of these manpower reports were issued under the aegis of distinguished committees and commissions, the information presented was almost without exception inadequate for the policy conclusions that were drawn. The authors were protagonists in a conflict over policy. Wittingly or not, they used the information they had collected and analyzed to support the policy they wanted to promulgate.

Manpower is a new discipline, and standards of criticism have not been developed. A democracy can afford competition and conflict in the marketplace of facts and ideas, just as it prospers under a system of competition in the production of goods and services. But just as conventional competition requires competent and informed consumers, the production of facts and figures must be subjected to the purifying consequences of incisive criticism. We need a critical tradition in manpower as a discipline, and the rate of innovation in manpower policy should be conditioned at least in part by the growth of this tradition.

There is one further dimension of manpower policy in a democracy which is implicit in all that has been said, but which warrants more specific delineation. We started this book by stating that manpower policy is concerned with the relation of human beings to their role in economic development—the part they play and will play in the production of goods and services. But the human being, the manpower resource present or potential, is more than that. He is a man, a man with a concept of the type of person he wants to be and the type of life he wants to lead. Of course the realization of his hopes and aspirations is a result of the success he achieves in the development of his potential for the world of work—the success he achieves in making use of his skills and competences. While every man is a worker, no worker is a complete man. The final challenge to manpower policy in a democracy is to reduce waste in the acquisition and utilization of skill without jeopardizing other important values. Manpower policy must aim to enrich both the individual and the society. It can never be an end in itself.

Sources

1. Based on a presentation to the All-University Honors Colloquium, University of Rhode Island, October, 1965.
2. Based on a presentation to *Time* Conferences on "The Environment of Change," held at Sterling Forest, New York, in January, 1966, and Airlie House, Virginia, in September, 1966.
3. Based on a presentation to the Second International Conference on Automation, Rationalization and Technological Progress, held at Oberhausen, Germany, March 16–19, 1965, under the auspices of Industrie-Gewerkschaft Metall (German Metal Workers Union). Slightly reduced and revised version of the chapter "Technischer Fortschritt und Beschäftigung in den USA," in *Automation Risiko und Chance,* Redaktion: Günter Friedrichs, Europäische Vierlagsanstalt, Frankfurt, A.M., Band I, 1965, pp. 151ff.
4. Slightly revised version of an article appearing in the *Columbia Journal of World Business,* Summer, 1966, pp. 133ff.
5. Substantially revised version of an article in the *New South,* Southern Regional Council, Spring, 1966, pp. 60ff.
6. Substantially revised version of an article in *Outlook,* National Women's League, Winter, 1965, pp. 5ff.
7. Slightly revised version of a background paper prepared for the Chamber of Commerce of the United States, Washington, D.C., 1967.
8. Revision of the consultant's paper prepared for the White House Conference on Education, July 20–21, 1965. Printed in: *White House Conference on Education,* prepared for the Subcommittee on Education of the Committee on Labor and Public Welfare, U.S. Senate, 89th Cong., 1st Sess., Washington, D.C., 1965, pp. 18ff.
9. Substantially reduced version of the draft of chapter 4 of the *Manpower Report of the President,* March, 1966, prepared by the Conservation of Human Resources staff at the request of the

U.S. Department of Labor, under the direction of Dr. Marcia K. Freedman, in consultation with Prof. Ivar E. Berg, and with the assistance of Carol A. Brown and Roberta B. Handwerger.

10. Substantially reduced version of the consultant's chapter produced for the President's Commission on Crime in the District of Columbia. Printed in the Appendix volume of *The Report of the President's Commission on Crime in the District of Columbia.* The assistance of Ivar E. Berg, Carol A. Brown, Marcia K. Freedman, and John L. Herma of the Conservation of Human Resources staff is gratefully acknowledged.

11. Substantial revision of an article in *Our Troubled Children: Our Community's Challenge,* Edwin Gould Foundation for Children, Columbia University Press, 1967, pp. 25ff.

12. Slight revision of an article in the *Journal of College Placement,* October–November, 1966, pp. 22ff.

13. "The Case for a Lottery," reprinted from *The Public Interest,* no. 5, Fall, 1966, pp. 83ff.

14. Reprinted with minor changes from the *New England Journal of Medicine,* vol. 275, July, 1966, pp. 85–87.

15. Substantial revision of a presentation at the Conference on Job Development and Training for Workers in Health Services, sponsored by the Departments of Labor and HEW. Printed in *Training Health Service Workers: The Critical Challenge,* 1966, pp. 16ff.

16. Slightly revised version of chapter 12 in *Talent and Performance,* by Eli Ginzberg and John L. Herma, with Ivar E. Berg, Carol A. Brown, Alice M. Yohalem, James K. Anderson, and Lois Lipper, Columbia University Press, 1964, pp. 219ff.

17. Slightly revised version of chapter 12 in *Life Styles of Educated Women,* by Eli Ginzberg with Ivar E. Berg, Carol A. Brown, John L. Herma, Alice M. Yohalem, and Sherry Gorelick, Columbia University Press, 1966, pp. 179ff.

18. Slightly revised version of an article in *American Psychologist,* vol. 21, no. 6, June, 1966, pp. 549ff.

19. Prepared originally in the summer of 1965 in response to a request of the Executive Office of the President. Revised for publication.

Index

Index